PENTAGON PRESS

COMMITTED TO SERVE THE ARMED FORCES

AFTER ABBOTTABAD

Terror to Turmoil in Pakistan

AFTER ABBOTTABAD

Terror to Turmoil in Pakistan

ANIL BHAT

Foreword by

Mujahid Hussain

PENTAGON PRESS

First Published in 2012

Published by
PENTAGON PRESS
206, Peacock Lane, Shahpur Jat,
New Delhi-110049
Phones: 011-64706243, 26491568
Telefax: 011-26490600
email: rajan@pentagonpress.in
website: www.pentagonpress.in

Cataloging in Publication Data—DK
Courtesy: D.K. Agencies (P) Ltd. <docinfo@dkagencies.com>

Bhat, Anil, 1951-
After Abbottabad: terror to turmoil in Pakistan / Anil Bhat ; foreword by Mujahid Hussain.
p. cm.
Includes bibliographical references, index.
ISBN 9788182746718

1. Bin Laden, Osama, 1957-2011. 2. Terrorists—Saudi Arabia—Biography. 3. Qaida (Organization)—Biography. 4. Terrorism—Religious aspects—Islam. 5. Terrorism—Pakistan. 6. Islamic fundamentalism—Pakistan. I. Title.

DDC 363.325092 23

Printed at Avantika Printers Private Limited, New Delhi.

Contents

Foreword

This writing by Anil Bhat brings forward in quite a vivid manner the dangers surrounding the present days' world due to fanatic mind-sets. Al-Qaeda, the most dreaded terrorist network of religious extremists is not a single outfit but a group or an umbrella organisation for all the elements that utilize garb of religious ideology in order to materialise their ulterior motive of creating a reign of terror in the name of a caliphate and sharia laws. Itself an offshoot of Arab imperialism, its aim has been quite lucky and its target has been made easier in the sense that an enemy called Western or more specifically American Imperialism was readily available to it. Certain circles rightly put it in this way that Al-Qaeda is not a terrorist outfit in a traditional sense but a mind-set that is bent upon to eventually disrupt and shatter all the progress made by any human civilization anywhere in the world.

This endeavour by Anil Bhat is quite laudable in the sense that it explains the basic elements of Al-Qaeda, its ideology and its present network along with all the detailed features that constitute one of most dangerous organisation of the world. Maximum effort has been made to bring its linkages to limelight. This work is also appreciable in the sense that presentation of his study is in total contrast to the tradition ways of Indian writers who generally turn into a 'patriot Indian' than an objective researcher while writing about Pakistan & Afghanistan or Al-Qaeda, Taliban and other militant outfits of the region while a general tendency is also noted among them that they either ignore the inescapable realities or resort to a politician like partiality that has the sole purpose of gaining political mileage. This approach might be suitable when it comes to mutual tussle of certain factions but it is totally counterproductive for impartial readership. So the academic and intellectual objectivity on the part of Mr. Bhat is commendable.

Unluckily Pakistan is among the few countries of the world where overt as well as covert activities of Al-Qaeda and its affiliated outfits have not only been extended full support by the state machinery but there has also been an overwhelming sense of tacit approval by the masses. There are so many factors behind these public sentiments but the factors that are the main contributors of such a situation could be summed up as following:

- Establishment's narrative of Pakistan being such a security state that has always faced grave dangers from a perennial and powerful enemy;
- A skewed rather distorted version of history taught through textbooks to (at least three) generations of Pakistanis where their country is presented as an eternal victim of aggression by a hostile neighbor as well as various global powers; and
- The perception created during previous three decades or so that Pakistan (partially due to its arsenal of nuclear warheads) has emerged as a 'fortress of Islam' that always has been a target of the conspiracies by the Hindus, Jews and Christians etc.

In this scenario an overwhelming 'moral support' extended to Al- Qaeda like ideologies should be quite comprehensible. Furthermore a quite negative and very dangerous development has taken place post 9/11 that the renowned intellectual and analyst Khaled Ahmed has narrated in these words:

> "In the year 2011, it is clear that Pakistan Army will not fight the Taliban and Al-Qaeda the way the world wants it to. The reason is Punjab. Many will find this a strange formulation but the fact is that Al-Qaeda has been rendered impregnable by the shift of allegiance of Punjab's 'non-state actors' from Pakistan Army to Al-Qaeda. The basis of Al-Qaeda's impregnability is in the persistence of Pakistan Army's designation of these 'non-state actors' as state assets and any attack on Al-Qaeda and the Taliban in the Tribal Areas will lead to a backlash in the country's biggest province.
>
> The situation turns more complicated as the state has not abandoned its past policy of using the terrorists as 'non-state actors' in a foreign policy of covert 'proxy war' in Afghanistan and India even after alignment of these elements with Al-Qaeda and the Taliban. The use of fully armed non-state actors in deniable wars has tended to create multiple centres of power in Pakistan, meaning that the state has abdicated a large portion of its claim on the 'monopoly of violence' in the Weberian sense. Parts of the state handling these clerically headed non-state organisations have

> suffered a split from the decision-making apparatus of the state, in this case the military and the intelligence agencies.
>
> The security institutions of the state are indoctrinated to link the survival of Pakistan to conflict with India. This gives rise to an ambivalence that undermines the fight against terrorism. There is a tendency to blame terrorism on India in the face of clear evidence that violence is being perpetrated by the non-state actors trained by the state as jihadi organisations to fight India. Psychologically, this is the most dangerous hurdle in the national effort to overcome terrorism and normalize the state. The conflict with India is embedded in Pakistan's nationalism, based on textbooks and the message from the media, which Pakistan lacks the intellectual suppleness to remove".

Apart from the situation in South Asian region when we look at the prevailing atmosphere of Anti-American and anti-Western sentiments in the Muslim world, it does not present a rosier picture either. Post Arab-Israel war of 1967 circumstances have served as a catalyst for extremist sentiments to prevail converting the purely nationalist cause of Palestinian people into a narrower Islamists agenda and these conscious and subconscious efforts at indoctrination towards a Pan-Islamist militancy finally culminate into Afghan Jihad where Muslim warriors from Arab and African countries (a number of newly converted Mujahedeen from Western world as well) flock towards Afghanistan, financed by the US and Saudi Arabia while accommodated and facilitated by Pakistan in the holy war against the infidel Soviet Union. What we see around us is just a continuation of the same mirage of a Caliphate. At present the core of Al-Qaeda does not comprise of Arab warriors only and it is now a multinational in the true sense of the word. Its manpower also includes expatriates from Muslim world who no longer integrate in their host. Western societies or the Muslims workers from South Asian countries working in oil rich Gulf countries. Whatever the composition of human resources of Al-Qaeda, every type of them either imbibed terrorism from clerics or they were radicalized due to prevailing Wahhabi edition of Islam in the host countries and developed a sense of alienation for their 'pro-West' ruling elites.

When talking in the Pakistani perspective we must not ignore the fact that Al-Qaeda has proved itself a tough opponent in its insurgency against Pak Army and it has its reinforcement from various quarters like local militants, Taliban of every category, hundreds of thousands of students from madrasahs, millions of sympathizers in the masses and above all a strong circle of well-wishers among officials of security institutions. The initial investigations of all the attacks by Al-Qaeda into Pakistani territories reveal that it has a very large pool of volunteers and sympathizers. For example all those spots were hit quite accurately where Pakistani officers were thought to have been engaged in joint investigations along with the US or NATO officials. Outfits like Sipah-e-Sahaba and Lashkar-e-Jhangvi are the greatest armed support of Al-Qaeda in Pakistan while Jaish-e-Muhammad and Lashkar-e-Tayyba also from time to time provide it with support in various ways. It has also been proven during investigations that Al-Qaeda quite successfully has utilized the serving officials from Pak Army and Air Force in two fatal attacks on (then) President and Chief of Army Staff General Pervez Musharraf. It seems quite strange that Al-Qaeda got all the basic information from the same places that it had selected for its suicide attacks as it already had its sympathizers and collaborators at these places and these deadly attacks had a success rate of almost one hundred per cent.

The grasp of Al-Qaeda over religious and sectarian outfits of Pakistan and its overall influence is not a matter that could be easily ignored. There are a number of evidences that points towards the grim reality that ALQaeda is not a "guest" organisation anymore and its Pakistani branch has turned nto a powerful and well-connected institute which can muster financial and material resources anywhere, anytime without much of difficulty. The people treating it as an Arabic outfit are in fact still hostage to its Yemeni, Sudanese and Iraqi background and find it hard to perceive that non-Arabs could also be its active members. A lot of Pakistani militants from various sectarian and jihadist outfits like Maulana Fazalur-Rahman Khalil to Ilyas Kashmiri and Major Haroon etc. are busy in fortifying the setup of Al-Qaeda in Pakistan and have very strong ties with local jihadist and sectarian elements. These relations are being actively utilised for targeting the security forces of Pakistan and there offices and other installations.

Al-Qaeda is engaged in a global jihad under its specific beliefs and perceptions in various countries including Pakistan and Afghanistan. For example in Pakistan it has its total impetus on 'pre-emptive jihad' i.e. initiate the strikes on 'enemy' and pounce into its territories when (these non-believers) are not even in preparations for assault against Muslims. According to the sketch of jihad brought forward by Sheikh Abdullah Azzam the founding father of Al-Qaeda, at present the organisation is participating in jihad under the both concepts of Udoo-al-Qareeb (eminent and ready to strike enemy) and Udoo-al-Baeed (potential and far off enemy) and it perceives both types of enemies equally dangerous for its causes whereas jihad against every type of enemy has become 'Wajib' (mandatory).

Under the same concepts it is engaged in war against the army as well as civil dispensation as both of them are supporting and reinforcing the forces of evil (Western powers). Neither it is hard to imagine the turns this jihad will take in near future nor could the security of India, Pakistan and Afghanistan be assured for the days to come. The Indo-Pakistan hostilities are also playing a considerable role for aggravation of situation while gradually a soft corner for Al-Qaeda has started to emerge in India as well that should be a matter of serious concern for India. There is a dire need of a paradigm shift in India so that it could see the rise of extremism and terrorist activities in the region not merely as a handiwork of Pakistani intelligence apparatus but as a graver and a devastating common threat for the whole region. The public sympathies for Al-Qaeda in Pakistan are not difficult to gauge as the list of deadly enemies of Pakistan compiled by the deep state has Western countries on its top after India and Israel. For generations after generations brought up under propaganda and eternal hate for a perceived enemy, it would not be difficult for jihadist outfits to find their staunch supporters in the society. This book by Anil Bhat informs us of the wrath of Al-Qaeda and its future plans; if it goes on with its planning it is not hard to imagine the plight of South Asia in the days to come.

Brussels **Mujahid Hussain**

Preface

Having written extensively on Pakistan army and ISI and some papers on Afghanistan post 9/11, as well as many articles on US-Af-Pak for over two decades, in the weeks following Osama bin Laden's (OBL) killing by US special forces, I wrote a series of six articles, followed by a few more over the past few months. Shortly after OBL's killing, Mr. Rajan Arya of Pentagon Press approached me to write a book. While I am not a specialist on OBL as such, but I had maintained in some of my articles since around 2004 at least, that OBL could not have been moving up and down mountains and caves. He was bound to be in Pakistan and that Pak army and the Inter Services Intelligence agency (ISI) knew of his whereabouts.

The arrangement of OBL living with his family near Pakistan Military Academy at Abbottabad and not in some cave in the mountains as many had guessed, could simply not have been possible without not only the knowledge of Pak army and ISI, but with effective assistance from both.

Since its inception in 1947, Pak army had begun to specialize in the strategy of raising proxy fighter groups using terrorism as force multipliers rather than committing its own troops/also use the raised groups as cannon fodder instead of its own soldiers. This modus was majorly developed by Pak army by the time it began fighting the Soviet Russian forces in Afghanistan. The advent of OBL and Al Qaeda in Pakistan for the purpose of supporting Pak army's operations against Soviet Russian forces in Afghanistan was a turning point. It was since then that Pak army's terrorism connections became enhanced and beginning to get almost global. However it remained a firm ally of the US and after 9/11 it officially-and most ironically so-became its "main frontline ally in US' war against terror". And it took the US ten years of chasing OBL, while Pak army and ISI continued to play the double game of "assisting" US and coalition forces, while supporting or sheltering some of the very terrorist groups responsible for thousands of fatal casualties of coalition troops and destruction of scores of NATO supply vehicles in umpteen attacks on its convoys.

While the public line of the Obama administration was that no evidence had emerged to suggest OBL had high-level help inside Pakistan, ISI is reported to have said that his long and comfortable existence in the country was an "intelligence failure." But suspicions increased following recent disclosures by one of OBL's wives in a police interrogation report that the al Qaeda leader lived in five houses while on the run and fathered four children, two of whom were born in Pakistani government hospitals.

"I just find the idea that he lived in a place like Abbottabad without the ISI's knowledge strains credibility. It is ridiculous that he wasn't being protected" Shawn Gregory, director of the Pakistan Security Research Unit at Bradford University, U.K, is reported to have said. Since the raid, Pakistan has undergone an unprecedented kinds of and combination of changes. Pakistan army's aura and power within the country got dented like never before, its relationship with the US nosedived and its equation with Pakistan's civilian government changed drastically. The residence in a town of Haripur was one of five safe houses used by the slain al Qaeda leader while on the run in Pakistan. In an ornate but not lavish two-storey house tucked away at the end of a mud clogged street in Haripur is where OBL is believed to have lived for nearly a year until he moved into the villa in which he was eventually killed.

The residence in the frontier town of Haripur was one of five safe houses used by the slain al Qaeda leader while on the run in Pakistan, according to information revealed by his youngest wife, who has been detained. However, the best information appears to have come from Amal Ahmed Abdel-Fatah al-Sada, a 30-year-old Yemeni, who has been in Pakistani custody since May 02, 2011, when US Navy SEALs overran the Abbottabad compound, killing OBL and four other people inside. Sada is believed to be OBL's favourite wife, who travelled with him since his escape from Afghanistan's eastern Tora Bora mountain range in 2001. Since then, the ISI, has been trying to uncover the trail that brought him to Abbottabad villa in the summer of 2005.

According to an Afghan officer, an ISI operative Syed Akbar Sabir is reported to have escorted OBL from Pakistan's Chitral region to Peshawar. ISI could have provided protection to OBL for a period of time, as per 'The New Yorker' magazine. Former Afghan intelligence chief Amrullah Saleh told the magazine' writer Dexter Filkins, a Pulitzer prize winner, that an ISI operative Syed Akbar Sabir had escorted OBL from the

Pakistani region of Chitral to Peshawar, passing through Kunar Province, in Afghanistan, along the way.

A week after the raid in Abbottabad, US President Barack Obama is reported to have told a media agency that OBL had a "support network" in Pakistan and that it must investigate how he evaded capture. Pakistan responded by announcing the formation of a committee to investigate bin Laden's presence in Pakistan as well as the circumstances surrounding the U.S. raid. Soon after it began its work, the head of the committee said he was sure that security forces were not hiding OBL. Other statements since then have also suggested the report will be more of a whitewash than a genuine probe. The committee spokesman, retired Col. Mohammad Irfan Naziri reportedly said that its findings were being written but they might not be released publicly. "We're disappointed," said a U.S. official about the investigation. "They promised to do it, but they haven't yet."

Ever since Pak army's duplicitous post 9/11 u-turn of hunting with the hounds and running with the hare, while the US giving it the status of "frontline ally in the war against terror", kept giving it arms and monetary aid, this writer often asked how long this flawed equation could continue. Most of the arms Pakistan received from the US were not applicable for counter-terrorism operations and got added to Pak army's arsenal meant for use against India. It took ten years and the loss of almost 2,800 coalition casualties for the US to decide upon course-correction vis-a-vis Pak army and Inter Services Intelligence (ISI) agency. The fissures following the killing of Osama bin Laden in the meticulously planned operation by US special forces on May 2, 2011, at Abbottabad, widened over the months, causing serious problems between Pakistan's ever powerful army and its civilian leadership and yet altering the equation between them that Pak army has not again ousted the civilian government and taken charge.

By July 2011, the strain in US-Pak relations increased after US Chairman, Joint Chiefs of Staff Admiral Mike Mullen reportedly said that Pakistan government had "sanctioned" the kidnap, torture and murder of journalist Saleem Shahzad. Later in September, prior to his retirement, Admiral Mullen while addressing a US Senate panel accused Pakistan's Inter Services Intelligence (ISI) of supporting the Jalaluddin Haqqani militant network which attacked the U.S. Embassy in Kabul.

Pakistan was reported to have subsequently arrested military officers suspected of spying for US intelligence agencies and decided to expel more than a 100 US military trainers and tighten the process of granting visas to US military personnel.

That move provoked an immediate reaction of slashing US aid, already a subject of heated debate within the US administration since the killing of bin Laden. Expressing increasing frustration with Pakistan's efforts in the war against terror, US lawmakers reportedly made numerous proposals to make US aid to Pakistan conditional on more cooperation in fighting militants such as the Haqqani network, which Washington believes operate out of Pakistan and attacks US troops in Afghanistan.

Unfortunately the area from which the Haqqani network operates in the tribal northern region of Waziristan is one where the tribal overlords are far more powerful than the Pakistani government. As a consequence the long time pending demand of the US to launch a military operation and flush out the terrorists there has been met with constant denial by the Pakistan government. They simply cannot afford to open up another front to the multifaceted battle that is already ravaging the nation.

However the patience of the US and Afghanistan is being severely tested as fresh evidence of Pakistan based terror operatives causing mayhem in Kabul comes in. The Afghanistan security forces recently held 5 insurgents with 10 tonnes of explosives in the capital. National Directorate Security spokesman Shafiqullah Tahiri said that the three Pakistani and two Afghan terrorists had been caught placing explosives under bags of potatoes in a truck on Kabul's outskirts. The five had confessed to being trained by key commanders of the Pakistani Taliban, Noor Afzal and Mohammad Omar. President Hamid Karzai's response to the incident was that the Taliban may have the ability to launch attacks, to explode IEDs (improvised explosive devices), to send suicide bombers, but that they are not capable to come and take over the country and take it backward, as they had in the years before 9/11. His claims that Afghanistan has moved forward, that it will defend itself and that Afghan people will not allow the progress made to be put back or reversed is easier said than done, as recent attacks in Afghanistan have proved.

Finally, a year after the killing of OBL in Abbottabad, came a firmer financial punishment. A far-reaching legislation reported to have been introduced in the US Congress aims to deduct $50 million from the aid to Islamabad for every American killed by terrorists operating from Pakistan. "Pakistan has for decades leveraged radical terrorist groups to carry out attacks in India and Afghanistan," Congressman Dana Rohrabacher said introducing the Pakistan Terrorism Accountability Act of 2012. The legislation would require the department of defence to list all Americans killed by terrorist groups operating inside Pakistan and Afghanistan supported by elements of Pakistani government. For each person killed, $50 million would be subtracted from US foreign assistance to Pakistan and given to the victim's family. "For too long America has funded the Pakistani government, giving it free money, while elements of the ISI and Pakistan's military operate radical Islamic groups that are actively murdering Americans. Americans will not accept this," Rohrabacher, chairman of the House foreign affairs oversight and investigations subcommittee, said. Within a few days of this report followed another from Washington, that prominent US legislators urged the Obama administration to cut off every cent of its aid to Pakistan, referring to it as a "black hole where the US has 'sunk' a huge sum of $ 24 billion since 2004.

A more direct snub was awarded to the Pakistan Prime Minister Asif Ali Zardari by Obama when he initially refused to meet him on the sidelines of the NATO summit in Chicago, only to have two brief interactions with him later to offer his discontent, subsequently. The criticism was a result of the restriction that the Pakistan government has imposed over the movement of NATO supply lines through Pakistan into Afghanistan. The restriction was imposed by Pakistan as fallout of the NATO air strike last November that killed 24 Pakistani soldiers. The US has been hoping to reestablish that supply route ever since. President Obama said that they did not anticipate the supply line issue would be resolved by this summit, but that they were making diligent progress on it.

The brief meeting between Obama and Zardari took place as they were walking into the summit. Obama told Zardari that Pakistan had to be part of the solution in Afghanistan. He added that it was in their national interest to see a Pakistan that was democratic, prosperous and stable. He added that they had a common enemy in the extremists and that they needed to work through the tensions that had arisen after 10 years of military presence in the region. The second brief conversation that Obama had with Zardari was in the presence of Afghanistan President Hamid Karzai underlining the focus of the US.

Pakistan Army Chief General Ashfaq Pervez Kayani said that expectations of both the NATO and Pakistan were not met in the summit. While he did not define the expectations of either side he added that the situation would become clearer once the Pakistan delegation came back from Chicago. That there is clear unrest in both the civil and military leadership regarding US relations was further emphasized by the statement of PPP Chairman Bilawal Bhutto Zardari, the son of the late Benazir Bhutto and present Prime Minister Asif Ali Zardari. Bilawal urged

Obama to show some courage. He understood that Obama was running for reelection but added that the future of the NATO mission in Afghanistan should be more important than poll numbers. He added that Pakistan deserved an apology.

With Pakistan wanting to regain its dignity but not able to do so owing to no control over all hues of terrorists/jihadis, mostly sponsored and supported by its army and the ISI and the US being more focused on the ongoing negotiations to reopen the ground line of communication that they shut down, it is easy to see that the mutual relationship between the US and Pakistan is still far from comfortable.

The marriage was on the rocks, got rocked quite a bit, but one suspected that it would not break. And sure enough the time came in July 2012 only 14 months after the historic killing of Bin Laden and about eight months after the NATO strike killing 24 Pakistani soldiers, when Hillary Clinton finally worded an apology in consultation with the sauve Pak foreign minister Hina Rabani Khar.

Whatever the US finally decides about its presence in Afghanistan, what is very clear is that if it eventually implements the exit of its forces from there it will have a major negative impact on Afghanistan and Pakistan, whereas India will have much more to worry about. In 2006 when then US Chief of Staff General Peter Pace visited India, while addressing a select gathering at the Services Institution of India, on a query by this writer, had said that US would "stay the course in Afghanistan". It now remains to be seen how the US will achieve that aim as it must to avoid a situation where the various anti-US, anti-India terrorist groups will get more space and freedom to operate against Afghanistan and India and ironically, even against Pakistan's army and dragging Pakistan's people further towards fundamentalism and bloodshed.

As this book went to print in mid 2012, Senator Rand Paul announced that he would introduce a legislation in the US Senate to strip Pakistan of all the US aid and grant Pakistani doctor Shakil Afridi US citizenship for his help in hunting OBL. The other news was about the possibility of US deploying its 7th Fleet littoral combat ships in Southeast Asia by 2013 to defend American freedom of navigation through the Strait of Malacca, a move which if implemented will have major varying impacts on Pakistan, Afghanistan and India.

New Delhi — ANIL BHAT

CHAPTER 1

Beginnings

"I have sworn to only live free. Even if I find bitter the taste of death, I don't want to die humiliated or deceived," said Osama bin Laden, the worst and the most publicised terrorist the world suffered in recent times. As events transpired, neither did his claim prove true and nor was his wish fulfilled because after being on the run for a decade, he was effectively stalked, hunted, killed and his body committed to a watery grave.

Saudi Arabia, the country in which Osama was born and brought up, is an ancient land but very young as a state. In 1905, the Arabian Peninsula consisted of numerous Bedouin tribes. The western sides of the country, along the coastal strip surrounding the holy cities of Mecca and Medina and the city of Jeddah, were dominated and ruled by the Hashemite family. The northeastern region around Riyadh was controlled by Abdul Aziz Ibn Saud. The British supported the Hashemite rebellion against the Ottoman Turks during World War I, but later they changed sides. In 1920, Ibn Saud started expanding his kingdom conquering Mecca in 1924 and Medina in 1925. In 1932, he renamed his kingdom Saudi Arabia.

Saudi Arabia was never a kingdom of concern for the Europeans till oil was discovered there in the 1930s. This became the most valuable resource of the twentieth century lying beneath the barren desert kingdom. Saudi Arabia was a backward country which used to rely on foreign engineers, businessmen and other experts for the extraction of petroleum and manage its refinement and sale.[1]

Waking up to this discovery, caused a sea change in the Western world's view of Saudi Arabia, which was a backward country in every respect. European engineers and workers with knowledge of extracting petroleum and refining it to its consumable state started pouring in. Rather than improving the infrastructure to ameliorate the lot of common people, the country's founder, Abdul Aziz and his successors spent most of the resources in building palaces and living the high life The entry of western culture caused a conflict of interests between those wanting to preserve the conservative way of life and those who felt the need to modernise thus giving rise to a conservative Islamic movement termed as Islamism.

It was this extreme form of Muslim revival movement during Osama's formative years that inspired him and which eventually put him on the path leading towards a terrorist campaign against the government of his native land and the United States.

The wealthy bin Laden family, intimately connected with the Saudi royal family, has financial interests represented by the Saudi Bin Laden Group, a global oil and equity management conglomerate grossing $5 billion U.S. dollars annually, and one of the largest construction firms in the Islamic world, with offices in London and Geneva. According to an American diplomat, the bin Laden family owns part of Microsoft and Boeing, among other companies. This family was thrown into media spotlight mainly through the activities of one of its members, Osama bin Laden, a name that featured frequently whenever the terrorist world was discussed.

Osama bin Laden also spelled as Usama bin Ladin, whose full name was Osama bin Muhammad bin Awad bin Laden ("bin" means "son" in Arabic), also denoted his genealogy. Osama, the son of Muhammad and grandson of Awad, was born in 1957 in Riyadh, Saudi Arabia's capital. He was the only son of Muhammed bin Laden's tenth wife, Hamida al-Attas, who was of Syrian origin. He was the 17th of over 54 children born to his Yemeni father, Muhammad bin Laden.

FAMILY BACKGROUND

The family traces its origins to a poor, uneducated Hadhrami named Awad bin Laden, a Kendah tribesman from Yemen, who died in 1919. His son Mohammed bin Awad bin Laden, born in 1908, poor and uneducated, worked as a porter and emigrated from Hadhramaut, on the south coast of Yemen, to the Red Sea port of Jeddah, Saudi Arabia, prior to World War I.

Beginning his life in Jeddah as a porter, he rose to found his own company and began his construction business for the Arabian American

Oil Company and later on secured government contracts. It was his ability to work both with foreign investors and the monarchy that earned him his fortune. Set up in 1930, his construction company came to Abdul Aziz ibn Saud's attention through construction projects and was later awarded contracts for major renovations to the mosque of the Prophet in Medina and the grand Mosque in Mecca. He made his initial fortune from exclusive rights to all construction of mosques and other religious buildings not only in Saudi Arabia, but as far as Ibn Saud's influence reached. Until his death, Mohammed bin Awad bin Laden had exclusive control over restorations at the Al-Aqsa Mosque in Jerusalem. Soon the bin Laden corporate network extended far beyond construction sites. Mohammed further built his fortune as a building contractor for the Saudi royal family during the 1950s. In his later years, the bin Laden corporate network diversified its activities beyond construction, largely in foreign investment and oil. Sheikh Mohammed bin Ladin was on way to attend his 23rd wedding when his plane crashed. The sheikh, who was 59, died in the crash.

Mohammed's closeness with the monarchy was inherited by his younger bin Laden generation. His sons attended Victoria College, Alexandria, Egypt and thereby became schoolmates of King Hussein of Jordan, Zaid Al Rifai, the Khashoggi brothers (whose father was one of the king's physicians), Kamal Adham (who ran the General Intelligence Directorate under King Faisal) etc.

Despite his close association with royal families and great wealth, Mohammed bin Laden lived a relatively simple and devout life compared to many wealthy Saudis, demanding that his children observe a strict religious and moral code. He had at least 22 wives but divorced many, having only four wives at a time, in accordance with Muslim law. Muhammad fathered 54 children from his 22 wives, of which Osama bin Laden was born as the 17th child from his 10th wife. He divorced Osama's mother Hamida al-Attas soon after Osama was born. Osama was 11 years old when Muhammad died in 1967 in an airplane crash in Saudi Arabia caused by his American pilot misjudging a landing.

Following Muhammad his eldest son Salem bin Laden took over the family enterprises and changed the name from bin Laden Brothers for Contracting and Industry to Saudi Bin Laden Group, as it is now known, and continued to expand their late father's company until it employed more than 40,000 people. This group is now involved in construction, engineering, manufacturing, and telecommunications. Construction projects include airports, housing complexes, tunnels and bridges. The group is also involved in city planning and real estate development. The Saudi Bin Laden Group is Egypt's largest private foreign company and negotiated with the Lebanese government to rebuild part of central Beirut under a $50 million U.S. dollar contract. Salem bin Laden died of an accident in 1988.

Osama bin Laden's mother, Hamida al-Attas, also known as Alia Ghanem was born in 1934 in a Sunni Syrian family with two brothers and a sister. She was married to Mohammed bin Laden in Latakia, the principal port city of Syria, in 1956 and moved with him to Saudi Arabia. She was the tenth wife of Mohammed bin Laden, but it is believed that she was a concubine rather than wife.[2]

More cosmopolitan than Mohammed's first three Wahhabi[3] Saudi wives, after being divorced from Muhammad bin Laden, she remarried Mohammed al-Attas in 1958 and had other children, including Ahmad Mohammed. Osama bin Laden, her only child with Mohammad bin Laden, grew up with his mother, stepfather and their three other children.

EDUCATION AND POLITICIZATION

Raised as a devout Wahhabi, Osama was schooled in the Saudi port city, Jeddah. His family's wealth gave him access to the elite Al Thagher Model School, which he attended from 1968–1976. The school combined British style secular education with daily Islamic worship. In the 1960s, King Faisal started appointing exiled teachers from Syria, Egypt and Jordan, so that by the early seventies it was common to find members of the Muslim Brotherhood teaching at Saudi schools and universities. During that time, Osama became a member of the Brotherhood and attended its political teachings in the after-school Islamic study groups.

His introduction to Islam was on the basis of political and potentially violent activism through informal sessions run by the Al Thagher's teachers, as reported by Steve Coll in *The New Yorker*. He came under the influence of his Syrian Physical Education teacher with Islamist sympathies, who invited him to join the small Islamic study group and thus influenced him with extremely conservative ideas that advocated a return to traditional Muslim values and the merging of politics and religion. These ideas appealed to Osama's conservative bend of mind and he played an important role in the activities of the school religious committee.[4]

At King Abdul Aziz University in Jeddah, while Osama earned a degree in civil engineering in 1979, he also studied business

Muhammad bin Laden - Osama bin Laden's father

With 22 family members in Sweden in 1971. Inset right top - Osama bin Laden

administration, economics and public administration, but it is his enthusiasm in religious debates and activities, that he is remembered for. Religion being his main interest, at the university, Osama was involved in both "interpreting the Quran and jihad" and charitable work. A close friend recalls that he was most impressed by late Sayyid Qutb, author of *Ma'alim fi-l-Tariq*, or *Milestones*, one of the most influential tracts on the importance of jihad against all that is un-Islamic in the world and his brother, Muhammad Qutb, who publicised his work and lectured regularly at the university. So did another charismatic Muslim Brotherhood member, Abdallah Azzam, an Islamic scholar from Palestine who was instrumental in building pan-Islamic fervour for jihad against the Soviets in Afghanistan and in drawing Muslims (like bin Laden) from all over the Middle East to fight there.

Osama was described by a University friend, Jamal Khalifa, as extremely religious. He neither watched movies nor listened to music, because such activities were supposed to be against the teachings of the Quran. During his University career he witnessed many world-changing events, especially in 1979. First he watched the Iranian Revolution, in which Ayatollah Khomieini successfully overthrew Iran's Western supported government to install an Islamist state. Then he saw the seizure of the Grand Mosque in Mecca by radicals in Saudi Arabia and the Saudi government's response, based on its dependence on Western power. It was only with the assistance of French Special Forces that the government was able to regain control of Mecca's holiest site. Disgusted with his government's lack of ability to protect the sacred city, bin Laden began to see the royal family more and more as corrupt. In 1979 he left to fight against invading Soviets in Afghanistan.

In deference to his Islamic learning, Osama was sometimes referred to as "sheikh," connoting one who is "well versed in the classical scriptures and traditions of Islam" and was said to have been mentored by scholars such as Musa al-Qarni. Having had no formal training in Islamic jurisprudence however, he was criticised by Islamic scholars as having no standing to issue *fatwas* (religious opinions).

In 1994, the bin Laden family disowned Osama and the Saudi government revoked his passport and stripped him of his citizen, for publicly speaking out against it after it permitted U.S. troops to be based in Saudi Arabia prior to and for the 1991 Gulf War.

EARLY ADULTHOOD

Marriages

Bin Laden is reported to have married at least five women, although he later divorced the first two. Three of his wives were from distinguished families, highly educated and university lecturers and according to Wisal al Turabi, the wife of Sudan's ruler Hassan Turabi, bin Laden married them because they were "spinsters,"[5] who "were going to go without marrying in this world. So he married them for the Word of God". His known wives were:

1. **Najwa Ghanhem,** born in 1960 in Syria, also known as *Umm* Abdullah (mother of Abdullah). Osama's mother, Hamida, accompanied with Laden often spent summers at her brother Naji's home in Latakia till he was 17. Najwa Ghanem, Hamida's brother's daughter was married to Osama, as earlier promised, in 1974, when she was 14 and Osama was 18. After the birth of their first son, Abdullah, they moved from his mother's house to a building in the Al-Aziziyah district of Jeddah. She is the mother of Saad bin Laden, as well as at least 10 more children. She co-authored *Growing up bin Laden* with her son Omar. She was the youngest and least educated of Osama's wives. Her children did not like life in Khartoum and even less so the tough life in Afghanistan. She left bin Laden around 2001, about the same time as his marriage to Amal al-Sadah. She returned to Syria and was last reported living in Latakia. Her father is the brother of Osama's mother, Hamida al-Attas (born Alia Ghanem), as mentioned earlier.
2. **Khadijah Sharif** (born 1948) also known as Umm Ali (mother of Ali), was a university lecturer who studied and worked in Saudi Arabia. Umm Ali bin Laden spent holidays in Khartoum, Sudan, where Osama later settled during his years of exile—1991 to 1996. As per Wisal al Turabi, Umm Ali taught Islam to some families in Riyadh, an upscale neighborhood in Khartoum. According to Abu Jandal, bin Laden's former chief bodyguard, while living in Sudan, Umm Ali asked Osama for a divorce because she said that she "could not continue to live in an austere way and in hardship".
3. **Khairiah Sabar**, also known as Umm Hamza (mother of Hamza), a child psychologist with a PhD in Islamic studies, was reportedly Osama's favourite wife, and the most mature, being seven years

his senior. She had only one child, a son. Though frail and not beautiful, she was from "a wealthy and distinguished family," exuded a "regal quality," and "was deeply committed to the jihadi cause".

4. **Siham Sabar**, Osama's fourth wife, also known as Umm Khaled (mother of Khaled), was a teacher of Arabic grammar, who kept her university job and commuted to Saudi Arabia during their time in Sudan. News reports suggest that she was also living in bin Laden's compound in Abbottabad, Pakistan, at the time of his death.
5. **Amal Ahmed al-Sadah**. Osama's youngest wife, born in 1981 as Amal Ahmed Abdulfattah in Yemen, married Osama in 2000. However, according to a Yemeni passport, she was born in 1987. Her marriage to bin Laden was apparently part of a "political arrangement" between Osama and "an important Yemeni tribe, meant to boost al-Qaeda recruitment in Yemen". Osama authorised Rashad Mohammed Saeed Ismael to choose the bride and arrange the marriage. She was reprtedly his favourite wife at the time of his death and was in the infamous compound in Abbottabad.

News reports suggest that Siham Sabar, Khairiah Sabar and Amal al-Sadah were living with bin Laden in the compound mansion in Abbottabad, Pakistan, at the time he was attacked and killed by U.S. Special Forces. Amal al-Sadah was injured in the calf during the raid.[6]

Children

Osama bin Laden is believed to have fathered up to 24 children. The children of his wife, Najwa, included Abdallah, Omar, Saad and Mohammed. Mohammed bin Laden married the daughter of the former Al-Qaeda military chief Mohammed Atef (aka Abu Haf) in January 2001, in Khandhar, Afghanistan.

IMPORTANT MEMBERS OF BIN LADEN FAMILY

Shaikha al-Attas (born c. 1960), half-sister of Osama, daughter of Hammida Al-Attas and Muhammad al-Attas, married **Mohammed Jamal Khalifa**. He was the founder of Benevolence International Foundation, in the Philippines in 1988. During this period, Khalifa is believed to have received large donations of cash from outside the country, some of which, intelligence officials suspect, may have been funnelled to him by Al-Qaeda. He also ran the International Relations and Information Centre, by which embezzled money was funnelled to Ramzi Yousef. In 1993, his business cards were found in the Jersey City, New Jersey apartment that Yousef stayed in while he was involved with the 1993 World Trade Center bombing plot. Khalifa was first arrested on December 14, 1994, in Mountain View, California, placed in solitary confinement and the contents of his luggage were logged and edited. In 1995 Khalifa was arrested in San Francisco on charges of violating United States immigration laws. He was detained while the Justice Department tried but failed to gather enough information to charge him in connection with suspected terrorist activities. Eventually, he was deported on May 5, 1995, to Jordan, which had an outstanding warrant for him on charges stemming from the bombing of movie theatres in Amman in 1994, for which he had been under a possible death sentence, convicted in absentia. Later a new trial acquitted him. In 1996, Khalifa returned to Saudi Arabia, where he was again arrested after 9/11, but later released. After 9/11 he publicly condemned Osama bin Laden and was assassinated in 2007 in Madagascar.

Abdallah bin Osama bin Mohammed bin Awad bin Laden, son of Osama from his first wife, Najwa Ghanem, was involved in the Annandale, Virginia office of the World Assembly of Muslim Youth (WAMY), an organisation long suspected of terrorism links by the FBI. Investigative reporter Greg Palast revealed shortly after the 9/11 attacks: "On this unremarkable street, at 3411 Silver Maple Place, we located the former home of Abdullah and another brother, Omar, also an FBI suspect. It is conveniently close to WAMY....in a little room in the basement at 5613 Leesburg Pike. And here, just a couple blocks down the road at 5913 Leesburg, is where four of the hijackers that attacked New York and Washington are listed as having lived."

Abdallah, running his own firm in Jeddah called Fame Advertising, was closely watched by the Saudi government, which restricted his travel from the kingdom since 1996. Abdallah, who reportedly has never disowned his father, was known to dine occasionally with his father's half-brother, Saudi Binladin Group chairman Bakr bin Laden, at the Intercontinental Hotel in Jeddah.

Saad bin Laden (born 1979) son of Osama and Najwa, accompanied Osama on his exile to Sudan from 1991–96, and then to Afghanistan. Believed to be married to a woman from Yemen, Saad reportedly arrived in Iran in 2002, from Afghanistan with a fake Iranian passport using the name Saad Mahmoudian. He was believed to have been largely responsible for the bombing of a Tunisian synagogue on April 11, 2002. He was then implicated on May 12, 2003, for suicide bombing in Riyadh and the Morocco bombing four days later. He is also allegedly the perpetrator of the 2005 Qom bombings.

Occupying a position in Al-Qaeda, Saad accompanied his father on his exile to Sudan from 1991–96, and then followed him to Afghanistan. When Hamid Mir interviewed Osama, he noted that the 16-year-old Saad was carrying a gun and asked him whether he was following in the footsteps of his father, to which Saad replied, "No, I am following in the footsteps of my prophet".

He was believed to be married to a woman from Yemen, he was placed under house arrest in Iran and on being released is believed to have travelled to Pakistan in December 2008. On July 22, 2009, National Public Radio (NPR) reported that U.S. officials believe Saad bin Laden was killed by a CIA-administered unmanned aerial vehicle strike in Pakistan. A senior U.S. counter-terrorism official said U.S. spy agencies are "80 to 85 per cent" certain that Saad bin Laden is dead. According to NPR, American security officials were 80 to 85 percent certain Saad bin Laden was killed in a missile strike.

On July 24, 2009, *The Hindu* reported that senior Taliban spokesmen in Islamabad claimed Saad bin Laden was not killed, or even hurt, during the missile attack. According to *The Hindu*, a senior Punjabi Taliban commander claimed that he and some of his acquaintances saw him just a few days before reports of his death started circulating.

Omar bin Osama bin Mohammed bin Awad bin Laden, better known as **Omar bin Laden**, the fourth eldest son from Najwa, accompanied Osama on his exile to Sudan from 1991–96, and then to Afghanistan. He has said that he trained in Al-Qaeda camps beginning at the age of 14, but after training with Al-Qaeda for six years and sharing a house with Ayman al-Zawahiri, Al-Qaeda's second-in-command, he left it in 2000 because he did not want to be associated with killing civilians and his father did not object. He is married to Jane Felix Brown.

OMAR'S RELATIONSHIP WITH HIS FATHER AND AL-QAEDA

Some interesting, albeit contradictory observations/opinions about Osama emerge from an interview of his son, Omar by Nick Watt of ABC News, published on January 1, 2008: The family resemblance is unmistakable. Omar bin Laden is his father's son. Look past the long braids, the manicure, the leather jacket and the designer jeans, and there's a bin

Laden. No doubt we met in a Konovz café in Cairo, where Omar now lives with his English wife. They met while horseback riding in the shadow of Egypt's ancient pyramids. He is 26 years old. She's a 52-year-old grandmother. But his private life is not the most unusual thing about bin Laden. What comes out of his mouth is, in turn, bizarre, shocking, heartfelt and insightful.

"My father is very kind man," he told me. "And he very sorry when he do something like 11th September." If he's sorry, then why does Osama bin Laden order such atrocities?"Because he believe if he put two buildings down, maybe some people, little will die," explained Omar. "But millions other will (be) save (d). He believes that."Omar does not believe that. "I believe he did it the wrong," he told me in the sometimes broken English he learned from his wife.[7]

In a January 21, 2008, CNN interview, Omar said: *"I try and say to my father: 'Try to find another way to help or find your goal. This bomb, this weapons, it's not good to use it for anybody'* On the September 11 attacks he said, *"I don't think 9/11 was right personally, but it happened. I don't think ... [the war] in Vietnam was right. I don't think what's going on in Palestine is right. I don't think what's going on in Iraq is right. If we make what is right and not right, we will make a very big list."*

Omar stated that he had not been in contact with his father since leaving Afghanistan in 2000. He has said, *"The last time I saw my father was in 2000, 2001. I was in Saudi Arabia and felt a terrible sorrow for all the victims" (of the September 11 attacks). "My father has a kind heart,"* and *"I do not believe my father is dead, otherwise I would have known it; the world would have known it."* When asked whether he would tell the Americans if he found out where his father was living, he said with a smile *"Actually, I would hide him because he is my father."*

According to *Time Magazine*'s website, Omar has stated a desire to become an "ambassador of peace" between Muslims and the West. Omar has said that Osama bin Laden offered a truce to Europe in a 2004 videotape and a conditional truce with the United States in a 2006 videotape, and believes a truce is possible. *"My father is asking for a truce but I don't think there is any government (that) respects him. At the same time they do not respect him, why everywhere in the world, they want to fight him? There is a contradiction."* The truces offered in these videos of Osama bin Laden were rapidly rejected at the time.

Omar bin Laden and his mother Najwa published a book authored with Jean Sasson in late October 2009, titled *Growing Up Bin Laden*. According to media, the book details that "the kids grew up in Saudi

Omar bin Laden and Jane his wife

She took up Islam and a new name after marrying Omar - Zaina Alsabah Bin Laden

Arabia, Sudan and Afghanistan without laughter or toys, were routinely beaten, and lost their pets to painful death from poison gas experiments by their fathers' fighters." It states that Osama bin Laden tried to persuade Omar to volunteer for suicide missions and exposed his son to dangerous conditions while visiting training camps in Afghanistan and sending him to the front lines of the Afghan civil war. The book describes the family living in Jeddah without air conditioning or refrigeration, treating asthma with honeycombs and onions, and eventually moving to stone huts in Tora Bora without electricity or running water in 1996. Subsequent correspondence with the Associated Press indicated that 25 bin laden family members had moved to Iran following U.S. involvement in Afghanistan.

Widespread news coverage beginning with an Associated Press interview in Cairo, Egypt, on January 11, 2008, has featured Omar with dreadlocks and a black leather biker jacket promoting a 3,000-mile (4,800 km) horse race for peace across North Africa. The race was organised to provide money to benefit child victims of war and was described by Omar as an equine counterpart to the cancelled 2008 Paris-Dakar car rally, saying "I heard the rally was stopped because of Al-Qaida. I don't think they are going to stop me."

Mohammad bin Osama bin Laden (born c. 1983), son of Osama and Najwa, married the daughter of the late Al-Qaeda leader Mohammed Atef in January 2001, at Kandahar, Afghanistan, with footage broadcast by Al-Jazeera, where three of Osama's step-siblings and Osama's mother were in attendance.

Hamza bin Laden (1991), son of Osama. Senior member of Al-Qaeda in Afghanistan is better known as **Hamza bin Laden** or "Hamza Laden", is a son of Osama bin Laden, and a senior member of Al-Qaeda in Afghanistan. There is confusion as to whether he was the son who was killed in the 2011 Navy SEAL raid that killed his father.

In January 2001, Hamza (then ten years old), his father and other family members attended the wedding of his brother Mohammed bin Laden in the southern Afghan city of Kandahar. Video footage shot in the Ghazni province in November of the same year shows Hamza and some of his siblings handling U.S. helicopter wreckage and working alongside Taliban resistance.

In a 2005 video titled *The Mujahideen of Waziristan*, Hamza is shown participating in an Al-Qaeda assault on Pakistani security forces in the south Waziristan tribal region between Afghanistan and Pakistan. In

September 2007, it was reported that he was again in the tribal belt that encompasses the Pakistan/Afghanistan border region taking a senior role with Al-Qaeda forces.

In July 2008, *The Sun* published a translation of a poem said to be written by Hamza, which had been published on an extremist Islamic web site. In the poem Hamza wrote "Accelerate the destruction of America, Britain, France and Denmark". In response British MP Patrick Mercer dubbed Hamza bin Laden the *Crown Prince of Terror.*

Khaled bin Laden, son of Osama was killed along with his father at Abbottabad, Pakistan, May 2011.

APPEARANCE AND MANNERISM

Osama bin Laden is described as tall and thin between 6′4" and 6′6" (193–198 cm) in height and about 165 pounds (75kg) in weight. He had an olive green complexion, was left handed and used to walk with a cane. He used to wear a plain white turban instead of the traditional Saudi male headdress.

In terms of personality, bin Laden was described as a soft-spoken, mild mannered man. His soft voice was also a function of necessity. Interviews with reporters had often left his vocal cords inflamed. His bodyguard contends that Soviet chemical weapons were to blame for this malady; reporters have speculated that kidney disease was the cause.

Bin Laden's "wealth and generosity ... simplicity of ... behaviour, personal charm and ... bravery in battle" have been described as "legendary." According to Michael Scheuer, bin Laden claims to speak only Arabic. In a 1998 interview, he had the English questions translated into Arabic.[3, 4] But others, such as Rhimaulah Yusufzai and Peter Bergen, believe he understood English.

Bin Laden had been praised for his self-denial, despite his great wealth, or former great wealth. While living in Sudan, a lamb was slaughtered and cooked every evening at his home for guests, but bin Laden "ate very little himself, preferring to nibble what his guests left on their plates, believing that these abandoned morsels would gain the favor of God."

Bin Laden was said to have "consciously modeled himself" since childhood "on certain features of the Prophet's life", using "the fingers of his right hand," rather than a spoon when eating, believing it to be *Sunnah* "the way the Prophet did it, ... choosing to fast on the days that Prophet fasted, to wear clothes similar to those the Prophet may have worn, even to sit and to eat in the same postures that tradition ascribes to him."

At the same time, other actions of his were motivated by concern for appearances. He had dyed his beard to cover the streaks of gray. In 2001 he restaged a recitation of a poem intended for Arab television when he wasn't satisfied with the original video results done before an audience at his son's wedding dinner. The second take, done the next day after the wedding was over, had a handful of supporters crying in praise to simulate the noise of the full room the day before.[39] "His image management extended to asking one of the reporters, who had taken a digital snapshot, to take another picture because his neck was 'too full'."

BELIEFS AND IDEOLOGY OF OSAMA BIN LADEN

Osama bin Laden was a founder of Al-Qaeda, In conjunction with several other Islamic leaders, he issued two fatwas—in 1996 and then again in 1998—that Muslims should kill civilians and military personnel from the United States and allied countries until they withdraw support for Israel and withdraw military forces from Islamic countries. Bin Laden's ideological guides have proven to be Ibn Taymiyya, Ibn al-Qayyim al-Jawziyyah, and Sayyid Qutb. Although perceptions to the contrary abound, bin Laden has not been influenced greatly by Ibn Abd al-Wahhab or the Wahhabi school of thought, and he is not a good example of contemporary Wahhabi Islam as practiced in Saudi Arabia.

Sharia

Following an extreme form of Islamism, bin Laden believed that the restoration of God's law will set things right in the Muslim world—or as he put it, his hope that the revelation unto Mohammed will be resorted to for ruling. "When we used to follow Mohammed's revelation we were in great happiness and in great dignity, to Allah belongs the credit and praise."

He has been noted for his simplicity. He believed "the only Islamic country" in the Muslim world was Afghanistan under the rule of Mullah Omar's Taliban before that regime was overthrown in late 2001.

Differences with Wahhabi Ideology

Although bin Laden possessed views similar to Wahhabi Islam, his ideology was different in crucial ways. First, Wahhabi doctrine is very clear that only political leaders can call for *jihad*, making bin Laden's calls illegitimate. Secondly, Wahhabi Islam has positioned itself very clearly behind the Saudi royal family, in contradiction to bin Laden's repeated calls for the overthrow of the Saudi government, and it does not allow for disobedience to a ruler unless the rule commands that his/her subjects violate religious commandments. Furthermore, the basic goals of bin Laden are different. Bin Laden was most interested in "resisting western domination and combating regimes that fail to rule according to Islamic law." However, Wahhabism focuses on correct methods of worshipping God, removing idols, and ensuring adherence to Islamic law.

Wahabism : Its Origin and Meaning

Wahabism is named after its founder Muhammad ibn Abdal-Wahab who was born in1703 in Uyaynah, Central Arabia. Born in a family of religious judges and scholars, Wahab travelled extensively in other regions of Middle East. After his travels he returned to Uyaynah to preach his revolutionary ideas of religious reformation on fundamentalist lines.

Uthman ibn Mu'amar, the ruler of Uyaynah, readily embraced theWahab doctrine but on pressure from Wahab's opponents, was forced to dismiss Wahab from his territory. He then went to Ad-Diriyah, some 60 kms away which was the seat of local prince Muhammad ibn Saud since 1726. He found a willing ally in Prince Saud and thus their alliance prospered and by 1745, Wahab became famous and the prince embarked on military expeditions under the banner of Wahabism. Uyaynah came under Wahabi control. After the death of Muhammad ibn Saud, his son Abd al-Aziz worked in harmony with Wahab. He reigned from 1765 to 1803 and Wahabism flourished during his time.[8]

KEY INFLUENCES

Bin Laden's first influences were the Al Thagher teachers who offered extra-curricular Islam lessons. They were members of the Muslim Brotherhood, an Islamist political group begun in Egypt which, at that time, promoted violent means to achieve Islamic governance.

Another key influence was Abdullah Azzam, a Palestinian-born professor at King Abdul Aziz University, and a founder of Hamas, the Palestinian militant group. After the 1979 Soviet invasion of Afghanistan, Azzam solicited bin Laden to raise money and recruit Arabs to help the Muslims repel the Soviets, and he played an instrumental role in the early establishment of al-Qaeda.

Later, Ayman Al Zawahiri, the leader of Islamic Jihad in the 1980s, would play a significant part in the development of bin Laden's organisation, Al-Qaeda.

ORGANISATIONAL AFFILIATIONS

In the early 1980s, bin Laden worked with the Mujahideen, guerrillas fighting a self-proclaimed holy war to oust the Soviets from Afghanistan and from 1986–88, he himself fought.

In 1988, bin Laden formed Al-Qaeda (the Base), a militant transnational network whose original backbone was Arab Mujahideen who fought the Soviets in Afghanistan.

Ten years later, bin Laden forged the Islamic Front for Jihad against the Jews and Crusaders, a coalition of terrorist groups intending to wage war against Americans and battle their Middle Eastern military presence.

OBJECTIVES

Bin Laden expressed his ideological goals in both action and words, with his periodically videotaped public statements.

After founding Al-Qaeda, his objectives were the related goals of eliminating the Western presence in the Islamic/Arab Middle East, which included battling American ally, Israel, and overthrowing local allies of the Americans (such as the Saudis), and establishing Islamic regimes.[9]

His radical ideas were perhaps a culmination of his desire to prove that the American infidels needed to be shown the true religious path. His first wife Najwa recollects—

> One evening he [Osama] arrived home with a surprise announcement: "Najwa, We are going to travel to the United States. Our boys are going with us.
>
> I was worried about Abdul Rahman because he had become quite ill on the trip and was even suffering with a high fever. Osama arranged for us to see a doctor in Indianapolis. I relaxed after that kindly physician assured us that Abdul Rahman would soon be fine.
>
> ...I am sometimes questioned about my personal opinion of the country and its people. This is surprisingly difficult to answer. We were there for only two weeks, and for one of those weeks, Osama was away in Los Angeles to meet with some men in that city. The boys and I were left behind in Indiana with a girlfriend whom I would rather not name...
>
> My girlfriend was gracious and guided me on short trips...We even went into a big shopping mall in Indianapolis...

I came to believe that Americans were gentle and nice, people easy to deal with. As far as the country itself goes, my husband and I did not hate America, yet we did not love it.

There was one incident that reminded me that some Americans are unaware of other cultures. When the time came for us to leave America, Osama and I, along with our two boys, waited for our departure at the airport in Indiana. I was sitting quietly in my chair, relaxing, grateful that our boys were quiet....

I saw an American man gawking at me. I knew without asking that his unwelcome attention had been snagged by my black Saudi costume...

I took a side glance at Osama and saw that he was intently studying the curious man. I knew that my husband would never allow the man to approach me...

When my husband and I discussed the incident, we were both more amused than offended. That man gave us a good laugh, as it was clear he had no knowledge of veiled women...

We returned to Saudi Arabia none the worse for our experiences."

Not a particularly consequential experience, perhaps, but surely one that has a life in Osama's memory and imagination—and another indication, among many available in his life, that he should be understood not only as a self-isolating radical imbued with millenarian religious narratives, but also as a modern and globalised figure whose experiences and outlook belong very much to our age.[10]

TIMELINE OF SOME IMPORTANT YEARS IN OSAMA'S LIFE

1976: Osama enrolls as a student at the King Abdul Aziz University in Jeddah. He studies economics and management. Najwa says that her husband never studied engineering, although that is a popular myth. During these years the Muslim Middle East undergoes an Islamic awakening, called the *Salwa*, which came about after the 1967 war with Israel, when Egypt, Jordan and Syria suffered a demoralizing military defeat. Osama came of age during this political change.

1980: Osama responds to what he calls the invasion by "Godless communists" by organising charities to benefit the Afghan resistance fighters, known as the Mujahideen. His friend and mentor, Abdullah Azzam, establishes an organisation for this purpose. Osama, backed by his family wealth and the Saudi government's encouragement, becomes a chief financier.

1980: Osama begins the first of his travels to Pakistan to deliver supplies and offer assistance to his Afghan Muslim brothers. From this time on, Osama is heavily involved in the Afghan struggle against Russia, coordinating his trips to fit around his schooling and family responsibilities.

1980 or 1981: Due to his Jihadi responsibilities Osama drops out of the university, although he lacked only one semester to graduate.

1986: In order to introduce his firstborn to Jihad, Osama takes his eight-year-old son, Abdullah, with him to the fighting base Jaji. He receives unexpected criticism from family and other Jihadi leaders for exposing his young son to the danger of war. This is only the first of many instances when Osama will push his unenthusiastic sons to the forefront of his personal passion for Jihad.

1988: In August of 1988, Osama turns to a global crusade, founding Al-Qaeda al- Askariya (translates to "the military base," later shortened to Al- Qaeda, "the base," or "the foundation"). By this time Osama has achieved a high status in the Arab press. Due to Osama's prominence, fighters for his organisation are easily recruited.

1990: On August 2, 1990, Saddam Hussein invades Kuwait. Osama approaches the Saudi royal family, volunteering his military expertise and holy warriors to fight and defeat Saddam Hussein. Confident of his ability to convince the royal family of the wisdom of his plan, Osama prepares his forces to defend the kingdom.

1990: The Saudi government allows the United States to form a coalition of many countries, including many Muslim countries, to battle Saddam Hussein. The United States begins sending troops to Saudi Arabia.

1990: Osama is so enraged at what he considers a royal slight in allowing infidel troops on Islamic holy land that he begins to speak out and write treatises against the Saudi regime, leading to an end to their previous friendly relationship.

NOTES

[1] T.R. Mockaitis, *Osama bin Laden, A Biography*, Pentagon Security International, New Delhi, 2011.

[2] http://www.enotes.com/topic/Hamida_al-Attas#cite_note-CNN2002-5 and a transcript of CNN.com (Accessed January 22, 2012).

[3] Wahhabi: Wahhabism is a religious movement or a branch of Islam. It was developed by an 18th century Muslim theologian (Muhammad ibn Abd al-Wahhab) (1703–1792) from Najd, Saudi Arabia. Ibn Abdul Al-Wahhab advocated purging Islam of what he considered to be impurities and innovations. Wahhabism is the dominant form of Islam in Saudi Arabia. http://en.wikipedia.org/wiki/Wahhabi (Accessed January 22, 2012).

[4] T.R. Mockaitis, *Osama bin Laden, A Biography,* Pentagon Security International, New Delhi, 2011. See also http://en.wikipedia.org/wiki/Personal_life_of_Osama_bin_Laden (Accessed January 22, 2012).

[5] A spinster, or old maid, is an older, childless woman who has never been married. For a woman to be identified as a spinster, age is critical. A "spinster" is not simply a "single" woman, but a woman who has not formed a human pair bond by the time she is approaching or has reached menopause and the end of her reproductive lifespan, at http://en.wikipedia.org/wiki/Spinster (Accessed January 22, 2012).

[6] http://en.wikipedia.org/wiki/Personal_life_of_Osama_bin_Laden (Accessed January 22, 2012).

[7] N. Watt (2008), "Bin Laden's Son Wants to Make up for Father's Mistake," at http://abcnews.go.com/GMA/story?id=4168151&page=1#.TxvXo4GHrEE (Accessed January 22, 2012).

[8] R. Sharma, *Global Jihad,* Kaveri Books, New Delhi, 2006.

[9] http://terrorism.about.com/od/groupsleader1/p/OsamabinLaden.htm. (Accessed January 22, 2012).

[10] S. Coll (2009) "Osama in America: The Final Answer," at http://www.newyorker.com/online/blogs/stevecoll/2009/06/osama-in-america-the-final-answer.html (Accessed January 22, 2012).

CHAPTER 2

Al-Qaeda

Towards the end of the Soviet military mission in Afghanistan, some *Mujahideen* wanted to expand their operations to include Islamist struggles in other parts of the world, such as Israel and Kashmir. A number of overlapping and interrelated organisations were formed, to further those aspirations. One of these was the organisation that would eventually be called Al-Qaeda. Al-Qaeda alternatively spelled al-Qaida and sometimes al-Qa'ida, is a global militant Sunni Islamist group calling for global Jihad was found by Osama bin Laden with an initial meeting held on August 11, 1988.[1]

Osama bin Laden established this organisation to bring together Arabs who fought in Afghanistan against the Soviet Union and helped finance, recruit, transport, and train Sunni Islamic extremists for the Afghan resistance. Their goal is to establish a pan-Islamic Caliphate throughout the world by working with allied Islamic extremist groups to overthrow regimes it deems "non-Islamic" and expelling Westerners and non-Muslims from Muslim countries—particularly Saudi Arabia. Al-Qaeda also known as "the World Islamic Front for Jihad against the Jews and Crusaders" from the year 1998 says, it was the duty of all Muslims to kill U.S. citizens—civilian or military—and their allies everywhere. Al-Qaeda merged with Egyptian Islamic Jihad (Al-Jihad) in June 2001.

Al-Qaeda is a multi-national organisation, with members from almost all countries and with a worldwide presence. Senior leaders in the organisation are also senior leaders in other terrorist organisations, including those designated by the Department of State as foreign terrorist organisations, such as the Egyptian al-Gama'at al-Islamiyya and the Egyptian al-Jihad. Al-Qaeda's goal is radicalisation of existing Islamic groups and the creation of radical Islamic groups where none exist. Its ideology is "unite all Muslims and to establish a government which follows the rule of the Caliphs." Bin Laden has stated that the only way to establish the Caliphate is by force. Therefore, it suggests to overthrow nearly all Muslim governments, which are viewed as corrupt by them and to drive Western influence from those countries which will eventually result to abolish state boundaries.

Al-Qaeda instigated the sectarian violence among Muslims and was completely intolerant of the non-Sunni branches of Islam and declared them by calling them "takfir", which means a non-believer of Islam and thus excommunicated from the Muslim community. Al-Qaeda leaders regard liberal Muslims, Shias, Sufis and other sects as apostates and sometimes issue attacks on their mosques and gatherings. Examples of sectarian attacks include the Yazidi community bombings, Sadr City bombings, Ashoura Massacre and April 2007 Baghdad bombings.

Al-Qaeda supports Muslim fighters in Afghanistan, Bosnia, Chechnya, Tajikistan, Somalia, Yemen and Kosovo. It also trains members of terrorist organisations from such diverse countries as the Philippines, Algeria and Eritrea.

Al-Qaeda has attacked civilian and military targets in various countries, such as the September 11 attacks, 1998 U.S. embassy bombings and 2002 Bali bombings. The U.S. government responded by launching the War on Terror. Al-Qaeda has continued to exist and grow through the decade from 2001 to 2011.

Characteristic techniques include suicide attacks and simultaneous bombings of different targets. Activities ascribed to it may involve members of the movement, who have taken a pledge of loyalty to Osama bin Laden, or the much more numerous "al-Qaeda-linked" individuals who have undergone training in one of its camps in Afghanistan, Pakistan, Iraq or Sudan, but not taken any pledge.

MYSTERY BEHIND THE NAME AL-QAEDA

The etymology of the name Al-Qaeda stands for the Arabic noun *qâ'idah,* which means *foundation* or *basis* and the initial *al-* is the Arabic definite article *the,* which refers to the military base. Bin Laden explained the origin of the term Al-Qaeda in an interview with Al Jazeera journalist Tayseer Alouni in October 2001. According to him, the name "Al-Qaeda" was established a long time ago by mere chance. He said that "the late Abu Ebeida El-Banashiri established the training camps for our Mujahedeen against Russia's terrorism. We used to call the training camp Al-Qaeda [meaning "the base" in English]. And the name stayed."

There are also some controversial writings related to the name Al-Qaeda. Shortly before the premature death of the former British Foreign Secretary Robin Cook told to the House of Commons that "Al-Qaeda" was the name given to the computer database of the international Mujahideen and armed smugglers used by the CIA and Saudis to funnel arms, and money into Soviet-occupied Afghanistan. The *Guardian* article written by Robin Cook quotes as:

"Bin Laden was, though, a product of a monumental miscalculation by western security agencies. Throughout the 80s he was armed by the CIA and funded by the Saudis to wage jihad against the Russian occupation of Afghanistan. Al-Qaeda, literally "the database", was originally the computer file of the thousands of Mujahideen who were recruited and trained with help from the CIA to defeat the Russians. Inexplicably, and with disastrous consequences, it never appears to have occurred to Washington that once Russia was out of the way, Bin Laden's organisation would turn its attention to the west."[2]

IDEOLOGY

The radical Islamist movement in general and Al-Qaeda in particular developed during the Islamic revival and Islamist movement of the last three decades of the 20th century, along with less extreme movements.

Some have argued that "without the writings" of Islamic author and thinker Sayyid Qutb, "al-Qaeda would not have existed." Qutb preached that because of the lack of *sharia* law, the Muslim world was no longer Muslim, having reverted to pre-Islamic ignorance known as *jahiliyyah.*

To restore Islam, he said a vanguard movement of righteous Muslims was needed to establish "true Islamic states", implement *sharia,* and rid the Muslim world of any non-Muslim influences, such as concepts like socialism and nationalism. Enemies of Islam in Qutb's view included "treacherous Orientalists" and "world Jewry", who plotted "conspiracies" and "wickedly" opposed Islam.

In the words of Mohammed Jamal Khalifa, a close college friend of bin Laden:

> "Islam is different from any other religion; it's a way of life. We (Khalifa and bin Laden) were trying to understand what Islam has to say about how we eat, who we marry, how we talk. We read

Mohammed Jamal Khalifa

Abdel Bari Atwan

Sayyid Qutb. He was the one who most affected our generation."

Qutb had an even greater influence on bin Laden's mentor and another leading member of Al-Qaeda, Ayman al-Zawahiri. Zawahiri's uncle and maternal family patriarch, Mafouz Azzam, was Qutb's student, then protégé, then personal lawyer, and finally executor of his estate—one of the last people to see Qutb before his execution. "Young Ayman al-Zawahiri heard again and again from his beloved uncle Mahfouz about the purity of Qutb's character and the torment he had endured in prison."[3] Zawahiri paid homage to Qutb in his work *Knights under the Prophet's Banner.*[4]

One of the most powerful of Qutb's ideas was that many who said they were Muslims were not. Rather, they were apostates. That not only gave jihadists "a legal loophole around the prohibition of killing another Muslim," but made "it a religious obligation to execute" these self-professed Muslims. These alleged apostates included leaders of Muslim countries, since they failed to enforce *sharia* law.

The fatwa on terrorism is regarded as a direct assault on the ideology of Al-Qaeda which dismantles it from the sources of Quran and *sunnah*.

RELIGIOUS COMPATIBILITY

Abdel Bari Atwan writes that: While the leadership's own theological platform is essentially Salafi, the organisation's umbrella is sufficiently wide to encompass various schools of thought and political leanings. Al-Qaeda counts among its members and supporters people associated with Wahhabism, Shafi'ism, Malikism, and Hanafism. There are even some whose beliefs and practices are directly at odds with Salafism, such as Yunis Khalis, one of the leaders of the Afghan Mujahideen. He is a mystic who visits tombs of saints and seeks their blessings—practices inimical to bin Laden's Wahhabi-Salafi school of thought. The only exception to this pan-Islamic policy is Shi'ism. Al-Qaeda seems implacably opposed to it, as it holds Shi'ism to be heresy. In Iraq it has openly declared war on the Badr Brigades, who have fully cooperated with the U.S., and now considers even Shi'i civilians to be legitimate targets for acts of violence.

HISTORY

Researchers have described five distinct phases in the development of Al-Qaeda: the beginning in the late 1980s, the "wilderness" period in 1990–96, its "heyday" in 1996–2001, the network period of 2001–05, and a period of fragmentation from 2005 to today.

Jihad in Afghanistan

Mujahideen leader walks among his fighters

The origins of Al-Qaeda as a network inspiring terrorism around the world and training operatives can be traced to the Soviet War in Afghanistan (December 1979–February 1989).[5] The U.S. viewed the conflict in Afghanistan, with the Afghan Marxists and allied Soviet troops on one side and the native Afghan *Mujahideen*, some of whom were radical Islamic militants, on the other, as a blatant case of Soviet expansionism and aggression. The U.S. channeled funds through Pakistan's Inter-Services Intelligence agency to the Afghan Mujahideen fighting the Soviet occupation in a CIA program called Operation Cyclone.[6]

At the same time, a growing number of Arab *Mujahideen* joined the *jihad* against the Afghan Marxist regime, facilitated by international Muslim organisations, particularly the Maktab al-Khidamat,[62] whose funds came from some of the $600 million a year donated to the *jihad* by the Saudi Arabia government and individual Muslims—particularly independent Saudi businessmen who were approached by bin Laden.[7]

Maktab al-Khidamat (MAK), or the "Services Office", a Muslim organisation founded in 1980 to raise and channel funds and recruit foreign *Mujahideen* for the war against the Soviets in Afghanistan, was established by Abdullah Yusuf Azzam, a Palestinian Islamic scholar and member of the Muslim Brotherhood, and bin Laden in Peshawar, Pakistan, in 1984.

Omar Abdel-Rahman

From 1986, it began to set up a network of recruiting offices in the U.S., the hub of which was the Al Kifah Refugee Center at the Farouq Mosque in Brooklyn's Atlantic Avenue. Among notable figures at the Brooklyn center were "double agent" Ali Mohamed, whom FBI special agent Jack Cloonan called "bin Laden's first trainer,"[8] and "Blind Sheikh" Omar Abdel-Rahman, a leading recruiter of *Mujahideen* for Afghanistan. Al-Qaeda evolved from the MAK.

MAK organised guest houses in Peshawar, near the Afghan border, and gathered supplies for the construction of paramilitary training camps to prepare foreign recruits for the Afghan war front. Azzam persuaded bin Laden to join MAK. Bin Laden became a "major financier" of the *Mujahideen*, spending his own money and using his connections with "the Saudi royal family and the petro-billionaires of the Gulf" in order to improve public opinion of the war and raise more funds. Beginning in 1987, Azzam and bin Laden started creating camps inside Afghanistan.

U.S. government financial support for the Afghan Islamic militants was substantial. Aid to Gulbuddin Hekmatyar, an Afghan *Mujahideen* leader and founder and leader of the Hezb-e Islami radical Islamic militant faction, alone amounted "by the most conservative estimates" to $600 million. Hekmatyar "worked closely" with bin Laden in the early 1990s. In addition to hundreds of millions of dollars of American aid, Hekmatyar also received the lion's share of aid from the Saudis. There is evidence that the CIA supported Hekmatyar's drug trade activities by giving him immunity for his opium trafficking that financed operation of his militant faction.

The MAK and foreign *Mujahideen* volunteers, or "Afghan Arabs", did not play a major role in the war. While over 250,000 Afghan *Mujahideen* fought the Soviets and the communist Afghan government, it is estimated that were never more than 2,000 foreign *Mujahideen* in the field at any one time.[9] Nonetheless, foreign *Mujahideen* volunteers came from 43 countries, and the total number that participated in the Afghan movement between 1982 and 1992 is reported to have been 35,000. Bin Laden was one of the key players in organising training camps for the foreign Muslim volunteers.[10]

The Soviet Union finally withdrew from Afghanistan in 1989. To the surprise of many, Mohammad Najibullah's communist Afghan government hung on for three more years, before being overrun by elements of the *Mujahideen*. With *Mujahideen* leaders unable to agree on a structure for governance, chaos ensued, with constantly reorganising alliances fighting for control of ill-defined territories, leaving the country devastated.

Expanding operations

Towards the end of the Soviet military mission in Afghanistan, some *Mujahideen* wanted to expand their operations to include Islamist struggles in other parts of the world, such as Israel and Kashmir. A number of overlapping and interrelated organisations were formed, to further those aspirations.

One of these was the organisation that would eventually be called Al-Qaeda, formed by bin Laden with an initial meeting held on August 11, 1988.

Formation and structuring of Al-Qaeda from notes of a meeting of bin Laden and others on August 20, 1988 indicate that Al-Qaeda was a formal group by that time: "basically an organized Islamic faction, its goal is to lift the word of God, to make His religion victorious."

According to Wright, the group's real name wasn't used in public pronouncements because "its existence was still a closely held secret."[11] His research suggests that Al-Qaeda was formed on August 11, 1988, in a meeting between "several senior leaders" of Egyptian Islamic Jihad, Abdullah Azzam, and bin Laden, where it was agreed to join bin Laden's money with the expertise of the Islamic Jihad organisation and take up the jihadist cause elsewhere after the Soviets withdrew from Afghanistan.

Bin Laden wished to establish non-military operations in other parts of the world; Azzam, in contrast, wanted to remain focussed on military campaigns. After Azzam was assassinated in 1989, the MAK split, with a significant number joining bin Laden's organisation.

In November 1989, Ali Mohamed, a former special forces Sergeant stationed at Fort Bragg, North Carolina, left military service and moved to California. He traveled to Afghanistan and Pakistan and became "deeply involved with bin Laden's plans."

A year later, on 8 November 1990, the FBI raided the New Jersey home of Ali Mohammed's associate El Sayyid Nosair, discovering a great deal of evidence of terrorist plots, including plans to blow up New York City skyscrapers. Nosair was eventually convicted in connection to the 1993 World Trade Center bombing, and for the murder of Rabbi Meir Kahane on November 5, 1990. In 1991, Ali Mohammed is said to have helped orchestrate bin Laden's relocation to Sudan.[12]

Organisation

Al-Qaeda's management philosophy has been described as "centralization of decision and decentralization of execution." Following the War on Terror, it is thought that Al-Qaeda's leadership has "become geographically isolated", leading to the "emergence of decentralized leadership" of regional groups using the al-Qaeda "brand".[13]

Many terrorism experts do not believe that the global jihadist movement is driven at every level by bin Laden and his followers. Although bin Laden still had huge ideological sway over some Muslim extremists, experts argue that Al-Qaeda has fragmented over the years into a variety of disconnected regional movements that have little connection with each other. Marc Sageman, a psychiatrist and former Central Intelligence Agency (CIA) officer, said that Al-Qaeda would now just be a "loose label for a movement that seems to target the West". "There is no umbrella organisation. We like to create a mythical entity called [Al-Qaeda] in our minds, but that is not the reality we are dealing with."[14]

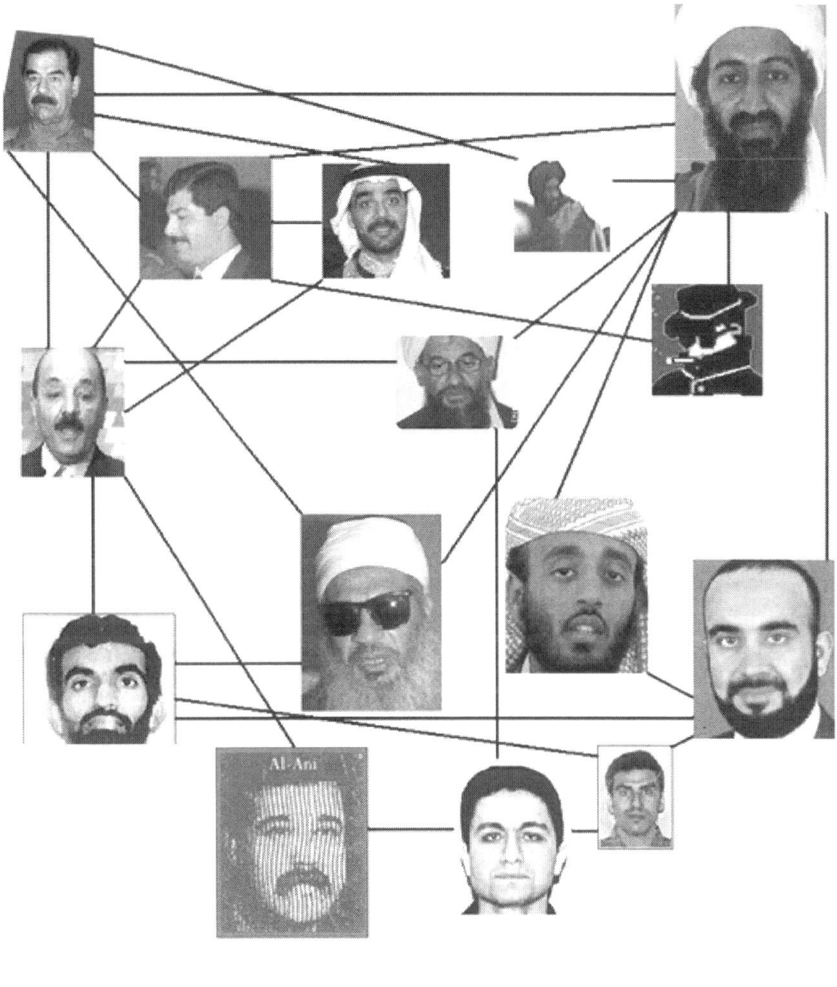

The Ring of Terror led by Osama bin Laden

Indeed this view mirrors the account given by Osama bin Laden in his October 2001 interview by Tayseer Allouni:

"...this matter isn't about any specific person and...is not about the al-Qai`dah Organization. We are the children of an Islamic Nation, with Prophet Muhammad as its leader, our Lord is one...and all the true believers [mu'mineen] are brothers. So the situation isn't like the West portrays it, that there is an "organization" with a specific name (such as "al-Qai`dah") and so on. That particular name is very old. It was born without any intention from us. Brother Abu Ubaida... created a military base to train the young men to fight against the vicious, arrogant, brutal, terrorizing Soviet empire... So this place was called "The Base" ["Al-Qai`dah"], as in a training base, so this name grew and became. We aren't separated from this nation. We are the children of a nation, and we are an inseparable part of it, and from those public demonstrations which spread from the far east, from the Philippines, to Indonesia, to Malaysia, to India, to Pakistan, reaching Mauritania... and so we discuss the conscience of this nation."

Others, however, see Al-Qaeda as an integrated network that is strongly led from the Pakistani tribal areas and has a powerful strategic purpose. Bruce Hoffman, a terrorism expert at Georgetown University said, "It amazes me that people don't think there is a clear adversary out there, and that our adversary does not have a strategic approach."

Al-Qaeda has the following direct franchises:

- Al-Qaeda in the Arabian Peninsula, which comprises
  - Al-Qaeda in Saudi Arabia, and
  - Islamic Jihad of Yemen
- Al-Qaeda in Iraq
- Al-Qaeda Organization in the Islamic Maghreb
- Al-Shabaab (Mujahideen Youth Movement) in Somalia
- Egyptian Islamic Jihad
- Libyan Islamic Fighting Group
- East Turkestan Islamic Movement in Xinjiang, China

Strategy

On March 11, 2005, *Al-Quds Al-Arabi* published extracts from Saif al-Adel's document "Al Quaeda's Strategy to the Year 2020".[15] Abdel Bari Atwan summarises this strategy as comprising five stages:

1. Provoke the United States into invading a Muslim country.
2. Incite local resistance to occupying forces.

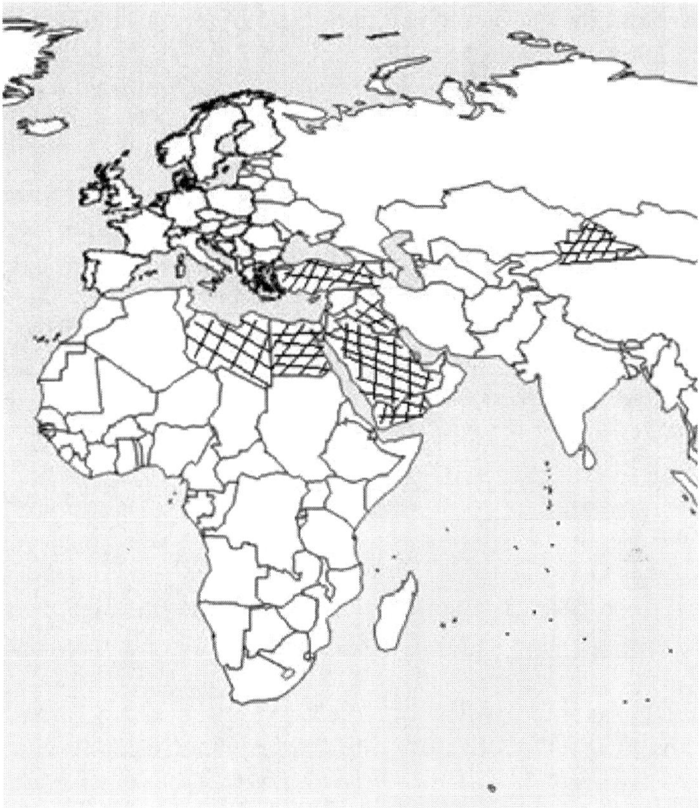

Al Qaeda's direct franchises

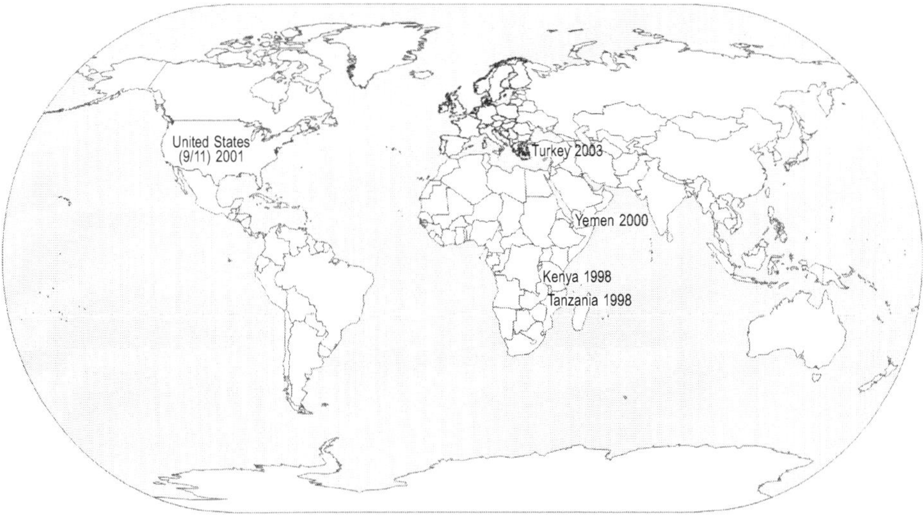

Major AL Qaeda Attacks

Sketches by Cashmere

3. Expand the conflict to neighboring countries, and engage the U.S. in a long war of attrition.
4. Convert Al-Qaeda into an ideology and set of operating principles that can be loosely franchised in other countries without requiring direct command and control, and via these franchises incite attacks against countries allied with the U.S. until they withdraw from the conflict, as happened with the 2004 Madrid train bombings, but which did not have the same effect with the 7 July 2005 London bombings.
5. The U.S. economy will finally collapse under the strain of too many engagements in too many places, similarly to the Soviet war in Afghanistan. Arab regimes supported by the U.S. will then collapse, and a Wahhabi Caliphate will be installed across the region.

Leadership

Information mostly acquired from Jamal al-Fadl provided American authorities with a rough picture of how the group was organised. While the veracity of the information provided Osama bin Laden was the most historically notable emir, or commander, and Senior Operations Chief of Al-Qaeda prior to his assassination on May 1, 2011 by U.S. forces. Ayman al-Zawahiri, Al-Qaeda's Deputy Operations Chief prior to bin Laden's death, has assumed the role of commander as announced by Al-Qaeda on June 16, 2011, replacing Saif al-Adel, who served as interim commander.[17]

As of August 6, 2010, the chief of operations was considered to be Adnan Gulshair el Shukrijumah, replacing Khalid Sheikh Mohammed.

Bin Laden was advised by a Shura Council, which consists of senior Al-Qaeda members, estimated by Western officials at about 20–30 people. Abu Musab al-Zarqawi was the senior leader of Al-Qaeda in Iraq, but his safe house was hit by U.S. missiles in a targeted killing, and Abu Ayyub al-Masri succeeded him who was also later killed by U.S. and Iraqi forces on 18 April 2010.

Al-Qaeda's network was built from scratch as a conspiratorial network that draws on leaders of all its regional nodes "as and when necessary to serve as an integral part of its high command."[18]

- The Military Committee is responsible for training operatives, acquiring weapons, and planning attacks.
- The Money/Business Committee funds the recruitment and training of operatives through the *hawala* banking system. U.S.-

Osama bin Laden

Ayman al Zawahiri

led efforts to eradicate the sources of terrorist financing were most successful in the year immediately following September 11; Al-Qaeda continues to operate through unregulated banks, such as the 1,000 or so *hawaladars* in Pakistan, some of which can handle deals of up to $10 million. It also provides air tickets and false passports, pays Al-Qaeda members, and oversees profit-driven businesses. In the 9/11 Commission Report, *it was estimated that Al-Qaeda required $30 million-per-year to conduct its operations.*

- The Law Committee reviews Sharia law, and decides whether particular courses of action conform to the law.
- The Islamic Study/*Fatwah* Committee issues religious edicts, such as an edict in 1998 telling Muslims to kill Americans.
- In the late 1990s there was a publicly known Media Committee, which ran the now-defunct newspaper *Nashrat al Akhbar (Newscast)* and handled public relations.
- In 2005, Al-Qaeda formed As-Sahab, a media production house, to supply its video and audio materials.

Command structure

When asked about the possibility of al-Qaeda's connection to the July 7, 2005 London bombings in 2005, Metropolitan Police Commissioner Sir Ian Blair said: "Al-Qaeda is not an organization. Al-Qaeda is a way of working ... but this has the hallmark of that approach ... Al-Qaeda clearly has the ability to provide training ... to provide expertise ... and I think that is what has occurred here."[19]

However, on August 13, 2005, *The Independent*, quoting police and MI5 investigations, reported that the 7 July bombers acted independently of an Al-Qaeda terror mastermind someplace abroad.

What exactly Al-Qaeda is, or was, remains in dispute. Author and journalist Adam Curtis contends that the idea of Al-Qaeda as a formal organisation is primarily an American invention. Curtis contends the name "Al-Qaeda" was first brought to the attention of the public in the 2001 trial of bin Laden and the four men accused of the 1998 U.S. embassy bombings in East Africa:

The reality was that bin Laden and Ayman al-Zawahiri had become the focus of a loose association of disillusioned Islamist militants who were attracted by the new strategy. But there was no organisation. These were militants who mostly planned their own operations and looked to bin Laden for funding and assistance. He was not their commander. There is also no evidence that bin Laden used the term "Al-Qaeda" to refer to the name of a group until after 11 September, when he realised that this was the term the Americans had given it.[20]

As a matter of law, the U.S. Department of Justice needed to show that bin Laden was the leader of a criminal organisation in order to charge him *in absentia* under the Racketeer Influenced and Corrupt Organizations Act, also known as the RICO statutes. The name of the organisation and details of its structure were provided in the testimony of Jamal al-Fadl, who said he was a founding member of the organisation and a former employee of bin Laden.[21] Questions about the reliability of al-Fadl's testimony have been raised by a number of sources because of his history of dishonesty, and because he was delivering it as part of a plea bargain agreement after being convicted of conspiring to attack U.S. military establishments.[22] Sam Schmidt, one of his defense lawyers, said:

"There were selective portions of al-Fadl's testimony that I believe was false, to help support the picture that he helped the Americans join together. I think he lied in a number of specific testimony about a unified image of what this organisation was. It made Al-Qaeda the new Mafia or the new Communists. It made them identifiable as a group and therefore made it easier to prosecute any person associated with Al-Qaeda for any acts or statements made by bin Laden."

Field operatives

The exact number of individuals in the organisation who have undergone proper military training, and are capable of commanding insurgent forces, are largely unknown. In 2006, it was estimated that Al-Qaeda had several thousand commanders embedded in 40 different countries.[23] As of 2009, was believed that no more than 200–300 members were still active commanders.

According to the award-winning 2004 BBC documentary *The Power of Nightmares*, Al-Qaeda was so weakly linked together that it was hard to say it existed apart from bin Laden and a small clique of close associates. The lack of any significant numbers of convicted Al-Qaeda members, despite a large number of arrests on terrorism charges, was cited by the documentary as a reason to doubt whether a widespread entity that met the description of Al-Qaeda existed.

Insurgent forces

According to Robert Cassidy, Al-Qaeda controls two separate forces deployed alongside insurgents in Iraq and Pakistan. The first, numbering in the tens of thousands, was "organized, trained, and equipped as insurgent combat forces" in the Soviet-Afghan war. It was made up primarily of foreign *Mujahideen* from Saudi Arabia and Yemen. Many went on to fight in Bosnia and Somalia for global *jihad*. Another group, with strength of approximately 10,000, lives in western states and has received rudimentary combat training.

Other analysts have described Al-Qaeda's rank and file as changing from being "predominantly Arab," in its first years of operation, to "largely Pakistani," as of 2007. It has been estimated that 62 per cent of Al-Qaeda members have university education.[24]

Financing

The majority of financing for Al-Qaeda in the 1990s and 2000s came from the personal wealth of Osama bin Laden which was estimated at around $300 million. Other sources of income include the heroin trade and donations from supporters.[25]

Formation and structuring of Al-Qaeda

By 1988, bin Laden had split from Maktab al-Khidamat. While Azzam acted as support for Afghan fighters, bin Laden wanted a more military role. One of the main points leading to the split and the creation of Al-Qaeda was Azzam's insistence that Arab fighters be integrated among the Afghan fighting groups instead of forming a separate fighting force. Notes of a meeting of bin Laden and others on August 20, 1988, indicate Al-Qaeda was a formal group by that time: "Basically an organized Islamic faction, its goal is to lift the word of God, to make His religion victorious." A list of requirements for membership itemised the following: listening ability, good manners, obedience, and making a pledge (*bayat*) to follow one's superiors.

According to Wright, the group's real name wasn't used in public pronouncements because "its existence was still a closely held secret." His research suggests that Al-Qaeda was formed at an August 11, 1988, meeting between "several senior leaders" of Egyptian Islamic jihad, Abdullah Azzam, and bin Laden, where it was agreed to join Osama bin Laden's money with the expertise of the Islamic Jihad organisation and take up the jihadist cause elsewhere after the Soviets withdrew from Afghanistan.

Following the Soviet Union's withdrawal from Afghanistan in February 1989, Osama bin Laden returned to Saudi Arabia in 1990 as a hero of jihad, who along with his Arab legion "had brought down the mighty superpower" of the Soviet Union.[26]

He was set to take on the next superpower, the United States. Bin Laden's offer was rebuffed, and after the Saudi monarchy invited the deployment of U.S. troops in Saudi territory,[27] Osama publicly denounced Saudi Arabia's dependence on the U.S. military. Osama believed the presence of foreign troops in the "land of the two mosques" (Mecca and Medina) profaned sacred soil. Bin Laden's criticism of the Saudi monarchy led that government to make an attempt to silence him.

Shortly after Saudi Arabia invited U.S. troops into Saudi Arabia, bin Laden turned his attention to attacks on the West. On November 8, 1990, the FBI raided the New Jersey home of El Sayyid Nosair, an associate of Al-Qaeda operative Ali Mohamed, discovering copious evidence of terrorist plots, including plans to blow up New York City skyscrapers.

This marked the earliest discovery of Al-Qaeda terrorist plans outside of Muslim countries. It was here that the organization stepped out of the Muslim world and targeted the United States directly. Nosair was eventually convicted in connection to the 1993 World Trade Center bombing, and later admitted guilt for the murder of Rabbi Meir Kahane in New York on November 5, 1990.

Bin Laden continued to speak publicly against the Saudi government for harbouring American troops, for which the Saudis banished him. In what was to become an often repeated pattern of switching countries of residence he went to live in exile in Sudan, in 1992, in a deal brokered by Ali Mohamed.[28]

ACTIVITIES

In Iraq

Al-Qaeda is Sunni, and often attacked the Iraqi Shia majority in an attempt to incite sectarian violence and greater chaos in the country.[29] Al-Zarqawi purportedly declared an all-out war on Shiites while claiming responsibility for Shiite mosque bombings.[30]The same month, a statement claiming to be by AQI rejected as "fake" a letter allegedly written by al-Zawahiri, in which he appears to question the insurgents' tactic of indiscriminately attacking Shiites in Iraq. In a December 2007 video, al-Zawahiri defended the Islamic State in Iraq, but distanced himself from the attacks against civilians committed by "hypocrites and traitors existing among the ranks".[31]

U.S. and Iraqi officials accused AQI of trying to slide Iraq into a full-scale civil war between Iraq's majority Shiites and minority Sunni Arabs, with an orchestrated campaign of civilian massacres and a number of provocative attacks against high-profile religious targets.[32]

With attacks such as the 2003 Imam Ali Mosque bombing, the 2004 Day of Ashura and Karbala and Najaf bombings, the 2006 first al-Askari Mosque bombing in Samarra, the deadly single-day series of bombings in which at least 215 people were killed in Baghdad's Shiite district of Sadr City, and the second al-Askari bombing in 2007.

They provoked Shiite militias to unleash a wave of retaliatory attacks, resulting in death squad-style killings and spiraling further sectarian violence which escalated in 2006 and brought Iraq to the brink of violent anarchy in 2007.[33] In 2008, sectarian bombings blamed on Al-Qaeda killed at least 42 people at the Imam Husayn Shrine in Karbala in March, and at least 51 people at a bus stop in Baghdad in June.

Somalia and Yemen

The percentage of terrorist attacks in the West originating from the Afghanistan–Pakistan (AfPak) border declined considerably from almost 100 per cent to 75 per cent in 2007 and to 50 per cent in 2010, as Al-Qaeda shifted to Somalia and Yemen.[34] While Al-Qaeda leaders are hiding in the tribal areas along the AfPak border, the middle-tier of the movement display heightened activity in Somalia and Yemen. "We know that South Asia is no longer their primary base," a U.S. defense agency source said. "They are looking for a hideout in other parts of the world, and continue to expand their organisation".

In Somalia, Al-Qaeda agents closely collaborate with the Shahab group, actively recruit children for suicide-bomber training, and export young people to participate in military actions against Americans at the AfPak border. In January 2009, Al-Qaeda's division in Saudi Arabia merged with its Yemeni wing to form Al-Qaeda in the Arabian Peninsula. Centered in Yemen, the group takes advantage of the country's poor economy, demography and domestic security.

In August 2009, they made the first assassination attempt against a member of the Saudi royal dynasty in decades. President Obama asked his Yemen counterpart Ali Abdullah Saleh to ensure closer cooperation with the U.S. in the struggle against the growing activity of Al-Qaeda in Yemen, and promised to send additional aid. Because of the wars in Iraq and Afghanistan, the U.S. is unable to pay sufficient attention to Somalia and Yemen, which may cause the U.S. some serious problems in the near future.[35] Al-Qaeda in the Arabian Peninsula claimed responsibility for the 2009 bombing attack on Northwest Airlines Flight 253 by Umar Farouk Abdulmutallab. The group released photos of Abdulmutallab smiling in a white shirt and white Islamic skullcap, with the Al-Qaeda in Arabian Peninsula banner in the background.

Africa

An article on the front page of *The Guardian Weekly* on the eighth anniversary of the September 11 attacks claimed that Al-Qaeda's activity is "increasingly dispersed to 'affiliates' or 'franchises' in Yemen and North Africa."

Al-Qaeda involvement in Africa has included a number of bombing attacks in North Africa, as well as supporting parties in civil wars in Eritrea and Somalia. From 1991 to 1996, bin Laden and other Al-Qaeda leaders were based in Sudan.

Islamist rebels in the Sahara calling themselves Al-Qaeda in the Islamic Maghreb have stepped up their violence in recent years.[36] French officials say the rebels have no real links to the Al-Qaeda leadership, but this is a matter of some dispute in the international press and amongst security analysts. It seems likely that bin Laden approved the group's name in late 2006, and the rebels "took on the Al-Qaeda franchise label", almost a year before the violence began to escalate.[37]

Europe

In 2003, Islamists carried out a series of bombings in Istanbul killing 57 people and injuring 700. Seventy-four people were charged by the Turkish authorities. Some had previously met Bin Laden, and though they specifically declined to pledge allegiance to Al-Qaeda they asked for its blessing and help.

In 2009, three Londoners, Tanvir Hussain, Assad Sarwar and Ahmed Abdullah Ali, were convicted of conspiring to detonate bombs disguised as soft drinks on seven airplanes bound for Canada and the U.S. The massively complex police and MI5 investigation of the plot involved more than a year of surveillance work conducted by over 200 officers. British and U.S. officials said the plan—unlike many recent homegrown European terrorist plots—was directly linked to Al-Qaeda and guided by senior Islamic militants in Pakistan.[38]

Arab world

Following Yemeni unification in 1990, Wahhabi networks began moving missionaries into the country in an effort to subvert the capitalist north. Although it is unlikely bin Laden or Saudi Al-Qaeda were directly involved, the personal connections they made would be established over the next decade and used in the *USS Cole* bombing. Concerns grow over Al-Qaeda's group in Yemen.[39]

In Iraq, Al-Qaeda forces loosely associated with the leadership were embedded in the Jama'at al-Tawhid wal-Jihad organisation commanded by Abu Musab al-Zarqawi. Specialising in suicide operations, they have been a "key driver" of the Sunni insurgency.[40]

Although they played a small part in the overall insurgency, between 30 per cent and 42 per cent of all suicide bombings which took place in the early years were claimed by Zarqawi's organisation.[41] Reports have indicated that oversights such as the failure to control access to the Qa'qaa munitions factory in Yusufiyah have allowed large quantities of munitions to fall into the hands of Al-Qaida. In November 2010, the Islamic State of Iraq militant group, which is linked to Al-Qaeda in Iraq, threatened to "exterminate Iraqi Christians".[42]

Significantly, it was not until the late 1990s that Al-Qaeda began training Palestinians. This is not to suggest that resistance fighters are underrepresented in the network as a number of Palestinians, mostly coming from Jordan, wanted to join and have risen to serve high-profile roles in Afghanistan.[204] Rather, large groups such as Hamas and Palestinian Islamic Jihad—which cooperate with Al-Qaeda in many respects—have had difficulties accepting a strategic alliance, fearing that Al-Qaeda will co-opt their smaller cells. This may have changed recently, as Israeli security and intelligence services believe Al-Qaeda has managed to infiltrate operatives from the Occupied Territories into Israel, and is waiting for the right time to mount an attack.[43]

Kashmir

Bin Laden and Ayman al-Zawahiri consider India to be a part of the 'Crusader-Zionist-Hindu' conspiracy against the Islamic world.[44] According to the 2005 report 'Al-Qaeda: Profile and Threat Assessment' by Congressional Research Service, bin Laden was involved in training militants for Jihad in Kashmir while living in Sudan in the early nineties. By 2001 Kashmiri militant group Harkat-ul-Mujahideen had become a part of the Al-Qaeda coalition.[45] According to the United Nations High Commissioner for Refugees, Al-Qaeda is thought to have established bases in Pakistan-administered Kashmir during the 1999 Kargil War and continues to operate there with tacit approval of Pakistan's Intelligence services.

Many of the militants active in Kashmir were trained in the same Madrasas as Taliban and Al-Qaeda. Fazlur Rehman Khalil of Kashmiri militant group Harkat-ul-Mujahideen was a signatory of Al-Qaeda's 1998 declaration of Jihad against America and its allies. In a 'Letter to American People' written by bin Laden in 2002 he stated that one of the reasons he was fighting America is because of her support to India on the Kashmir issue.[46][47]

In November 2001 Kathmandu airport went on high alert after threats that bin Laden planned to hijack a plane from there and crash it into a target in New Delhi. In 2002 U.S. Secretary of Defense Donald Rumsfeld, on a trip to Delhi, suggested that Al-Qaeda was active in Kashmir though he did not have any hard evidence.[48][49] He proposed hi-tech ground sensors along the line of control to prevent militants from infiltrating into Indian administered Kashmir.[49]

An investigation in 2002 unearthed evidence that Al-Qaeda and its affiliates were prospering in Pakistan-administered Kashmir with tacit approval of Pakistan's National Intelligence agency Inter-Services Intelligence · In 2002 a special team of Special Air Service and Force was sent into Indian Administered Kashmir to hunt for bin Laden after reports that he was being sheltered by Kashmiri militant group Harkat-ul-Mujahideen, which had previously been responsible for the 1995 kidnapping of tourists from the West in Kashmir.[50] Britain's highest ranking Al-Qaeda operative Rangzieb Ahmed had previously fought in Kashmir with the group Harkat-ul-Mujahideen and spent time in Indian prison after being captured in Kashmir.

U.S. officials believe that Al-Qaeda was helping organise a campaign of terror in Kashmir in order to provoke conflict between India and Pakistan. Their strategy was to force Pakistan to move its troops to the border with India, thereby relieving pressure on Al-Qaeda elements hiding in northwestern Pakistan. In 2006 Al-Qaeda claimed they had established a wing in Kashmir; this has worried the Indian government.

However the Indian Army Lt. Gen. H.S. Panag, GOC-in-C Northern Command, said to reporters that the army has ruled out the presence of Al-Qaeda in Indian-administered Jammu and Kashmir; furthermore he said that there is nothing that can verify reports from the media of Al-Qaeda presence in the state. However, he stated that Al-Qaeda had strong ties with Kashmiri militant groups Lashkar-e-Taiba and Jaish-e-Mohammed based in Pakistan. It has been noted that Waziristan has now become the new battlefield for Kashmiri militants fighting NATO in support of Al-Qaeda and Taliban.[52][53] Dhiren Barot, who wrote the *Army of Madinah In Kashmir* and was an Al-Qaeda operative convicted for involvement in the 2004 financial buildings plot, had received training in weapons and explosives at a militant training camp in Kashmir.[54]

Maulana Masood Azhar, the founder of another Kashmiri group Jaish-e-Mohammed, is believed to have met bin Laden several times and received funding from him.[55] In 2002 Jaish-e-Mohammed organised the kidnapping and murder of Daniel Pearl in an operation run in conjunction with Al-Qaeda and funded by bin Laden. According to American counter-terrorism expert Bruce Riedel, Al-Qaeda and Taliban were closely involved in the 1999 hijacking of Indian Airlines Flight 814 to Kandahar which led to the release of Maulana Masood Azhar and Ahmed Omar Saeed Sheikh from an Indian prison in exchange for the passengers. This hijacking, Riedel stated, was rightly described by then Indian Foreign minister Jaswant Singh as a 'dress rehearsal' for September 11 attacks.[56]

Bin laden personally welcomed Azhar and threw a lavish party in his honour after his release, according to Abu Jandal, bodyguard of bin Laden.[56] Ahmed Omar Saeed Sheikh, who had been in Indian prison for his role in 1994 kidnappings of Western tourists in India, went on to murder Daniel Pearl and was sentenced to death by Pakistan. Al-Qaeda operative Rashid Rauf, who was one of the accused in 2006 transatlantic aircraft plot, was related to Maulana Masood Azhar by marriage.[57]

Lashkar-e-Taiba, a Kashmiri militant group which is thought to be behind 2008 Mumbai attacks, is also known to have strong ties to senior Al-Qaeda leaders living in Pakistan.[58] In late 2002 top Al-Qaeda operative Abu Zubaydah was arrested while being sheltered by Lashkar-e-Taiba in a safe house in Faisalabad.[59] The FBI believes that Al-Qaeda and Lashkar have been 'intertwined' for a long time while the CIA has said that Al-Qaeda funds Lashkar-e-Taiba.[59] French investigating magistrate Jean-Louis Bruguière, who was the top French counter-terrorism official, told Reuters in 2009 that 'Lashkar-e-Taiba is no longer a Pakistani movement with only a Kashmir political or military agenda. Lashkar-e-Taiba is a member of Al-Qaeda.'[60][61]

In a video released in 2008, senior Al-Qaeda operative Adam Yahiye Gadahn stated that "victory in Kashmir has been delayed for years; it is the liberation of the jihad there from this interference which, Allah willing, will be the first step towards victory over the Hindu occupiers of that Islam land."[62]

In September 2009 a U.S. Drone strike reportedly killed Ilyas Kashmiri who was the chief of Harkat-ul-Jihad al-Islami, a Kashmiri militant group associated with Al-Qaeda.[63] Kashmiri was described by Bruce Riedel as a 'prominent' Al-Qaeda member[64] while others have described him as head of military operations for Al-Qaeda.[65] Kashmiri was also charged by the U.S. in a plot against Jyllands-Posten, the Danish newspaper which was at the center of Jyllands-Posten Muhammad cartoons controversy. U.S. officials also believe that Kashmiri was involved in the Camp Chapman attack against the CIA.[66] In January 2010 Indian authorities notified Britain of an Al-Qaeda plot to hijack an Indian airlines or Air India plane and crash it into a British city. This information was uncovered from interrogation of Amjad Khwaja, an operative of Harkat-ul-Jihad al-Islami, who had been arrested in India.

In January 2010 U.S. Defense secretary Robert Gates, while on a visit to Pakistan, stated that Al-Qaeda was seeking to destabilise the region and planning to provoke a nuclear war between India and Pakistan.

Early attacks and aid for attacks

It is believed that the first bombing attack involving bin Laden was the December 29, 1992 bombing of the Gold Mihor Hotel in Aden in which two people were killed.[67]

It was after this bombing that Al-Qaeda was reported to have developed its justification for the killing of innocent people. According to a fatwa issued by Mamdouh Mahmud Salim, the killing of someone standing near the enemy is justified because any innocent bystander will find their proper reward in death, going to *Jannah* (Paradise) if they were good Muslims and to *Jahannam* (hell) if they were bad or non-believers.[68] The fatwa was issued to Al-Qaeda members but not the general public.

In the 1990s bin Laden's Al-Qaeda assisted jihadis financially and sometimes militarily in Algeria, Egypt and Afghanistan. In 1992 or 1993 bin Laden sent an emissary, Qari el-Said, with $40,000 to Algeria to aid the Islamists and urge war rather than negotiation with the government. Their advice was heeded but the war that followed killed 150,000–200,000 Algerians and ended with Islamist surrender to the government.

Bin Laden funded the Luxor massacre of November 17, 1997,[69][70][71] which killed 62 civilians, but outraged the Egyptian public. In mid-1997, the Northern Alliance threatened to overrun Jalalabad, causing bin Laden to abandon his Nazim Jihad compound and move his operations to Tarnak Farms in the south.

Another successful attack was carried out in the city of Mazar-e-Sharif in Afghanistan. Bin Laden helped cement his alliance with the Taliban by sending several hundreds of Afghan Arab fighters along to help the Taliban kill between five and six thousand Hazarasoverrunning the city.[72]

In February 1998, Osama bin Laden and Ayman al-Zawahiri co-signed a *fatwa* in the name of the World Islamic Front for Jihad Against Jews and Crusaders which declared the killing of North Americans and their allies an "individual duty for every Muslim" to "liberate theal-Aqsa Mosque [in Jerusalem] and the holy mosque [in Mecca] from their grip".[73] At the public announcement of the fatwa bin Laden announced that North Americans are "very easy targets". He told the attending journalists, "You will see the results of this in a very short time."[74]

In December 1998, the Director of Central Intelligence Counterterrorist Center reported to President Bill Clinton that Al-Qaeda was preparing for attacks in the USA, including the training of personnel to hijack aircraft.

Bin Laden and Al-Zawahiri organised an Al-Qaeda congress on June 24, 1998.[75]

The 1998 U.S. Embassy bombings were a series of attacks that occurred on August 7, 1998, in which hundreds of people were killed in simultaneous truck bomb explosions at the United States embassies in the major East African cities of Dar-es-Salaam, Tanzania and Nairobi, Kenya. The attacks were linked to local members of the Egyptian Islamic Jihad, brought Osama bin Laden and Ayman al-Zawahiri to the attention of the U.S. public for the first time, and resulted in the U.S. Federal Bureau of Investigation placing bin Laden on its Ten Most Wanted list.

At the end of 2000, Richard Clarke revealed that Islamic militants headed by bin Laden had planned a triple attack on January 3, 2000, which would have included bombings in Jordan of the Radisson SAS Hotel in Amman and tourists at Mount Nebo and a site on the Jordan River, the sinking of the destroyer USS *The Sullivans* in Yemen, as well as an attack on a target within the United States. The plan was foiled by the arrest of the Jordanian terrorist cell, the sinking of the explosive-filled skiff intended to target the destroyer, and the arrest of Ahmed Ressam.[76]

Balkan wars

A former U.S. State Department official in October 2001 described Bosnia and Herzegovina as a safe haven for terrorists, after it was revealed that militant elements of the former Sarajevo government were protecting extremists, some with ties to Osama bin Laden.[77] In 1997, *Rzeczpospolita*, one of the largest Polish daily newspapers, reported that intelligence services of the Nordic-Polish SFOR Brigade suspected that a center for training terrorists from Islamic countries was located in the Bocina Donja village near Maglaj in Bosnia and Herzegovina. In 1992, hundreds of volunteers joined an "all-mujahedeen unit" called El Moujahed in an abandoned hillside factory, a compound with a hospital and prayer hall.

According to Middle East intelligence reports, bin Laden financed small convoys of recruits from the Arab world through his businesses in Sudan. Among them was Karim Said Atmani who was identified by authorities as the document forger for a group of Algerians accused of plotting the bombings in the USA. He is a former roommate of Ahmed Ressam, the man arrested at the Canadian–U.S. border in mid-December 1999 with a car full of nitroglycerin and bomb-making materials. He was convicted of colluding with Osama bin Laden by a French court.

A Bosnian government search of passport and residency records, conducted at the urging of the United States, revealed other former Mujahideen who were linked to the same Algerian group or to other groups of suspected terrorists, and had lived in the area 60 miles (97 km) north of Sarajevo, the capital, in the past few years. Khalil al-Deek, was arrested in Jordan in late December 1999 on suspicion of involvement in a plot to blow up tourist sites; a second man with Bosnian citizenship, Hamid Aich, lived in Canada at the same time as Atmani and worked for a charity associated with Osama bin Laden. In its June 26, 1997, Report on the bombing of the Al Khobar building in Riyadh, Saudi Arabia, *The New York Times* noted that those arrested confessed to serving with Bosnian Muslims forces. Further, the captured men also admitted to ties with Osama bin Laden.

In 1999 it was revealed that bin Laden and his Tunisian assistant Mehrez Aodouni were granted citizenship and Bosnian passports in 1993 by the government in Sarajevo. This information was denied by the Bosnian government following the 9/11 attacks, but it was later found that Aodouni was arrested in Turkey and that at that time he possessed the Bosnian passport. Following this revelation, a new explanation was given that bin Laden "did not personally collect his Bosnian passport" and that officials at the Bosnian embassy in Vienna, which issued the passport, could not have known who bin Laden was at the time.[78][79][80] The Bosnian daily *Oslobođenje* published in 2001 that three men, believed to be linked to bin Laden, were arrested in Sarajevo in July 2001. The three, one of whom was identified as Imad-El-Misri, were Egyptian nationals. The paper said that two of the suspects were holding Bosnian passports.

In 1998 it was reported that bin Laden was operating his Al-Qaeda network out of Albania. *The Charleston Gazette* quoted Fatos Klosi, the head of the Albanian intelligence service, as saying a network run by Saudi exile Osama bin Laden sent units to fight in the Serbian province of Kosovo. Confirmation of these activities came from Claude Kader, a French national who said he was a member of bin Laden's Albanian network.

By 1998 four members of Egyptian Islamic Jihad (EIJ) were arrested in Albania and extradited to Egypt.[81]

September 11 attacks

> "Allah knows it did not cross our minds to attack the towers but after the situation became unbearable and we witnessed the injustice and tyranny of the American-Israeli alliance against our people in Palestine and Lebanon, I thought about it. And the events that affected me directly were that of 1982 and the events that followed – when America allowed the Israelis to invade Lebanon, helped by the U.S. Sixth Fleet. As I watched the destroyed towers in Lebanon, it occurred to me punish the unjust the same way (and) to destroy towers in America so it could taste some of what we are tasting and to stop killing our children and women."
>
> – *Osama bin Laden*, 2004

After repeated denials,[82] in 2004, Osama bin Laden claimed responsibility for the September 11, 2001, attacks on the United States.[83] The attacks involved the hijacking of four commercial passenger aircraft, the subsequent destruction of those planes and the World Trade Center in New York City, New York, severe damage to The Pentagon in Arlington, Virginia, and the deaths of 2,974 people and the 19 hijackers.[84] In response to the attacks, the United States launched a War on Terror to depose the Taliban regime in Afghanistan and capture Al-Qaeda operatives, and several countries strengthened their anti-terrorism legislation to preclude future attacks. The CIA's Special Activities Division was given the lead in tracking down and killing or capturing bin Laden.[85]

The Federal Bureau of Investigation has stated that classified[86] evidence linking Al-Qaeda and bin Laden to the attacks of September 11 is clear and irrefutable.[87] The UK Government reached a similar conclusion regarding Al-Qaeda and Osama bin Laden's culpability for the

September 11, 2001, attacks although the government report notes that the evidence presented is insufficient for *a prosecutable case*. Bin Laden initially denied involvement in the attacks. On September 16, 2001, bin Laden read a statement later broadcast by Qatar's Al Jazeera satellite channel denying responsibility for the attack.

In a videotape recovered by U.S. forces in November 2001 in Jalalabad, bin Laden was seen discussing the attack with Khaled al-Harbi in a way that indicates foreknowledge. The tape was broadcast on various news networks on December 13, 2001. The merits of this translation have been disputed. Arabist Dr. Abdel El M. Husseini stated: "This translation is very problematic. At the most important places where it is held to prove the guilt of bin Laden, it is not identical with the Arabic."[88]

In the 2004 Osama bin Laden video, bin Laden abandoned his denials without retracting past statements. In it he stated he had personally directed the 19 hijackers.[89] In the 18-minute tape, played on Al-Jazeera, four days before the American presidential election, bin Laden accused U.S. President George W. Bush of negligence on the hijacking of the planes on September 11.

According to the tapes, bin Laden claimed he was inspired to destroy the World Trade Center after watching the destruction of towers in Lebanon by Israel during the 1982 Lebanon War.

In two other tapes aired by Al Jazeera in 2006, Osama bin Laden announces,

> *I am the one in charge of the nineteen brothers [...] I was responsible for entrusting the nineteen brothers [...] with the raids [5 minute audiotape broadcast May 23, 2006], and is seen with Ramzi bin al-Shibh, as well as two of the 9/11 hijackers, Hamza al-Ghamdi and Wail al-Shehri, as they make preparations for the attacks (videotape broadcast September 7, 2006).*[90]

Major Attacks

Map of recent major attacks attributed to Al-Qaeda:

1. The Pentagon, U.S.A. – Sep 11, 2001
2. World Trade Center, U.S.A. – Sep 11, 2001
3. Istanbul, Turkey – Nov 15, 2003; Nov 20, 2003
4. Aden, Yemen – Oct 12, 2000
5. Nairobi, Kenya – Aug 7, 1998
6. Dar-es-Salaam, Tanzania – Aug 7, 1998

Al-Qaeda has carried out a total of six major terrorist attacks, four of them in its jihad against America. In each case the leadership planned the attack years in advance, arranging for the shipment of weapons and explosives and using its privatised businesses to provide operatives with safehouses and false identities. Al-Qaeda usually does not disburse funds for attacks, and very rarely makes wire transfers.[91]

On December 29, 1992, Al-Qaeda's first terrorist attack took place as two bombs were detonated in Aden, Yemen. The first target was the Movenpick Hotel and the second was the parking lot of the Goldmohur Hotel. The bombings were an attempt to eliminate American soldiers on their way to Somalia to take part in the international famine relief effort, Operation Restore Hope.

Internally, Al-Qaeda considered the bombing a victory that frightened the Americans away, but in the U.S. the attack was barely noticed. No Americans were killed because the soldiers were staying in a different hotel altogether, and they went on to Somalia as scheduled. However little noticed, the attack was pivotal as it was the beginning of Al-Qaeda's change in direction, from fighting armies to killing civilians.[92]

Two people were killed in the bombing, an Australian tourist and a Yemeni hotel worker. Seven others, mostly Yemenis, were severely injured. Two fatwas are said to have been appointed by the most theologically knowledgeable of Al-Qaeda's members, Mamdouh Mahmud Salim, to justify the killings according to Islamic law. Salim referred to a famous fatwa appointed by Ibn Taymiyyah, a 13th-century scholar much admired by Wahhabis, which sanctioned resistance by any means during the Mongol invasions.[93]

Ramzi Yousef

In 1993, Ramzi Yousef used a truck bomb to attack the World Trade Center in New York City. The attack was intended to break the foundation of Tower One knocking it into Tower Two, bringing the entire complex down.

Yousef hoped this would kill 250,000 people. The towers shook and swayed but the foundation held and he succeeded in killing only six people (although he injured 1,042 others and caused nearly $300 million in property damage).[94][95]

After the attack, Yousef fled to Pakistan and later moved to Manila. There he began developing the Bojinka Plot plans to implode a dozen American airliners simultaneously, to assassinate Pope John Paul II and

President Bill Clinton, and to crash a private plane into CIA headquarters. He was later captured in Pakistan.[94]

None of the U.S. government's indictments against bin Laden have suggested that he had any connection with this bombing, but Ramzi Yousef is known to have attended a terrorist training camp in Afghanistan. After his capture, Yousef declared that his primary justification for the attack was to punish the U.S. for its support for the Israeli occupation of Palestinian territories and made no mention of any religious motivations.[95]

1998 Nairobi embassy bombing

In 1996, bin Laden personally engineered a plot to assassinate Clinton while the president was in Manila for the Asia Pacific Economic Cooperation. However, intelligence agents intercepted a message just minutes before the motorcade was to leave, and alerted the U.S. Secret Service. Agents later discovered a bomb planted under a bridge.[96]

The 1998 U.S. embassy bombings in East Africa, resulting in upward of 300 deaths, mostly locals. A barrage of cruise missiles launched by the U.S. military in response devastated an Al-Qaeda base in Khost, Afghanistan, but the network's capacity was unharmed.

In October 2000, Al-Qaeda militants in Yemen bombed the missile destroyer *U.S.S. Cole* in a suicide attack, killing 17 U.S. servicemen and damaging the vessel while it lay offshore. Inspired by the success of such a brazen attack, Al-Qaeda's command core began to prepare for an attack on the U.S. itself.

AFTERMATH OF THE SEPTEMBER 11 ATTACKS

The September 11, 2001, attacks were the most devastating terrorist acts in American history, killing approximately 3,000 people. Two commercial airliners were deliberately flown into the World Trade Center towers, a third into The Pentagon, and a fourth, originally intended to target the U.S. Capitol, crashed in a field in Shanksville, Pennsylvania.

The attacks were conducted by Al-Qaeda, acting in accord with the 1998 *fatwa* issued against the U.S. and its allies by military forces under the command of bin Laden, al-Zawahiri, and others. Evidence points to suicide squads led by Al-Qaeda military commander Mohamed Atta as the culprits of the attacks, with bin Laden, Ayman al-Zawahiri, Khalid Shaikh Mohammed, and Hambali as the key planners and part of the political and military command.

Messages issued by bin Laden after September 11, 2001, praised the attacks, and explained their motivation while denying any involvement. Bin Laden legitimised the attacks by identifying grievances felt by both mainstream and Islamist Muslims, such as the general perception that the U.S. was actively oppressing Muslims.

Bin Laden asserted that America was massacring Muslims in 'Palestine, Chechnya, Kashmir and Iraq' and that Muslims should retain the 'right to attack in reprisal'. He also claimed the 9/11 attacks were not targeted at women and children, but 'America's icons of military and economic power'.

Evidence has since come to light that the original targets for the attack may have been nuclear power stations on the east coast of the U.S. The targets were later altered by Al-Qaeda, as it was feared that such an attack "might get out of hand".

CRIMINAL CHARGES

On March 16, 1998, Libya issued the first official Interpol arrest warrant against bin Laden and three other people. They were charged for killing two German citizens in Libya on March 10, 1994, one of whom is thought to have been a German counter-intelligence officer. Bin Laden was still wanted by the Libyan government at the time of his death. Osama bin Laden was first indicted by the United States on June 8, 1998, when a grand jury indicted Osama bin Laden on charges of killing five Americans and two Indians in the November 14, 1995, truck bombing of a US-operated Saudi National Guard training center in Riyadh.

Bin Laden was charged with "conspiracy to attack defense utilities of the United States" and prosecutors further charged that bin Laden is the head of the terrorist organisation called Al-Qaeda, and that he was a major financial backer of Islamic fighters worldwide. Bin Laden denied involvement but praised the attack.

On November 4, 1998, Osama bin Laden was indicted by a Federal Grand Jury in the United States District Court for the Southern District of New York, on charges of *Murder of US Nationals Outside the United States, Conspiracy to Murder US Nationals Outside the United States, and Attacks on a Federal Facility Resulting in Death*[97] for his alleged role in the 1998 United States embassy bombings in Kenya and Tanzania.

The evidence against bin Laden included courtroom testimony by former Al-Qaeda members and satellite phone records, from a phone purchased for him by Al-Qaeda procurement agent Ziyad Khaleel in the

U.S. Bin Laden became the 456th person listed on the FBI Ten Most Wanted Fugitives list, when he was added to the list on June 7, 1999, following his indictment along with others for capital crimes in the 1998 embassy attacks. Attempts at assassination and requests for the extradition of bin Laden from the Taliban of Afghanistan were met with failure prior to the bombing of Afghanistan in October 2001.

In 1999, U.S. President Bill Clinton convinced the United Nations to impose sanctions against Afghanistan in an attempt to force the Taliban to extradite him. Years later, on October 10, 2001, bin Laden appeared as well on the initial list of the top 22 FBI Most Wanted Terrorists, which was released to the public by the President of the United States George W. Bush, in direct response to the attacks of 9/11, but which was again based on the indictment for the 1998 embassy attack. Bin Laden was among a group of thirteen fugitive terrorists wanted on that latter list for questioning about the 1998 embassy bombings. Bin Laden remains the only fugitive ever to be listed on both FBI fugitive lists.

Despite the multiple indictments listed above and multiple requests, the Taliban refused to extradite Osama bin Laden. It wasn't until after the bombing of Afghanistan began in October 2001 that the Taliban finally did offer to turn over Osama bin Laden to a third-party country for trial, in return for the U.S. ending the bombing and providing evidence that Osama bin Laden was involved in the 9/11 attacks. This offer was rejected by George W Bush stating that this was no longer negotiable with Bush responding that "there's no need to discuss innocence or guilt. We know he's guilty."

Syed Saleem Shahzad's book *Inside Al-Qaeda & Taliban—Beyond Bin Laden & 9/11* (published in UK by Pluto Press/ distributed in India by Pentagon Press, 2011) is a damning account of ISI's nefarious connections with terrorist groups as well as many other facts about and cross connections between them.Shahzad said, "26/11 was scripted by ISI, approved by Al-Qaeda commanders and executed by Lashkar-e-Taiba (LeT).

From Al-Qaeda the main player was Ilyas Kashmiri and from LeT it was Haroon Ashik. The common link between Ashik and Kashmiri is that they were both from Pakistan Army, which "has been embedding terror outfits with its own men, especially in the operations and planning department so that there is close co-ordination with what Pakistan Army & ISI demands and its seamless execution by these terror outfits."

The book and Saleem's last article published in the publication he worked for, in all likelihood proved to be his nemesis. An excerpt of this article reads: "Al-Qaeda carried out the brazen attack on PNS Mehran naval air station in Karachi on May 22 after talks failed between the navy and al-Qaeda over the release of naval officials arrested on suspicion of al-Qaeda links".

The latest status of Al-Qaeda is reflected in some news reports. One is datelined Dera Ismail Khan, Pakistan, stating that prominent Al-Qaeda and Afghan Taliban fighters asked Pakistani militants in two rare meetings, to set aside their differences and step up support for the battle against U.S.-led forces in Afghanistan. The meetings were held in Pakistan's tribal region in November and December at the request of the Afghan Taliban's leadership council. They could indicate the militants are struggling in Afghanistan, or conversely, that they want to make sure they hit U.S. forces hard as the Americans accelerate their withdrawal this year. That could give the Taliban additional leverage in any peace negotiations[98].

The other is about recent arrests and killings of top Al-Qaeda members, which according to some Pakistani defence and security analysts have fractured the terrorist organisation and will ultimately weaken its capabilities to plan and launch attacks inside and outside Pakistan. "The arrest of Younas al-Mauritani and two other affiliates after the death of the al-Qaeda second-in-command, Atiya Abdel Rahman, in an (aerial strike) is a major setback for al-Qaeda," senior security analyst and author Dr. Ayesha Siddiqa told centralasiaonline.com.

Al-Mauritani was considered Al-Qaeda's foreign minister. His capture and Rahman's death on the heels of Osama bin Laden's death on May 2, 2011, have splintered Al-Qaeda, she said. The Directorate for Inter-Services Intelligence, in co-ordination with the Balochistan Frontier Corps, captured al-Mauritani, who was mainly responsible for planning and conducting international operations in Quetta, in August but announced the capture on September 5th. Authorities also captured his colleagues Abdul Ghaffar al-Shami and Messara al-Shami. "Through this critical arrest, yet another fatal blow has been delivered to al-Qaeda," Inter Services Public Relations said on September 5, 2011, regarding al-Mauritani's capture.[99]

Be that as it may, it must not be taken for granted that Al-Qaeda is out. While it may be down organisationally, it certainly is not so ideologically and there is no saying when or how it may re-emerge and become organised enough to launch terrorist attacks. In fact as this writer has often stressed, all countries that may not have been affected by Al-

Qaeda's global reach must be watchful not only of this group but also those which have closely associated with it in the past.

Al-Qaeda is struggling to raise funds for terrorist attacks and training following the killing last May of leader Osama bin Laden, analysts said.

The series of pro-democracy demonstrations in several Middle East countries last year, known as the Arab Spring, have also blunted the terrorist group's ability to raise funds, analysts said. The strength of the demonstrations showed that the majority of people in the Arab street did not support Al-Qaeda's policy of using violence to advocate for change. The demonstrations also showed that many Arabs rejected al-Qaeda's rationales for attacking the West.[100]

NOTES

[1] http://en.wikipedia.org/wiki/Al-Qaeda#cite_note-al-Fadl-16 (Accessed December 19, 2011).

[2] http://www.guardian.co.uk/uk/2005/jul/08/july7.development (Accessed December 19, 2011).

[3] A.B. Atwan, *The Secret History of Al-Qaeda*, University of California Press, California, 2006, p.221

[4] S. Ulph (2005), "Al-Qaeda's Strategy Until 2020," *The Jamestown Foundation*, http://www.jamestown.org/index.php?id=148.

[5] O. Roy, *Islam and Resistance in Afghanistan*, Cambridge University Press: Cambridge, U.K, 1990, p. 118.

[6] L. Grau, *"The Soviet-Afghan War: A Superpower Mired in the Mountains,"* Foreign Military Studies Office Publications, 2004. Retrieved December 19, 2011. "The Soviet-Afghan War: A Superpower Mired in the Mountains," *Journal of Slavic Military Studies* 17(1),March *2004*, pp.129–51 and p.139.

[7] J.B. Amstutz, *Afghanistan: The First Five Years of Soviet Occupation*, NDU Press, Washington D.C.,1986, p. 127.

[8] E. Swenson (2006), "How Did Syed Qutub Influence Osam Bin Laden?" 2006, at http://gemsofislamism.tripod.com/qutb_milest_influence_obl.html (Accessed December 19, 2011).

[9] J.K. Cooley, *"Unholy Wars: Afghanistan, America and International Terrorism"* Pluto Press, London, 2003, p. 247.

[10] N. Dixon (2001), "How the CIA Created Osama bin Laden," at http://www.greenleft.org.au/node/24198, 2001 (AccessedDecember 19, 2011).

[11] M. Sageman, *Understanding Terror Networks*,University of Pennsylvania Press, Philadelphia, 2004, p.35.

[12] L. Wright, *The Looming Tower: Al-Qaeda and the Road to 9/11*, New York Press, New York, 2006, p.137.

[13] R. Gunaratna, *Inside Al-Qaeda* (1st ed.), C. Hurst & Co., London, 2002, pp. 95–96.

[14] L. Merriam, "The al-Qaeda Brand Died Last week," *Forbes*,September 6, 2011 at http://www.forbes.com/sites/realspin/2011/10/06/the-al-qaeda-brand-died-last-week/ (Accessed on December 20, 2011).

[15] J. Bennetto and H. Ian, "London bombings: The truth emerges," *The Independent*, UK,August 13, 2005.

[16] L. Wright, no. 12, pp.107-108, 185, 270-271.

[17] L. Wright, no. 12, p. 270.

[18] M. Ranstorp, *Unconventional Weapons and International Terrorism,* Routledge, Abingdon, Oxon, U.K., 2009, pp. 33.

[19] J. Feiser (2004), "Evolution of Al-Qaeda Brand Name," at http://www.atimes.com/atimes/Middle_East/FH13Ak05.html (Accessed December 20, 2011).

[20] J. Blitz, "A threat transformed," *Financial Times*, 2010, at http://www.ft.com/cms/s/0/af31e344-0499-11df-8603-00144feabdc0.html#axzz1h3aouIRT (Accessed December 20, 2011).

[21] J. McGeary, "A Traitor's Tale," *TIME*, Vol. 157 (7), 2001, pp. 36–37.

[22] S. Shane (2011), "Qaeda Selection of Its Chief Is Said to Reflect Its Flaws" at http://www.nytimes.com/2011/06/17/world/asia/17qaeda.html?scp=1&sq=Al-Qaida%20Says%20Al-Zawahri%20Has%20Succeeded%20Bin%20Laden%22,&st=cse (Accessed December 20, 2011).

[23] C. Anderson (2010), "New Al-Qaeda Leader Lived in U.S. for Years," 2010, at http://www.usatoday.com/news/world/2010-08-06-al-qaeda-leader_N.htm (Accessed on December 20, 2011).

[24] M. Basile, "Going to the Source: Why Al-Qaeda's Financial Network Is Likely to Withstand the Current War on Terrorist Financing," *Studies in Conflict and Terrorism,* Vol. 27 (3), 2004, pp. 169–185.

[25] B. Hoffman, "The Emergence of the New Terrorism," in Tan, Andrew; Ramakrishna, Kumar *The New Terrorism: Anatomy, Trends, and Counter-Strategies*, Eastern Universities Press, Singapore, 2002, pp. 30–49.

[26] B.A. Abdel, *The Secret History of Al-Qaeda*, University of California Press, Los Angeles, California, p. 233

[27] J. Burke, and P. Allen (2009), "The Five Ages of Al-Qaeda," *The Guardian* (UK), at http://www.guardian.co.uk/world/interactive/2009/sep/10/al-qaida-five-ages-terror-attacks.

[28] J.K. Cooley, "Unholy Wars: Afganistan, America and International Terrorism". *Demokratizatsiya*, 2003.

[29] L. Napoleoni, *Modern Jihad: Tracing the Dollars Behind the Terror Networks*, Pluto Press, London, 2003, pp. 121–123.

[29] M. Akacem, "Review: Modern Jihad: Tracing the Dollars behind the Terror Networks," *International Journal of Middle East Studies* Vol. 37 (3), 2005, pp. 444–445.

[30] D. Eisenberg (2001), "Secrets Of Brigade 055," *Time* at http://www.time.com/time/magazine/article/0,9171,1101011105-181591,00.html (Accessed December 20, 2011).

[31] B. Roggio (2008), "Taliban have not split from al-Qaeda: sources" *The Long War Journal*, 2008, at http://www.longwarjournal.org/archives/2008/10/taliban_have_not_spl.php (Accessed on December 21, 2011).

[32] J. Partlow (2009), "In Afghanistan, Taliban surpasses al-Qaeda," at http://www.washingtonpost.com/wp-dyn/content/article/2009/11/10/AR2009111019644.html (Accessed December 21, 2011).

[33] M. Sageman, *Understanding Terror Networks*, University of Pennsylvania Press, Philadelphia, 2004, pp. 48, 51.

[34] Y. Trofimov, *Faith At War: A Journey On the Frontlines of Islam, From Baghdad to Timbuktu*, Picador, New York, 2006, p. 282.

[35] B.A. Abdel, *The Secret History of Al-Qaeda*, University of California Press, Los Angeles, California, 2006, pp. 168–169.

[36] Russia Outlaws 17 Terror Groups; Hamas, Hezbollah Not Included". Archived from the original on November 14, 2006,at http://web.archive.org/web/20061114154904/http://www.mosnews.com/news/2006/07/28/russiaterrorlist.shtml (Accessed December 21, 2011).

[37] Korean Foreign Ministry (2007), "Seoul confirms release of two Korean hostages in Afghanistan". Archived from the original on December 15, 2007, athttp://web.archive.org/web/20071215153000/http://www.korea.net/news/news/NewsView.asp?serial_no=20070813015&part=102 (Accessed December 21, 2011).
[38] United States Department of State, "Foreign Terrorist Organizations (FTOs)," Archived from the original on June 28, 2006, at http://web.archive.org/web/20060628111524/http://www.state.gov/s/ct/rls/fs/37191.htm (Accessed December 21, 2011).
[39] "Blair to Taliban: Surrender bin Laden or surrender power," Canadian Broadcasting Corporation, October 3, 2001, http://www.cbc.ca/news/world/story/2001/10/02/blair_war011002.html. (Accessed December 21, 2011). essed on 21st December, 2011 .
[40] "U.S. Releases Videotape of Osama bin Laden," December 13, 2001, Archived from the original on June 25, 2006, at http://web.archive.org/web/20060625223529/http://www.defenselink.mil/releases/2001/b12132001_bt630-01.html (Accessed December 21, 2011)..
[41] S. Morris (2001), "US urged to detail origin of tape," *The Guardian* (UK) at http://www.guardian.co.uk/world/2001/dec/15/september11.afghanistan (Accessed December 21, 2011).
[42] S. Shane (2008), "Inside the interrogation of a 9/11 mastermind," *The New York Times*, 2008, pp. A1, A12–A13, http://www.nytimes.com/2008/06/22/washington/22ksm.html (Accessed December 21, 2011).
[43] I. Black and T.R. Norton, "Al-Qaida weakened by global recruitment woes," *The Guardian Weekly (London)*, Vol. 181 (14), 2009, pp. 1–2. http://www.guardian.co.uk/world/2009/sep/10/al-qaida-recruitment-crisis (Accessed December 21, 2011).
[44] Y. Trofimov, "Islamic rebels gain strength in the Sahara," *The Wall Street Journal*, Vol. 254 (39), 2009, p. A9.
[44] Y. Trofimov, "Islamic rebels gain strength in the Sahara," *The Wall Street Journal Europe* Vol. 27 (136), 2009, p. 12.
[44] Y. Trofimov, "Islamic rebels gain in the Sahara," *The Wall Street Journal Asia* Vol. 33 (245), 2009, p. 12.
[45] B. Riedel *The Search for al-Qaeda: Its Leadership, Ideology, and Future*, Brookings Institution Press, Washington, D.C., 2008, p. 126.
[46] D. Gardham (2009) "Gang is brought to justice by most complex operation since the war," *The Daily Telegraph* (London), 2009, p. 2, at http://www.telegraph.co.uk/news/uknews/terrorism-in-the-uk/6152185/Airline-bomb-plot-investigation-one-of-biggest-since-WW2.html (Accessed December 21, 2011).
[46] D. Gardham, "Complex operation brings gang to justice," *The Weekly Telegraph* (Australian edition), 947, 2009, p. 9.
[47] C. Milmo (2009), "Police watched the plot unfold, then pounced," *The Independent* (London), 2009, pp. 2–4, http://www.independent.co.uk/news/uk/crime/police-watched-the-plot-unfold-then-pounced-1783388.html (Accessed December 21, 2011).
[48] D. Sandford (2009), "UK | Airline plot: Al-Qaeda connection," BBC News, at http://news.bbc.co.uk/2/hi/uk_news/8221375.stm (Accessed December 21, 2011).
[49] J. Burke, *Al-Qaeda: Casting a Shadow of Terror*, I.B. Tauris, New York, 2003, pp. 128–129.
[50] B. Riedel, *The Search for al-Qaeda: Its Leadership, Ideology, and Future*, Brookings Institution Press, Washington, D.C., 2008, p .100.
[51] D. Streatfeild (2011), "How the US let al-Qaida get its hands on an Iraqi weapons factory". *The Guardian* (UK), http://www.guardian.co.uk/world/2011/jan/07/iraq-weapons-factory-al-qaida-us-failure (Accessed December 21, 2011).
[52] Terrorism in India and the Global Jihad, Brookings Institution, November 30, 2008,

http://www.brookings.edu/articles/2008/1130_india_terrorism_riedel.aspx (Accessed December 21, 2011).

[53] R. Gunaratna, *Inside Al-Qaeda*, C. Hurst & Co, London, 2002, p.150.

[54] United Nations High Commissioner for Refugees (2008) "Freedom in the World 2008—Kashmir [Pakistan]" http://www.unhcr.org/refworld/topic,463af2212,469f2dcf2,487ca21a2a,0.html (Accessed December 23, 2011).

[55] B. Riedel, no. 50, p.126.

[56] (2002), "bin Laden's 'letter to America' ", at http://www.guardian.co.uk/world/2002/nov/24/theobserver (Accessed December 23, 2011). .

[57] Z. Abbas (2002), "Analysis: Is al-Qaeda in Kashmir?" at http://news.bbc.co.uk/2/hi/2043800.stm (Accessed December 23, 2011).

[58] (2002), "Rumsfeld offers US technology to guard Kashmir border," at http://www.smh.com.au/articles/2002/06/13/1023864326179.html (Accessed December 23, 2011).

[59] P. Smucker (2002), "Al-Qaeda thriving in Pakistani Kashmir," at http://www.csmonitor.com/2002/0702/p01s02-wosc.html (Accessed December 23, 2011).

[60] M. Smith (2002), "SAS joins Kashmir hunt for bin Laden," at http://www.telegraph.co.uk/news/worldnews/asia/india/1385795/SAS-joins-Kashmir-hunt-for-bin-Laden.html (Accessed December 23, 2011).

[61] D. Gradham (2008), "Al-Qaeda terror trial: Rangzieb Ahmed was highest ranking al-Qaeda operative in Britain," at http://www.telegraph.co.uk/news/uknews/3832366/Al-Qaeda-terror-trial-Rangzieb-Ahmed-was-highest-ranking-al-Qaeda-operative-in-Britain.html (Accessed December 23, 2011).

[62] (2002), "Bin Laden's finger on Kashmir trigger?" at http://edition.cnn.com/2002/WORLD/asiapcf/south/06/12/kashmir.qaeda/ (Accessed December 23, 2011).

[63] J. Diamond (2002), "Taliban, al-Qaeda linked to Kashmir," at http://www.usatoday.com/news/world/2002/05/29/taliban-kashmir.htm (Accessed December 23, 2011).

[64] A. Gentleman (2006), "Al-Qaeda claim of Kashmir link worries India - Asia – Pacific," *International Herald Tribune*, http://www.nytimes.com/2006/07/13/world/asia/13iht-india.2194572.html (Accessed December 23, 2011).

[65] (2007), "No Al-Qaeda presence in Kashmir: Army," at http://www.hindu.com/2007/06/18/stories/2007061801191400.htm (Accessed December 23, 2011).

[66] (2008), "Kashmiri militants move to Waziristan, open training camps," at http://www.indianexpress.com/news/kashmiri-militants-move-to-waziristan-open/390569/ (Accessed December 23, 2011).

[67] Lawrence Wright, *The Looming Tower: Al-Qaeda and the Road to 9/11*, Knopf, New York, 2006, p. 137.

[68] A. Khan (2006), "The War on Terror and the Politics of Violence in Pakistan," http://web.archive.org/web/20061208102951/http://www.jamestown.org/news_details.php?news_id=54 (Accessed December 23, 2011).

[69] P. Klebnikov (2001), "Who Is Osama bin Laden?" http://www.forbes.com/2001/09/14/0914whoisobl.html (Accessed December 23, 2011).

[70] J. Bruke (1999), "Frankenstein the CIA created," http://www.guardian.co.uk/world/1999/jan/17/yemen.islam (Accessed December 23, 2011).

[71] M. Scehuer, "Marching Towards Hell," Free Press, 2008, p. 10.

[72] Lawrence Wright, no. 67, pp. 133–134.

[73] Ibid, p. 260.

[74] Ibid, p. 181.

[75] S. Emerson (2007), "Osama bin Laden: The Past," at http://www.iacsp.com/itobli3.html (Accessed December 23, 2011).

[76] D. Jehl (2001), "A NATION CHALLENGED: SAUDI ARABIA; Holy War Lured Saudis As Rulers Looked Away," at http://www.nytimes.com/2001/12/27/world/a-nation-challenged-saudi-arabia-holy-war-lured-saudis-as-rulers-looked-away.html(Accessed December 23, 2011).

[77] Bruce Riedel, *The Search for al-Qaeda: Its Leadership, Ideology, and Future*, Brookings Institution Press, Washington, D.C., 2008, p. 52.

[78] M. Ijaz (2001), "Clinton Let Bin Laden Slip Away and Metastasize," http://articles.latimes.com/2001/dec/05/opinion/oe-ijaz05 (Accessed December 23, 2011).

[79] T. Camey and M. Ijaz (2002), "Intelligence Failure? Let's Go Back to Sudan," at http://www.washingtonpost.com/ac2/wp-dyn/A64828-2002Jun29 (Accessed December 23, 2011).

[80] D. Rose (2002), "The Osama Files," at http://www.vanityfair.com/politics/features/2002/01/osama200201?currentPage=1 (Accessed December 23, 2011).

[81] M. Belz (2003), "Clinton did not have the will to respond," http://www.worldmag.com/articles/8206 (Accessed December 23, 2011).

[82] Ahmed Rashid, *Taliban: Militant Islam, Oil and Fundamentalism in Central Asia*, Yale University Press, New Haven, (2002) [2000].

[83] D. Eisenberg (2001), "Secrets Of Brigade 055," at http://www.time.com/time/magazine/article/0,9171,1101011105-181591,00.html (Accessed December 23, 2011).

[84] J. Partlow (2009), "In Afghanistan, Taliban leaving al-Qaeda behind," at http://www.washingtonpost.com/wp-dyn/content/article/2009/11/10/AR2009111019644.html (Accessed December 23, 2011).

[85] Marc Sageman, *Understanding Terror Networks*, University of Pennsylvania Press, Philadelphia, 2004, pp. 48, 51.

[86] Yaroslav Trofimov, *Faith At War: A Journey On the Frontlines of Islam, From Baghdad to Timbuktu*, Picador, New York, 2006, p. 282.

[87] (1996), "Bin Laden's Fatwa," at http://www.pbs.org/newshour/terrorism/international/fatwa_1996.html (Accessed December 23, 2011).

[88] D. Benjamin and S. Simon, "By issuing fatwas, bin Laden and his followers are acting out a kind of self-appointment as alim: they are asserting their rights as interpreters of Islamic law," *The Age of Sacred Terror*, Random House, New York, 2002, p. 117.

[89] J.R. Nyquist (2005), "Is Al-Qaeda a Kremlin Proxy?" at http://www.jrnyquist.com/nyquist_2005_0813.htm (Accessed December 23, 2011).

[90] D. Eggen (2006), "Bin Laden, Most Wanted For Embassy Bombings?" at http://www.washingtonpost.com/wp-dyn/content/article/2006/08/27/AR2006082700687.html (Accessed December 23, 2011).

[91] D.R. Griffin (2009), "Bin Laden and 9/11: The Evidence," at http://www.veteranstoday.com/2009/10/30/bin-laden-and-9-11-the-evidence/ (Accessed December 23, 2011).

[92] (2011), "Osama bin Laden never charged for 911 - Inside Job likely," at http://www.ibtimes.com/articles/140099/20110502/osama-bin-laden-never-charged-for-911-inside-job-likely-wtc7.htm (Accessed December 23, 2011).

[93] C. Bray (2011), "U.S. Formally Drops Charges Against bin Laden," at http://online.wsj.com/article/SB10001424052702304453304576391563524482274.html (Accessed December 23, 2011).

[94] (2006), "Bill Clinton: I got closer to killing bin Laden," at http://web.archive.org/web/20061005001828/http://www.cnn.com/2006/POLITICS/09/24/clinton.binladen/index.html (Accessed December 23, 2011).

[95] (2001), "Report: Clinton Targeted Bin Laden," at http://www.cbsnews.com/stories/2001/09/16/national/main311490.shtml (Accessed December 23, 2011).

[96] B. Wodward and T.E. Ricks (2001), 'CIA Trained Pakistanis to Nab Terrorist But

Military Coup Put an End to 1999 Plot', http://www.washingtonpost.com/wp-dyn/content/article/2007/11/18/AR2007111800629.html(Accessed December 23, 2011).

[97] H. Phil (2006), "9/11 jurors face complex life or death decisions," at http://articles.cnn.com/2006-04-25/justice/moussaoui.trial_1_qaeda-conspirator-zacarias-moussaoui-penalty-phase-jury-returns?_s=PM:LAW (Accessed December 23, 2011).

[98] Ishtiaq Mahsud And Sebastian Abbot, "Al-Qaida, Taliban Ask Pakistani Militants For Help," at http://www.huffingtonpost.com/2012/01/02/al-qaeda-taliban-pakistan_n_1179366.html (Accessed December 23, 2011).

[99] Yasir Rehman, "Al-Qaeda on verge of collapse, observers say," at http://al-shorfa.com/cocoon/meii/xhtml/en_GB/features/meii/features/main/2011/09/12/feature-01 (Accessed December 23, 2011).

[100] Rajeh Said "Al-Qaeda struggling to raise money following death of Osama bin Laden," *Asia Pacific Defense Forum* at http://apdforum.com/en_GB/article/rmiap/articles/online/features/2012/02/01/al-qaeda-funding (Accessed December 23, 2011)

CHAPTER 3

Planning and Implementation of 9/11

On September 11, 2001, 19 hijackers took control of four airplanes and targetted The World Trade Center in New York, The Pentagon near Washington, D.C., and the United States Capitol Building. Two planes hit the World Trade Center. One hit the Pentagon; however, one plane never arrived at its target, the Capitol Building. Almost 3,000 people died, making it the most deadly terrorist attack in U.S. history. It was carefully planned by Al-Qaeda, who sent 19 terrorists to take over Boeing 757 and Boeing 767 aircraft, operated by American Airlines and United Airlines.

In 1991, Bin Laden moved to the Sudan, where he led operations in East Africa, including the 1993 assault on American troops at Mogadishu in Somalia. Under international pressure, the Sudanese forced Bin Laden out of Sudan in 1996, and he returned to Afghanistan.

The Iraqi invasion of Kuwait in 1990 marked a point where bin Laden turned his attention towards the United States. He strongly urged the Saudi regime not to host the 500,000 American troops, instead advocating the use of a Mujahideen force to oust the Iraqis. Bin Laden strongly opposed the continued presence of American troops in Saudi Arabia. He interpreted the Prophet Muhammad as banning the "permanent presence of infidels in Arabia".[1] This is why bin Laden attacked American military targets in Saudi Arabia. Also, the date chosen for the 1998 African embassy bombings (August 7), was eight years to the day that American troops were sent to Saudi Arabia.

Bin Laden viewed the House of Saud (royal family) as apostates. In

Islam, apostasy refers to Muslims who have become non-believers and rejected Islam and is a very serious charge, which may result in capital punishment in many Muslim countries (especially for males). He also objected to American alliances with the governments of Kuwait, Jordan, and Egypt.

Viewing Israelis as infidels, not welcome in "Muslim land", bin Laden condemned U.S. foreign policy with regards to Israel. He observed that key figures, Madeline Albright, Sandy Berger, and William Cohen who were all Jewish, "drove Washington's undoubtedly pro-Israel policy" during the Clinton administration.

FATWAS

In 1996, bin Laden issued a *fatwa*, calling for American troops to get out of Saudi Arabia. It is interesting to note that in Islam, a *fatwa* can only be given by an Islamic scholar. Bin Laden was a political fighter who used Islam to motivate his fighters. The 1998 United States Embassy bombings were the turning point, which made him intent on attacking the United States.[8] Bin Laden issued another fatwa in February 1998, together with Ayman al Zawahiri, declaring war against Americans. Bin Laden stated "We do not have to differentiate between military or civilian. As far as we are concerned, they [Americans] are all targets." Bin Laden cited grievances including the presence of American infidels (troops) in the Saudi holy land, suffering of Iraqi people due to sanctions imposed after the Gulf War, and U.S. support of Israel. In the December 1999 interview with Rahimullah Yusufzai, bin Laden reiterated his ideology and objected to America's military presence in Saudi Arabia. He proclaimed that Americans were "too near to Mecca". He considered this a provocation to the entire Muslim world.[9] He also believed Israel "was killing and punishing Palestinians with American money and American arms."[2]

ORIGINS OF 9/11

According to the intelligence authorities in the United States and the Philippines, the September 11 attacks originated with Operation Bojinka (a plan that was not executed), which was conceived by Khalid Sheikh Mohammed (K.S.M) and his nephew, Ramzi Yousef. The first stage would be the assassination of Pope John Paul II, Bill Clinton, Pervez Musharraf, Benazir Bhutto and the bombing of eleven airliners. The second and third stages called for small airplanes loaded with explosives to be crashed into the CIA headquarters and other targets. The plot was discovered by

Khalid Sheikh Mohammed

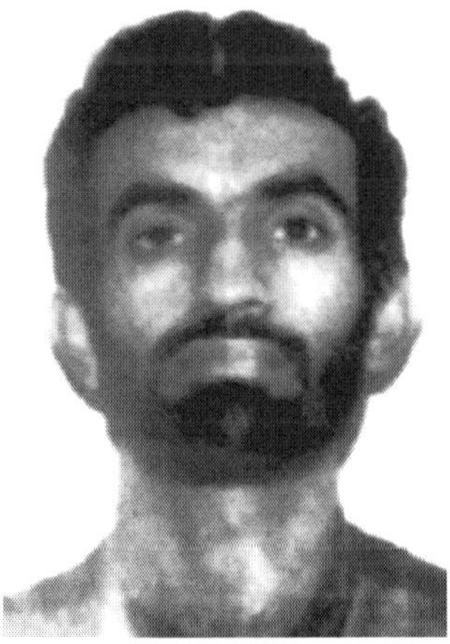

Ramzi Yousef

Hani Hanjour

Manila police on January 6, 1995, and Abdul Hakim Murad was arrested. Ramzi Yousef was arrested in Pakistan in February 1995. Wali Khan Amin Shah escaped after his arrest, but was re-arrested in Malaysia in December 1995. Khalid Sheik Mohammed escaped, and Riduan Isamuddin, also known as Hambali, was overlooked.

Khalid Sheikh Mohammed first presented the idea for the September 11 plot to Bin Laden in 1996 in Afghanistan.[3] However, nothing came of the idea at the time. At that point, Bin Laden and Al-Qaeda were in a period of transition, having just relocated back to Afghanistan from Sudan.

Mohammed moved to Qatar. Before the government there could arrest him (after a request by the United States), he fled to Afghanistan. The leaders of Al-Qaeda liked the idea of the modified Phases II and III Mohammed presented to them. Instead of using small airplanes loaded with explosives, as Murad planned to do, Mohammed planned to use commercial airliners. This method of attack was also outlined in Janet and Chris Morris 1984 book *The 40 Minute War*. Mohammed and Abu Zubaydah became the managers of the plot. During late 1996 and 1997, Khalid Sheik Mohammed stayed in the Czech Republic, as the Taliban allegedly did not approve of his womanising. German officials believe that the leaders of Al-Qaeda planned almost the entire September 11 plot in Afghanistan. Six of the hijackers that were chosen later down the line would have some say in the plot.

According to the September 11 Commission Khalid Shaikh Mohammed envisioned a hijacking of ten planes on both the East and West coasts, and for nine of them to be crashed into the World Trade Center, the Pentagon in Arlington, Virginia, either the White House or the United States Capitol, the tallest building in Los Angeles (the Library Tower, now known as the U.S. Bank Tower), the Sears Tower, both the Bank of America Tower and Space Needle in Seattle, Washington, and Empire State Building. The commission stated that Mohammed also wanted to personally hijack a tenth airliner, kill all of the adult males on board, land the plane in the U.S., make a political speech, and then free all of the women and children on the plane.

In December 1998, the Director of Central Intelligence Counterterrorist Center reported to the president that Al-Qaeda was preparing for attacks in the USA, including the training of personnel to hijack aircraft.

In late 1998 or early 1999, Bin Laden summoned Khalid Sheikh Mohammed to Kandahar and gave approval for Mohammed to go forward with the plot.[12] The plot was now referred to within Al-Qaeda as the "planes operation". In addition to flying planes into buildings, there was a plan to simultaneously crash additional planes in Asia, which could be done by operatives not granted a U.S. visa and without flight training.

Bin Laden cancelled the latter part of the planes operation in the spring of 2000, because of difficulties of coordination. The commission said that Khalid Sheikh Mohammed probably would have arranged to have six planes hijacked, even later on, if he was able to find more hijackers. He also considered a Phase II, but he and his colleagues spent so much time on the current plot that they could not plan a second phase.

A series of meetings occurred in spring of 1999, involving Khalid Sheikh Mohammed, Osama bin Laden, and his deputy Mohammed Atef.[4] Bin Laden recommended four individuals for the plot, including Nawaf al-Hazmi, Khalid al-Mihdhar, Walid Muhammad Salih Bin 'Attash (Khallad), and Abu Bara al-Taizi. Al-Hazmi and al-Mihdhar were both Saudi citizens, thus making it simple for them to obtain U.S. visas.

Khallad and al-Taizi were both Yemeni citizens, thus not able to easily obtain visas to the United States. The two Yemenis were assigned for the Asia component of the plot. When Mohamed Atta and other members of the Hamburg cell arrived in Afghanistan, Bin Laden was involved in selecting them for the plot, and assigning Atta to be the leader.[5]

Several Al-Qaeda members are said to have attended a meeting in Kuala Lumpur, Malaysia, from January 5 to January 8, 2000, that regarded the planning of the USS *Cole* bombing (which took place on October 12, 2000), and the forthcoming September 11, 2001 attacks. Hambali, Ramzi bin al-Shibh, Nawaf al-Hazmi, Khalid al-Mihdhar, and Tawfiq bin Attash attended the meeting.

The men were also photographed when they came out of the meeting. U.S. investigators did not identify these men until much later. The meeting was not wiretapped but it was videotaped.

Khalid Sheikh Mohammed was the head of Al-Qaeda's 'military committee'. He provided operational support, such as selecting targets and helping arrange travel for the hijackers.[4] Khalid Sheikh Mohammed explained to Fouda, "We had a large surplus of brothers willing to die as martyrs. As we studied various targets, nuclear facilities arose as a key option"... but the nuclear targets were dropped for concerns the plan would "get out of hand."

According to several captured Al-Qaeda members, the leaders decided that World Trade Center, The Pentagon, and the United States Capitol were the targets, and that leaders rejected the White House as it was too difficult to see from the air.

According to captured member Abu Zubaydah, the White House was the intended target of United Airlines Flight 93. According to his courtroom confession (which he recanted after being sentenced to life in prison) Zacarias Moussaoui intended to hijack a fifth plane with Richard Colvin Reid which would use GPS to find the White House.

HAMBURG CELL

Mohamed Atta, Ramzi bin al-Shibh, Marwan al-Shehhi and Ziad Jarrah came into the picture in 1999, when they arrived in Kandahar from Germany. The Hamburg cell was formed starting in 1998 shortly after Mohammed got approval by Al-Qaeda leadership for his plot. Mohamed Atta, Marwan al-Shehhi, Ziad Jarrah, Ramzi bin al-Shibh, Said Bahaji, Zakariyah Essabar, and fifteen others were all members.

Mohamed Atta was very religious, but not fanatically so when he came to Germany in fall 1992 to study urban planning at the Technical University of Hamburg.[6] While in Germany, he was drawn to Al Quds Mosque in Hamburg, which adheres to a "harsh, uncompromisingly fundamentalist, and resoundingly militant" version of Sunni Islam.[7] A friend of Atta's recalled meeting him at the Al-Quds mosque in 1993, though it is not known when he started going there. Atta had always lived as a strict Muslim.

Atta went to Mecca in 1995, and returned to Germany as more of a fanatical. Also in late 1997, Mohamed Atta told his roommate that he was going to Mecca, but he most likely instead went to Afghanistan. Atta had already taken his Mecca pilgrimage 18 months earlier. According to Al Jazeera journalist Yosri Fouda, Atta went to the mosque around this time period "not to pray but to sign his death will." He is known to have come for training Al-Qaeda camps in Afghanistan in 1999 and 2000.[8]

Ramzi bin al-Shibh, who also went under the name "Ramzi Omar", was a citizen of Yemen. In 1995, he came to Germany seeking asylum, claiming to be a political refugee from Sudan. The judge refused the asylum request, and bin al-Shibh returned to the Hadramawt region of Yemen. Bin al-Shibh later got a German visa under his real name, and came to Germany in 1997. There, he met Mohamed Atta, the leader of the Hamburg cell, at a mosque.[9] For two years, Atta and bin al-Shibh were roommates in Germany.[9]

In late 1999, bin al-Shibh traveled to Kandahar in Afghanistan, where he received training at Al-Qaeda training camps, and met others involved in planning the 9/11 attacks.[9] Original plans for the 9/11 attacks called for bin al-Shibh to be one of the hijacker pilots, along with Mohamed Atta, Marwan al-Shehhi, and Ziad Jarrah. From Hamburg, Germany, bin al-Shibh applied to take flight training in the United States. At that time, he also applied to Aviation Language Services, which provides language training for student pilots. Bin al-Shibh applied for an entry visa to the United States, four times, and was refused each time. He made visa applications in Germany on May 17, 2000, and again in June, on September 16, and October 25, 2000.

According to the 9/11 Commission, this refusal of a visa was out of general concern by U.S. officials that people from Yemen would illegally overstay their visit and seek work in the United States. His friend, Zakariyah Essabar, was also denied visas. After he failed to enter the United States, bin al-Shibh took on more of a "coordinator" role in the plot, and a link between Atta in the United States and Khalid Sheikh Mohammed in Afghanistan.[10]

Marwan al-Shehhi came to Bonn, Germany in 1996, on scholarship from the United Arab Emirates Army to study marine engineering. Al-Shehhi met Atta in 1997, and in 1998, he moved to Hamburg to join Atta and bin al-Shibh. As the son of a religiously trained father, al-Shehhi was very religious, well-educated in Islam, and adhered to a strict form of Islam. However, he had a friendlier, more humorous personality than Atta, who was very serious and more reclusive.

Ziad Jarrah came from Lebanon to Germany in April 1996, where he enrolled in a junior college in Greifswald. There, he met his girlfriend, Aysel Senguen, a medical student. By late 1996, Jarrah began turning radical. In September 1997, he transferred to the Technical University of Hamburg to study aircraft engineering. In the summer of that year, he worked at a paint shop factory for Volkswagen in Wolfsburg.

Other members of the Hamburg cell included Said Bahaji, who came to Germany in 1995. He had been born there, but moved to Morocco at age 9. In 1996, Said Bahaji enrolled in the electrical engineering program at the technical university. He spent weekdays at a student home and weekends at the home of his aunt, Barbara Arens. Arens, his "high tech aunt", kicked Bahaji out of the house when she saw his religious beliefs turn more radical.

SELECTION FOR 9/11 PLOT

In 1999, this group decided to go to Chechnya to fight. While still in Germany, they met Khalid al Masri who put the group in contact with Abu Musab in Duisburg, Germany. Abu Musab turned out to be Mohamedou Ould Slahi, an important Al-Qaeda operative. Slahi advised them that it would be difficult to get into Chechnya and advised them instead to go to Afghanistan for training first. In late 1999, the Hamburg group met with Bin Laden, and pledged loyalty to him.

They agreed to undertake a highly secret mission, and were told to go enroll in flight training. Atta was selected by Bin Laden to lead the group. Bin Laden met with Atta several more times for additional instructions. The selection of hijackers was entirely a decision made by Bin Laden, along with Mohammed Atef. The hijackers had not yet met with Khalid Sheikh Mohamed. At the time, the hijacking team also included Nawaf al-Hazmi and Khalid al-Mihdhar, who were selected in early 1999 by Osama bin Laden.

Atta, al-Shehhi, and Jarrah all obtained new passports, claiming the old ones were lost, before applying for U.S. visas. Atta, Jarrah, and bin al-Shibh returned to Hamburg, early in 2000, while al-Shehhi went back to the United Arab Emirates to get a new passport and U.S. visa. Once back in Germany, they made efforts to appear less radical—distanced themselves from others and stopped attending extremist mosques, changed their appearance and behavior, and Jarrah was behaving more the way he did when he first met Senguen.

HANI HANJOUR

Hani Hanjour arrived in San Diego on December 8, 2000, joining Hamzi there. Hani Hanjour had previously lived in the United States, attending some flight training in 1996 and 1997. In 1997, after three months of training in Arizona, he obtained his private pilot's license. With further training, Hanjour earned a commercial pilot's certificate, issued by the FAA, in April 1999. Hanjour aspired to become a commercial pilot, applying to a civil aviation school in Jeddah, in 1999, but was rejected.

In Spring 2000, Hanjour went to Afghanistan. At the Al Farouq training camp, he was identified as a trained pilot, and asked to report to Khalid Sheikh Mohammed. He returned to Saudi Arabia on June 20, and obtained a U.S. visa on September 25, 2000. He arrived back in San Diego on December 8, 2000. Hamzi and Hanjour then left for Mesa, Arizona, where Hanjour enrolled in refresher training at Arizona Aviation.

He had difficulties with multi-engine training, due to his poor English language skills. He did some training at Pan Am International Flight Academy, on a Boeing 737 simulator, but struggled there, as well. Though he struggled, Hanjour completed the initial training by the end of March 2001. At that point, they left Arizona and headed east. By April 4, they had arrived in Falls Church, Virginia.

ARRIVAL IN THE UNITED STATES

Al-Mihdhar and al-Hazmi arrived in Los Angeles on January 15, 2000. On January 18, Marwan al-Shehhi applied for a visa into the United States while he was in the United Arab Emirates. He was the first member to apply for a visa in the Hamburg cell.

By the end of June, Atta, Jarrah, and al-Shehhi left for the United States. Bin al-Shibh and Essabar wanted to join Atta, al-Shehhi, and Jarrah, but they were denied U.S. Visas several times. Bin al-Shibh's visa was denied since he was a citizen of Yemen. Bin al-Shibh decided to support the cell by sending money to it. Mohammed was making repeated trips to Indonesia and the Philippines in Southeast Asia at the time. Jarrah nearly abandoned his role in the plot and probably would have been replaced by Zacarias Moussaoui had he done so.

A man named Omar al-Bayoumi was in San Diego, California since 1995. He was raising a family and received a monthly stipend from his former employer, an aviation company in Saudi Arabia. He was seen regularly videotaping various locations. Al-Bayoumi was quick to house immigrants who needed housing. In 2000, he settled in Nawaf al-Hazmi and Khalid al-Mihdhar. According to al-Hazmi, al-Bayoumi met him and al-Mihdhar at a restaurant in Los Angeles. Al-Bayoumi offered a ride to San Diego after he heard the men speak Arabic. Al-Bayoumi threw the men a welcome party and al-Hazmi, who said he was in the United States to learn English, signed a six-month lease. He often surfed the Internet from the San Diego State University Library.

The first two months of the lease were paid for, yet the men complained that the lease was too expensive. In the spring, al-Hazmi told a friend that someone was going to wire $5000 to him, and that the money would come from Saudi Arabia. Al-Hazmi told his friend that he had no account. The friend allowed him to use his account, and later found that the money came from a man named "Ali", and that it didn't originate from the United States.

The two men wanted to take flight lessons, which is why they got the money. A friend took them to Montgomery Field and arranged lessons for them. They took a single flight lesson and did not return. Fereidoun "Fred" Sorbi, the instructor, recalled, "The first day they came in here, they said they want to fly Boeings. We said you have to start slower. You can't just jump right into Boeings."

Al-Hazmi had season passes to the San Diego Zoo and SeaWorld. The men frequented a men's club in San Diego called Cheetah's, which is near the Islamic Center. Al-Mihdhar and al-Hazmi frequently drove to Las Vegas in the Toyota sedan they bought.

FLIGHT TRAINING

In March 2000, Mohamed Atta contacted the Academy of Lakeland in Florida, via e-mail, inquiring about flight training, "Dear sir, we are a small group of young men from different Arab countries. Now we are living in Germany since a while for study purposes. We would like to start training for the career of airline professional pilots. In this field we haven't yet any knowledge but we are ready to undergo an intensive training program (up to ATP and eventually higher)." He sent 50-60 similar e-mails to other flight training schools in the United States.

On May 18, 2000, Atta applied for and received a U.S. visa. After obtaining his visa, Atta traveled to Prague before going to the United States. Atta, along with Marwan al-Shehhi arrived in Venice, Florida, and visited Huffman Aviation to "check out the facility." They explained that "they came from a flight school in the area, they were not happy and they were looking for another flight school". By December, Atta and al-Shehhi left Huffman Aviation, and on December 21, Atta received a pilot license.[11]

MUSCLE HIJACKERS

During the Summer and Fall of 2000, Bin Laden and other senior al-Qaeda leaders began selecting the "muscle" hijackers. With Hamzi and al-Mihdhar already selected, thirteen additional hijackers were selected. They were all from Saudi Arabia, except for Fayez Banihammad who was from the United Arab Emirates. They were all between age 20 and 28, most were unemployed with no more than a high school education, and were unmarried.

The muscle hijackers included Salem al-Hazmi, a younger brother of Nawaf al-Hamzi. They came to Afghanistan for training, to go fight in Chechnya. In the Summer and Fall of 2000, they were identified as candidates for the 9/11 operation, and brought before Bin Laden and Atef. Bin Laden personally selected the 13 hijackers from the candidates. They briefly left Afghanistan to acquire U.S. visas, and then returned for further training in late 2000 or early 2001. In late April 2001, the muscle hijackers began arriving in the U.S.

FINAL PREPARATIONS

The report by the September 11 Commission stated that Osama bin Laden aggressively pushed the September 11 plan as it formed, even when some of his closest aides were advising him to cancel the plans. Osama bin Laden envisioned an increase in recruiting and fundraising after the attacks would happen.

Hani Hanjour and Majed Moqed were photographed using an ATM in Maryland on September 5th, 2001 just 6 days prior to September 11th, 2001.

One week after he was given the money, Moussaoui came to Minnesota from Oklahoma. He paid $6,300 in cash to the Pan Am International Flight Academy on August 10. He was arrested for immigration violations on August 17. Some investigators think that this sparked the move to the attacks.

About three weeks prior to the attacks, the targets were assigned to four teams. The United States Capitol was called "The Faculty of Law". The Pentagon was dubbed "The Faculty of Fine Arts". Atta codenamed the World Trade Center as "The Faculty of Town Planning".

A conspirator named Abu Abdul Rahman sent a "love message" on an Internet chat room to his "German girlfriend", who was really Ramzi bin al-Shibh. The message said, "The first semester commences in three weeks. Two high schools and two universities ... This summer will surely be hot ...19 [the eventual number of hijackers] certificates for private education and four exams [the number of planes used]. Regards to the professor. Goodbye."

Between August 25 and August 28, the hijackers had bought their tickets. Some September 11 hijackers bought their reservations over the Internet on sites such as Travelocity, and some bought them in person at the airport.

Two of the United Airlines Flight 175 hijackers paid $4,500 for each of their tickets. Three of the other hijackers on that flight paid $1,600 and $1,760 for their tickets. Atta booked seat 8D. Waleed al-Shehri and Wail al-Shehri, who sat in seats 2B and 2A, used the same Hollywood post-

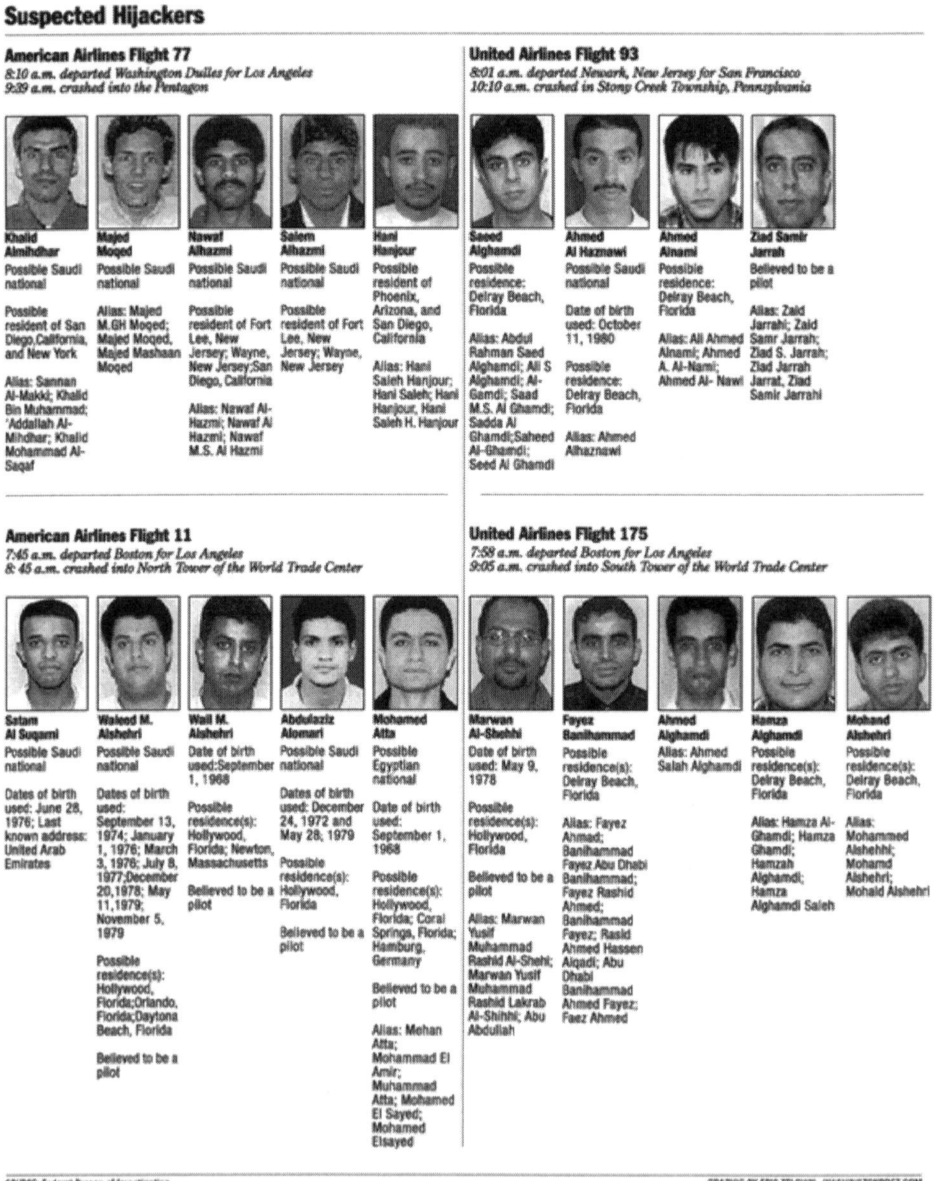

Suspected Hijackers

American Airlines Flight 77
8:10 a.m. departed Washington Dulles for Los Angeles
9:39 a.m. crashed into the Pentagon

Khalid Almihdhar — Possible Saudi national. Possible resident of San Diego,California, and New York. Alias: Sannan Al-Makki; Khalid Bin Muhammad; 'Addallah Al-Mihdhar; Khalid Mohammad Al-Saqaf

Majed Moqed — Possible Saudi national. Alias: Majed M.GH Moqed; Majed Moqed, Majed Mashaan Moqed

Nawaf Alhazmi — Possible Saudi national. Possible resident of Fort Lee, New Jersey; Wayne, New Jersey;San Diego, California. Alias: Nawaf Al-Hazmi; Nawaf Al Hazmi; Nawaf M.S. Al Hazmi

Salem Alhazmi — Possible Saudi national. Possible resident of Fort Lee, New Jersey; Wayne, New Jersey

Hani Hanjour — Possible resident of Phoenix, Arizona, and San Diego, California. Alias: Hani Saleh Hanjour; Hani Saleh; Hani Hanjour, Hani Saleh H. Hanjour

United Airlines Flight 93
8:01 a.m. departed Newark, New Jersey for San Francisco
10:10 a.m. crashed in Stony Creek Township, Pennsylvania

Saeed Alghamdi — Possible residence: Delray Beach, Florida. Alias: Abdul Rahman Saed Alghamdi; Ali S Alghamdi; Al-Gamdi; Saad M.S. Al Ghamdi; Sadda Al Ghamdi;Saheed Al-Ghamdi; Seed Al Ghamdi

Ahmed Al Haznawi — Possible Saudi national. Date of birth used: October 11, 1980. Possible residence: Delray Beach, Florida. Alias: Ahmed Alhaznawi

Ahmed Alnami — Possible residence: Delray Beach, Florida. Alias: Ali Ahmed Alnami; Ahmed A. Al-Nami; Ahmed Al- Nawi

Ziad Samir Jarrah — Believed to be a pilot. Alias: Zaid Jarrahi; Zaid Samr Jarrah; Ziad S. Jarrah; Ziad Jarrah Jarrat, Ziad Samir Jarrahi

American Airlines Flight 11
7:45 a.m. departed Boston for Los Angeles
8:45 a.m. crashed into North Tower of the World Trade Center

Satam Al Suqami — Possible Saudi national. Dates of birth used: June 28, 1976; Last known address: United Arab Emirates

Waleed M. Alshehri — Possible Saudi national. Dates of birth used: September 13, 1974; January 1, 1976; March 3, 1976; July 8, 1977;December 20,1978; May 11,1979; November 5, 1979. Possible residence(s): Hollywood, Florida;Orlando, Florida;Daytona Beach, Florida. Believed to be a pilot

Wail M. Alshehri — Date of birth used:September 1, 1968. Possible residence(s): Hollywood, Florida; Newton, Massachusetts. Believed to be a pilot

Abdulaziz Alomari — Possible Saudi national. Dates of birth used: December 24, 1972 and May 28, 1979. Possible residence(s): Hollywood, Florida. Believed to be a pilot

Mohamed Atta — Possible Egyptian national. Date of birth used: September 1, 1968. Possible residence(s): Hollywood, Florida; Coral Springs, Florida; Hamburg, Germany. Believed to be a pilot. Alias: Mohan Atta; Mohammad El Amir; Muhammad Atta; Mohamed El Sayed; Mohamed Elsayed

United Airlines Flight 175
7:58 a.m. departed Boston for Los Angeles
9:05 a.m. crashed into South Tower of the World Trade Center

Marwan Al-Shehhi — Date of birth used: May 9, 1978. Possible residence(s): Hollywood, Florida. Believed to be a pilot. Alias: Marwan Yusif Muhammad Rashid Al-Shehi; Marwan Yusif Muhammad Rashid Lakrab Al-Shihhi; Abu Abdullah

Fayez Banihammad — Possible residence(s): Delray Beach, Florida. Alias: Fayez Ahmad; Banihammad Fayez Abu Dhabi Banihammad; Fayez Rashid Ahmed; Banihammad Fayez; Rasid Ahmed Hassen Alqadi; Abu Dhabi Banihammad Ahmed Fayez; Faez Ahmed

Ahmed Alghamdi — Alias: Ahmed Salah Alghamdi

Hamza Alghamdi — Possible residence(s): Delray Beach, Florida. Alias: Hamza Al-Ghamdi; Hamza Ghamdi; Hamzah Alghamdi; Hamza Alghamdi Saleh

Mohand Alshehri — Possible residence(s): Delray Beach, Florida. Alias: Mohammed Alshehhi; Mohamd Alshehri; Mohald Alshehri

SOURCE: Federal Bureau of Investigation
GRAPHIC BY ERIC TELCHIN – WASHINGTONPOST.COM

September 11 Hijackers

office-box address to buy their tickets. Satam al-Suqami would pay in cash and sit in seat 10B. Abdulaziz al-Omari also planned to be on this flight.

On August 28, Mohamed Atta bought his ticket with his VISA card at the American Airlines website by using addresses in Coral Springs and Hollywood, Florida. He established an advantage frequent flyer miles account on August 25.

According to Ramzi bin al-Shibh, on August 29, Mohamed Atta notified bin al-Shibh after Moussaoui's capture in an early morning coded telephone message, "A mate of mine bothered me with this puzzle and I was hoping you would help me solve it. Two sticks, a dash and a cake with a stick down. What is it?"

"Did you wake me up to tell me this puzzle?" Ramzi bin al-Shibh replied. Atta meant that the attacks would be on September 11; he chose when the attack would happen. The date that the attacks would occur on was uncertain until the phone call happened. A report by the September 11 Commission stated that Atta chose the date "so that the United States Congress would be in session."

Salem al-Hazmi, Majed Moqed, and three other hijackers worked out at Gold's Gym, Greenbelt, Maryland from September 2 to September 6.

U.S. investigators say that Atta sent a package to Mustafa Ahmed, the alleged Al-Qaeda paymaster on September 4. Mustafa Ahmed was in the United Arab Emirates at the time.

Said Bahaji left Germany and flew to Karachi via Istanbul on September 4. German police found that two other men on the flight stayed with Bahaji at the Embassy Hotel in Karachi. The men had false identification papers. Zakariya Essabar disappeared around the same time. Investigators think that he may have been one of the passengers on the plane.

Ramzi bin al-Shibh returned to Spain on September 5, flying from Düsseldorf. Investigators say that he stayed at his private home in the Madrid area, and he never used his return ticket. He instead headed for Afghanistan.

Around this time, the FBI had been unable to access Moussaoui's computer. Agents were notified by the Central Intelligence Agency at this time that they needed to look for Khalid al-Mihdhar and Nawaf al-Hazmi.

Ziad Jarrah wrote a letter to his girlfriend and sent it to her on September 10. He wrote "I have done what I had to do" and "You should be very proud, it is an honor, and you will see the result, and everyone

The Pentagon

World Trade Center Towers

will be happy" as well as "Hold on to what you have until we meet each other again." The letter was returned to the U.S., as Jarrah made an error in writing the address.

Mohamed Atta spent September 10 with Abdulaziz al-Omari in South Portland and Scarborough, Maine. Atta called Khalid Sheik Mohammed that day. Intelligence officials think that Mohammed gave him a coded signal to proceed.

FINANCIAL SUPPORT

The 9/11 Commission stated in their final report that the "9/11 plotters eventually spent somewhere between $400,000 and $500,000 to plan and conduct their attack" but the "origin of the funds remains unknown." The Commission noted: "we have seen no evidence that any foreign government-or foreign government official-supplied any funding." Some people have claimed that the operation was financed by elements of the Pakistani government, specifically within the Inter-Services Intelligence (ISI), as well as agents of the Saudi Arabian government working from within the United States.

A senior-level U.S. government source told CNN in October 2001 that U.S. investigators believed Ahmed Omar Saeed Sheikh (Ahmed Umar Syed Sheikh), a long time ISI asset, using the alias Mustafa Muhammad Ahmad, sent more than $100,000 from Pakistan to Mohamed Atta, the suspected hijack ringleader of the September 11, 2001, attacks.

"Investigators said Atta distributed the funds to conspirators in Florida in the weeks before the deadliest acts of terrorism on U.S. soil that destroyed the World Trade Center, heavily damaged the Pentagon and left thousands dead [...] Syed also is described as a key figure in the funding operation of Al-Qaeda, the network headed by suspected terrorist mastermind Osama bin Laden."

The Pittsburgh Tribune notes *"There are many in Musharraf's government who believe that Saeed Sheikh's power comes not from the ISI, but from his connections with our own CIA."*[12]

CNN later confirmed that it was "Ahmed Umar Syed Sheikh, whom authorities say used a pseudonym to wire $100,000 to suspected hijacker Mohammad Atta, who then distributed the money in the United States."[13]

Soon after the money transfer was discovered, the head of Pakistan's Inter-Services Intelligence, General Mahmood (Mahmud) Ahmed, resigned from his position. Indian news outlets reported the Federal

Bureau of Investigation (FBI) was investigating the possibility that General Mahmood Ahmed ordered Saeed Sheikh to send the $100,000 to Atta, while most Western media outlets only reported his connections to the Taliban as the reason for his departure from the ISI.

The Wall Street Journal was one of the few Western news organisations to follow up on the story, citing the Times of India: "US authorities sought [Gen. Mahmud Ahmed's] removal after confirming the fact that $100,000 wired to WTC hijacker Mohamed Atta from Pakistan by Ahmad Umar Sheikh at the instance of Gen Mahmud." The best coverage came from *The Daily Excelsior*, reporting "The FBI's examination of the hard disk of the cellphone company Omar Sheikh had subscribed to led to the discovery of the "link" between him and the deposed chief of the Pakistani ISI, Gen. Mehmood Ahmed. And as the FBI investigators delved deep, sensational information surfaced with regard to the transfer of $100,000 to Mohamed Atta, one of the Kamikaze pilots who flew a Boeing into the World Trade Center. Gen. Mehmood Ahmed, the FBI investigators found, fully knew about the transfer of money to Atta."

According to the *Washington Post*, "on the morning of Sept. 11, [Porter] Goss and [Bob] Graham were having breakfast with a Pakistani general named Mahmud Ahmed—the soon-to-be-sacked head of Pakistan's intelligence service"[37] On September 12 and 13, Lt. Gen. Mahmood met with United States Deputy Secretary of State Richard Armitage, Senator Joseph Biden, the Chairman of the Senate Foreign Relations Committee, and Secretary of State Colin Powell. An agreement on Pakistan's collaboration in the new "war on terror" was negotiated between Mahmood and Armitage.

Lt Gen Mehmood Ahmed then led a six-member delegation to the Afghan city of Kandahar in order to hold crisis talks with the Taliban leadership, supposedly in an attempt to persuade them to hand over Osama bin Laden.

In June 2001, a "high-placed member of a US intelligence agency" told BBC reporter Greg Palast that "after the 2000 elections, the agencies were told to "back off" investigating the Bin Ladens and Saudi royals".[14]

In May 2002, former FBI Agent Robert Wright, Jr. delivered a tearful press conference apologizing to the families who lost loved ones on 9/11. He described how his superiors intentionally obstructed his investigation into Al-Qaeda financing.

Agent Wright would later tell ABC's Brian Ross: "September 11th is a direct result of the incompetence of the FBI's International Terrorism

Unit," specifically referring to the Bureau's hindering of his investigation into Yassin al-Qadi, whom Ross described as a powerful Saudi Arabian businessman with extensive financial ties in Chicago. One month after September 11, the U.S. government officially identified Yassin al-Qadi as one of Osama bin Laden's primary financiers and a Specially Designated Global Terrorist.

In an interview with Computerworld Magazine, a former business associate Zaidie described his relationship with al-Qadi: "I met him a few times and talked to him a few times on the telephone. He never talked to me about violence. Instead, he talked very highly of his relationship with [former President] Jimmy Carter and [Vice President] Dick Cheney."[15]

The Muwafaq Foundation, which U.S. authorities have confirmed was an arm of bin Laden's terror organisation, was headed by Yassin al-Qadi, who was also known as the owner of Ptech— a company that has supplied high-tech computer systems to the FBI, the Internal Revenue Service, the United States Congress, the United States Army, the Navy, the Air Force, the North Atlantic Treaty Organization, the Federal Aviation Administration (FAA), and the White House.

A former FBI counter-terrorism agent commented: "For someone like [al-Qadi] to be involved in a capacity, in an organisation, a company that has access to classified information, that has access to government open or classified computer systems, would be of grave concern." Also sitting on Ptech's board of directors was Yacub Mirza— "a senior official of major radical Islamic organizations that have been linked by the US government to terrorism." In addition, Hussein Ibrahim, the Vice President and Chief Scientist of Ptech, was vice chairman of a now defunct investment group called BMI, a company the FBI has named as a conduit used by al-Qadi to launder money to Hamas terrorists.

According to Senator Bob Graham, who was chairman of the Senate Intelligence Committee from June 2001 through the buildup to the Iraq war, "Two of the Sept. 11, 2001, hijackers had a support network in the United States that included agents of the Saudi government, and the Bush administration and FBI blocked a congressional investigation into that relationship," as reported by the *Miami Herald*.

"And in Graham's book, *Intelligence Matters*, obtained by The Herald Saturday, he makes clear that some details of that financial support from Saudi Arabia were in the 27 pages of the congressional inquiry's final report that were blocked from release by the administration, despite the pleas of leaders of both parties on the House and Senate intelligence committees."

FACE TO FACE WITH OSAMA

Millions of words have been written about bin Laden, but almost all of them by people who have never met him. One of the few who has is a distinguished Pakistani journalist Rahimullah Yusufzai. Here he describes his extraordinary meetings with the world's most wanted man, and tries to explain what makes him tick.

The fax rolled off the machine into the offices of Al-Jazeera Television on Sunday, and a world preparing for war paused for a moment to read it. Signed Osama bin Laden, it looked like a call to arms from the FBI's most wanted man, calling on "our beloved brothers" to "triumph over the infidel forces and the forces of tyranny, and to destroy the new Jewish-Christian crusader campaign on the soil of Pakistan and Afghanistan." Bin Laden, it seemed, was preparing for war.

We may never know if the fax came from his pen. But from my meetings and phone calls in recent years with him, I believe I have glimpsed his state of mind. It is three years ago now that the first call came to my office at The News in Peshawar, summoning me to a camp in southern Afghanistan.

The Pakistani border guards would not let us cross, so the Islamist militant group who had organised the meeting smuggled us in. We waited for three days until finally, on May 25 1998, we met Bin Laden - a softly spoken man who drank copious amounts of water, because of a kidney problem, as we later discovered.

He had brought me there to announce the launch of his International Islamic Front for Jihad Against the United States and Israel - but the Taliban had not approved the announcement, and were furious. Mullah Omar angrily insisted that there could only be one ruler of Afghanistan - Bin Laden or himself.

Bin Laden apologised, and for my next meeting with him, a one-to-one interview on December 23 the same year, he was sure to obtain the approval of his protectors. I had had one communication with him since our first meeting, on the day of America's attack in August 1998 in retaliation for the African embassy bombings.

The Egyptian Jihad leader Dr Ayman Al-Zawahiri had telephoned me at my office. Bin Laden was sitting next to him, Al-Zawahiri said, and wanted to stress that he was not involved in the bombings, though he was pleased by them. An hour after the US attack, he called back: they had survived the attack on Bin Laden's camp, Al-Zawahiri said, and were ready for war.

The second time I met him, he seemed the complete opposite of the man we have been led to imagine in recent weeks. He was polite, quiet, very civilised, and shy: after I had taken a few photographs, he begged me to stop. I particularly remember the softness of his hands. They spoke of a wealthy background, of never having done much physical work.

We talked for four hours, through the night, drinking tea. He carefully denied involvement in the US embassy bombings, but said he felt joy that they had happened, and I took that as an indirect admission. He said it was not his job to organise such attacks; it was his job to create awareness about the injustices done by the US to Muslims, to provoke and incite Muslims against America. And he was happy that his message seemed to be getting through. He would certainly say the same now about the attacks of September 11. But though he might want to contact the media, he cannot. That would infuriate the Taliban, and he needs them desperately.

At that second meeting, we spoke about what he was fighting for, and what he hated. At first, he told me, he had been opposed to the Americans because of their military presence in Saudi Arabia and because he felt they were too near to Mecca. That was a provocation to the entire Muslim world, he said.

But once those early encounters in his homeland had stoked his feelings, he came to concentrate more on America's involvement in the Middle East. He declared a jihad against America and Israel jointly, he said, because he believed Israel was killing and punishing Palestinians with American money and American arms.

There was, however, one significant element missing from his list of grievances: he did not say anything about the idea of America - its rights, its freedoms, its prosperity. It was in American foreign policy that he saw the greatest threat to Islam. Indeed, he criticised the West for supporting dictators and authoritarian regimes in Islamic countries simply because it suited their interests.

Whatever their origins, Bin Laden's views have caught part of the popular Muslim imagination. In the West, one view is heard - the elitist one which dismisses him as an extremist and a terrorist. But then there is the common view, held by people who do not read the English press, and they are fascinated by Bin *Laden because he has challenged America.*

The name Osama has always been rare in northern Pakistan. Now, though, it is growing fast in popularity among parents choosing names for their children. In Pakistani cities, firms are named after him, too: Osama Medical Stores; Osama Property Services.

But that support may meet its match in US military strength. The Taliban face losing their country because of their support for one person. And that will place pressure on the central political relationship in Afghanistan: that between Bin Laden and the Taliban's religious leader, Mullah Omar.

I first met Mullah Omar in Kandahar in March 1995, the first journalist to do so. He admitted me to his office, where he was seated on the ground with his fellow Taliban, although later, when he was made spiritual leader, they built a platform to elevate him above his compatriots.

He was a very simple man, a village clergyman: heavily built, not very articulate, a shy person who seemed to know little about the world. His right eye had been damaged by shrapnel after a battle with Soviet troops. He told me he had been a great marksman in his time, attacking Russian forces with anti-tank missiles. He said he was 35, though he looked older.

Mullah Omar - originally a small-time military commander - met Bin Laden in 1996, by which time the Saudi was renowned for his financial gifts to wounded Afghan soldiers. After some initial mutual suspicion, the Taliban allowed Bin Laden to stay. But I do not believe that the two were ever close friends. There have been rumours that Mullah Omar has married Bin Laden's daughter or sister, or vice versa. But though we have made endless enquiries, we have never obtained proof.

Mullah Omar might be relieved if Bin Laden left Afghanistan, but the Taliban have given their word, and they will be bound by it. The leader finds himself balancing the need to save his country with the need to uphold Afghan tradition regarding the hosting of such an honoured guest. And Bin Laden, of course, has nowhere to go.

What Mullah Omar and Bin Laden share, more than anything, is an absolute certainty that Allah will stay with them and support them no matter how great the superpower that attacks them. I have not spoken to Mullah Omar or to Osama bin Laden since the events of September 11, but I have spoken several times with senior Taliban figures.

I doubt their claims that 300,000 people have signed up to fight, and they will have difficulty convincing their exhausted people that they should fight another war. But an American attack would be an enormous provocation to the Afghan people, motivating many of those who would not normally support the leadership. Afghanistan is waiting for war.

NOTES

[1] P. L. Bergen, *Holy War Inc.* Simon & Schuster,2001, p. 3.

[2] R.Yusufzai, "Face to face with Osama" *The Guardian*, 2001, London. http://www.guardian.co.uk/world/2001/sep/26/afghanistan.terrorism3 (Accessed January 10, 2012).

[3] http://news.bbc.co.uk/2/hi/south_asia/3128802.stm (Accessed January 10, 2012)..

[4] National Commission on Terrorist Attacks Upon the United States. "Chapter 5". *9/11 Commission Report*. http://www.9-11commission.gov/report/911Report_Ch5.htm (Accessed January 10, 2012).

[5] P. Bergen, *The Osama bin Laden I Know*, Free Press, 2006, p. 283.

[6] Bergen, P.L. *Holy War Inc.* Simon & Schuster, (2001). p. 37.

[7] T. McDermott, *Perfect Soldiers*, Harper, 2005, pp. 2–3.

[8] "Atta trained in Afghanistan," (2002), at http://news.bbc.co.uk/2/hi/americas/2213701.stm (Accessed January 10, 2012)

[9] "Ramzi Binalshibh: al-Qaeda Suspect," (2002), at http://news.bbc.co.uk/2/hi/south_asia/2257456.stm (Accessed January 10, 2012)

[10] J.M. Mary (2009), "The Mastermind," at http://www.cbsnews.com/stories/2002/10/09/60II/main524947.shtml (Accessed January 10, 2012)

[11] J. Cloud, (2001), "Atta's Odyssey," *Time Magazine World*, at http://www.time.com/time/magazine/article/0,9171,1101011008-176917,00.html (Accessed January 10, 2012)

[12] March 3, 2002, "Did Pearl die because Pakistan deceived CIA?" at http://www.pittsburghlive.com/x/pittsburghtrib/s_20141.html (Accessed January 10, 2012)

[13] M.A. Ressa, (2001), "India wants terror spotlight on Kashmir," at http://archives.cnn.com/2001/WORLD/asiapcf/south/10/08/india.ressa/ (Accessed January 10, 2012).

[14] Has someone been sitting on the FBI? (2001), at http://news.bbc.co.uk/2/hi/events/newsnight/1645527.stm (Accessed January 10, 2012).

[15] D. Verton (2003), "Ptech workers tell the story behind the search," at http://www.computerworld.com/s/article/77682/Ptech_workers_tell_the_story_behind_the_search?taxonomyId=017 (Accessed January 10, 2012).

CHAPTER 4

Ten Years of Nine Lives

TRACKING OSAMA BIN LADEN

Twenty nine days after 9/11, on October 7, 2001, the official invasion by US, UK and coalition allied forces began with airstrikes over enemy targets in Afghanistan against the ruling Taliban and Al-Qaeda. Kabul, the capital city fell by mid-November. The remaining Al-Qaeda and Taliban remnants fell back to the rugged mountains of eastern Afghanistan, mainly Tora Bora, which Coalition forces focused on in December. Following which it is believed that bin Laden escaped into Pakistan during the battle.

The U.S. Senate Foreign Relations Committee completed a detailed look back at a crucial failure early in this battle against Al-Qaeda: the escape of Osama bin Laden from American forces in the Afghan mountains of Tora Bora in December 2001.

"Removing the Al-Qaeda leader from the battlefield eight years ago would not have eliminated the worldwide extremist threat," the committee's report concludes. "But the decisions that opened the door for his escape to Pakistan allowed bin Laden to emerge as a potent symbolic figure who continues to attract a steady flow of money and inspire fanatics worldwide."

The report, based in part on a little-noticed 2007 history of the Tora Bora episode by the military's Special Operations Command, asserts that the consequences of not sending American troops in 2001 to block bin Laden's escape into Pakistan are still being felt. The report blames the lapse for "laying the foundation for today's protracted Afghan insurgency and inflaming the internal strife now endangering Pakistan."

Its release came just as the Obama administration was preparing to announce an increase in forces in Afghanistan. The showdown at Tora Bora, a mountainous area dotted with caves in eastern Afghanistan, pitted a modest force of American Special Operations and C.I.A. officers, along with allied Afghan fighters, against a force of about 1,000 Qaeda fighters led by bin Laden.

The committee report, prepared at the request of Senator John Kerry of Massachusetts, the committee's Democratic chairman, concludes unequivocally that in mid-December 2001, bin Laden and his deputy, Ayman al-Zawahri, were at the cave complex, where bin Laden had operated previously during the fight against Soviet forces.

The news report suggests that a larger troop commitment to Afghanistan might have resulted in the demise not only of bin Laden and his deputy but also of Mullah Muhammad Omar, the leader of the Afghan Taliban. Mullah Omar, who also fled to Pakistan in 2001, has overseen the resurgence of the Taliban. Like several previous accounts, the committee's report blames Gen. Tommy R. Franks, then the top American commander, and Donald H. Rumsfeld, then the defense secretary, for not putting a large number of American troops there lest they fuel resentment among Afghans. General Franks, who declined to comment for the committee's report, has at times questioned whether bin Laden was even at Tora Bora in late 2001.

The report represents unfinished political business on the part of Mr. Kerry. Before and during his unsuccessful 2004 presidential campaign, he hammered on the failure to catch bin Laden. The Foreign Relations Committee's report draws on previous accounts, including books by two C.I.A. officers, Gary Berntsen and Gary Schroen, and by a commander in the Army's elite Delta Force who goes by the pen name Dalton Fury.

The analysis in their books of the flawed tactics at Tora Bora is generally echoed in the official Special Operations Command history. The 2007 history said that it "has been determined with reasonable certainty" that bin Laden was at Tora Bora in December 2001, but that the fewer than 100 American troops committed to the area were not enough to block his escape.

The Senate report was prepared by the Foreign Relations Committee's Democratic staff, whose chief investigator, Douglas Frantz, is a former journalist who has reported extensively on the hunt for bin Laden. The report describes how Americans at Tora Bora intercepted bin Laden's voice in radio transmissions to his fighters, as well as references to "the

Senator John Kerry of Massachusetts

General Tommy Ray Franks

Donald H. Rumsfeld

sheikh." The former Delta Force officer who uses the name Fury told staff members that C.I.A. officers "had a guy with them called Jalal and he was the foremost expert on bin Laden's voice."

"He worked on bin Laden's voice for seven years and he knew him better than anyone else in the West," the former officer said. "To him, it was very clear that bin Laden was there on the mountain." The report says some villagers who were paid to help in the fight were given global positioning system devices and told to push a button wherever they saw fighters or arms caches. The coordinates were then sent to American military spotters to call in airstrikes.[1]

Having been on the FBI's Ten Most Wanted Fugitives list since 1999, after evading capture at the Battle of Tora Bora, his whereabouts became unclear, and various rumours about his health, continued role in al-Qaeda, and location were circulated. Bin Laden also released several video and audio recordings during this time. Conflicting and unconfirmed reports variously indicated that bin Laden had died, by illness or through military attack, or was alive and living in various countries, including Pakistan, Afghanistan and Iran.

The most widespread theory among the general public was that bin Laden was hiding in the mountainous province of the Khyber Pakhtunkhwa region of Pakistan. Khyber Pakhtunkhwa, also known as the North-West Frontier Province of Pakistan, shares its border with Afghanistan, Gilgit-Baltistan, Pakistan occupied Kashmir and Punjab. Abbottabad is an important city of this province.

In the decade following his disappearance, there were many attempts made by the United States government to locate bin Laden, who had become a figurehead for Al-Qaeda and who, U.S. General Stanley McChrystal said, would need to be "captured or killed" in order for the U.S. to "finally defeat al-Qaeda."

In 2010, the CIA came closer to capturing or killing bin Laden's top deputy Ayman al-Zawahiri during a nine-year hunt than was previously known. The CIA missed a chance in 2003 in the north-west Pakistani city of Peshawar, where he met with another senior Al-Qaida leader, Khalid Sheikh Mohammed, who was apprehended the next day and sent to Guantanamo, according to U.S. intelligence officials. The Egyptian doctor may also have narrowly survived a bombing by Pakistani military planes in 2004, the officials added.[2]

In August 2010, the U.S. Central Intelligence Agency located a compound in Abbottabad in Pakistan and identified it as the likely location of bin Laden. On May 1, 2011, United States Navy SEALs of the Naval Special Warfare Development Group (DevGru) carried out an assault on the compound on orders from U.S. President Barack Obama.

During a 40-minute battle, bin Laden was hit by one bullet above the left eye and another to the chest. The SEALs overpowered the compound's remaining residents, killing several others, and extracted bin Laden's body (which was subsequently buried at sea) as well as computer hard drives, documents, and other material. After bin Laden's identity was positively confirmed, President Obama announced the operation in a national address.

ALLEGED SIGHTINGS

After the September 11 attacks, the U.S. government demanded that the Taliban government of Afghanistan deliver bin Laden to face charges of terrorism. The Taliban refused to surrender bin Laden without proof or evidence of his involvement in the September 11 attacks and made a counter-offer to try bin Laden in an Islamic court or extradite him to a third-party country. Both of those offers were rejected by the U.S. government.

Rumours surfaced that bin Laden was killed or fatally injured during U.S. bombardments, most notably near Tora Bora, or that he died of natural causes. According to Gary Berntsen, in his 2005 book, *Jawbreaker*, a number of al-Qaeda detainees later confirmed that bin Laden had escaped Tora Bora into Pakistan via an eastern route through snow covered mountains in the area of Parachinar, Pakistan.

The media reported that bin Laden suffered from a kidney disorder requiring him to have access to advanced medical facilities, possibly kidney dialysis. Ayman al-Zawahiri, Al-Qaeda's second-in-command and a close bin Laden associate, is a physician and may have provided medical care to bin Laden

2004

October 21: John Lehman, a member of the 9/11 Commission, reported that Osama bin Laden is indeed alive, and that the Pentagon knows exactly where he is. According to Lehman, bin Laden is living in South Waziristan in the Baluchistan Mountains of the Baluchistan region, surviving from donations from outside countries such as the United Arab Emirates and high-ranking ministers inside Saudi Arabia. "There is an American presence in the area, but we can't just send in troops," Lehman

WANTED

Dead or Alive

Usama bin Laden

for

Terrorism & Mass Murder

$50,000,000 Reward

Contact G. Bush, Washington, D.C.

said. "If we did, we could have another Vietnam, and the United States cannot afford that right now."

2005

June: Taliban commander Mullah Akhtar Usmani told Pakistani Geo News that bin Laden and Mullah Mohammed Omar were both alive and that Mohammad Omar was in direct command of Taliban forces in Afghanistan. He did not reveal anything about bin Laden's location, stating "All I can tell you is that Osama bin Laden is alive and well." Usmani declined to comment when asked about bin Laden's whereabouts. He further told the News station that "He is still our commander and we are still getting instructions from Omar. Rumours of his illness have been spread by our enemies." When the news person asked could he be sure that the instructions were from Omar, Usmani said: "I can listen to his voice ... I am sure he is alive." He did not elaborate.[3]

Further he said that the Taliban were getting increasing support from the Afghan people because of U.S. "brutality against Muslims and their bias against Muslim countries". "The Taliban are everywhere. In some places they are very dominant and in others they are not. They are dominant in the eastern, southern and southwestern provinces," he said. U.S. and Afghan army commanders say the Taliban are being defeated but insurgent attacks have been on the increase in recent months and 13 U.S. soldiers have been killed since late March. Dozens of government security men have also died in the fighting, as well as more than 150 insurgents, according to U.S. and Afghan government figures. A Taliban spokesman said Usmani's comments on bin Laden were his personal views. "We don't know anything about Osama," the spokesman, Abdul Latif Hakimi, said by telephone.

September 25: Americans fighting the war in Afghanistan have long harboured strong suspicions that Pakistan's military spy service has guided the Afghan insurgency with a hidden hand, even as Pakistan receives more than $1 billion a year from Washington for its help combating the militants, according to a trove of secret military field reports. The firsthand accounts of American anger at Pakistan's unwillingness to confront insurgents who launched attacks near Pakistani border posts, moved openly by the truckload across the frontier, and retreated to Pakistani territory for safety.

On the above said report Pakistani ISI counter-terrorism chief "Ali," whose true identity has not been publicly revealed, tells CBS News' *60 Minutes* that he believes that bin Laden is hiding in Afghanistan with a small group of supporters, possible with as few as 10 men do drew away the attention of the media about the connection of Pakistani ISI with Al-Queda. Some of the reports describe Pakistani intelligence working alongside Al-Qaeda to plan attacks. Experts cautioned that although Pakistan's militant groups and Al-Qaeda work together, directly linking the Pakistani spy agency, the Directorate for Inter-Services Intelligence, or ISI, with Al-Qaeda is difficult.[4]

October 4: The 2005 Kashmir earthquake strikes northeastern Pakistan and Pakistan-administered Kashmir. In November, Senate Minority Leader Harry Reid tells television news that "I heard today that he may have died in the earthquake that they had in Pakistan."Speaking on News 4's Nevada News Makers, Reid says he was informed today that bin Laden may have died in the October temblor. "I heard today that he may have died in the earthquake that they had in Pakistan, seriously." Reid says that if that is the case, "that's good for the world." When asked about Bin Laden during an exclusive News 4 interview, Reid said, "I'm not sure he is alive anymore. I think perhaps the earthquake took him down."

It's difficult to estimate the impact bin Laden's death would have on the War on Terror, the Bush Administration and on the American people as a whole. Bin Laden has been a powerful symbol of international terrorism, particularly since the September 11, 2001 tragedy, which he masterminded. The Bush Administration has been remarkably impotent in its pursuit of bin Laden. Of course, bin Laden has been quite useful to Bush/Cheney as a unifying symbol to incite voter fears, especially during the 2004 presidential campaign. So useful, that some wonder if Bush/Cheney would prefer to quietly contain bin Laden, rather than to publicly capture and imprison him. States blogger PW at leading liberal blog TPMCafe, "If Bush really wanted bin Laden, he'd have him by now.[5]

December 11: A letter to Abu Musab al-Zarqawi, dated December 11 and signed "Atiyah" (thought to be Atiyah Abd al-Rahman) is later intercepted and publicly reported in *The Washington Post* the following year. The letter indicates that bin Laden and the Al-Qaeda leadership were based in the Waziristan region of Pakistan at the time. In the letter, translated by the United States military's Combating Terrorism Center at West Point, "Atiyah" instructs Zarqawi to "send messengers from your end to Waziristan so that they meet with the brothers of the leadership ... I am now on a visit to them and I am writing you this letter as I am with them..." Al-Rahman also indicates that bin Laden and Al-Qaeda are "weak" and "have many of their own problems." The letter has been deemed authentic by military and counter-terrorism officials.

2006

January 9: Neo Conservative Commentator Michael Ledeen writes in a column in *National Review* that "according to Iranians I trust," bin Laden died of kidney failure in mid-December 2005 and was buried in Iran. Ledeen claimed that bin Laden has "spent most of his time since the destruction of al-Qaeda in Afghanistan" in Iran and wrote that, "I was told many months ago that Osama died in Iran last December, and is buried there, under a marker carrying a woman's name. In early January, Pakistan's President P. Musharaff announced bin Laden had died of kidney failure, which I took as pretty good confirmation. Meanwhile, there has been no bin Laden video for two years, only audios with a voice that might be his son's. Now French intelligence, which is a serious organization, has leaked a document citing Saudi sources (often not serious at all) saying Osama died recently in Pakistan of Typhoid fever. I think the circumstantial evidence of his death has been pretty good, especially the behavior of Zawahiri, who sure acts like a number 1, and secondarily the non-appearance of Osama for such a long time. It wouldn't be hard to conjure up explanations for all this, including a desire to convince us he was dead when he isn't, but all in the most reasonable conclusion is that he's dead. The misnamed Intelligence Community doesn't believe it, by the way. They think he's alive in Waziristan. And they're quite insistent about that."[6]

May 24: Alexis Debat of ABC News reported on rumours that bin Laden was sighted in the Kumrat Valley of Pakistan. While ABC News reports Kumrat Valley is in the Kohistan district, The Pakistan Guide from Satellite and the NWFP website indicate Kumrat Valley is in the Dir District, which resides on the Afghan border. The Afghan provinces of Kunar and Nurestan, and the Pakistani district of Bajaur border with Dir. Afghan and Coalition forces have gone on the offensive in the Pech River Valley of Kunar starting late April during *Operation Mountain Lion*. Pakistan's Bajaur district is the location of several Coalition and Pakistani air strikes, including the Predator drone attack on a meeting of Al-Qaeda and Taliban leaders, where Ayman al-Zawahiri was thought to be in attendance. Five senior commanders, including Abu Khabab al-Masri, the head of Al-Qaeda WMD committee are believed to have been killed in the strike. Bajaur appears to be a command and control center for Al-Qaeda and the Taliban, as well as a staging area into the northeastern provinces of Afghanistan.

The report, on ABC News's blog, was later removed due to doubts about the credibility of Debat's reporting.[7]

September 21: The French newspaper *L'Est Républicain* publishes an article by Laid Sammari which cited a September 21 French foreign intelligence document as reporting that Saudi officials received confirmation that bin Laden died August 23 of typhoid fever in Pakistan. U.S. intelligence officials stated that the reporting was unsubstantiated and that the U.S. had received no confirmation of that report. French President Jacques Chirac stated that the report was "in no way confirmed." Members of the bin Laden family also said they heard nothing to confirm the report.

Osama bin Laden is believed to be hiding out somewhere along the Afghan–Pakistani border but security analysts doubt he is in Waziristan, given the security forces' focus on the area. Several of bin Laden's Arab lieutenants have been killed in North Waziristan and U.S. drone aircraft have carried out missile strikes on Al- Qaeda targets from across the border in Afghanistan. Security officials say some Central Asian militants are also in the area. The first time when Musharraf decided to deploy Pakistan Army (PA) there in 2004, the initial reaction was reluctance, or backing out of its Pakhtun personnel.

The second was heavy casualties and capture of Pakistani troops by Taliban – Al-Qaeda (TAQ) and Waziri tribals. While the Pakhtuns of PA were let off, Punjabi soldiers were tortured, mutilated and killed. Musharraf had to announce amnesty and send a senior officer to negotiate the release of many PA soldiers held by TAQ and the tribesmen. This meant PA returning over 160 of TAQ captured and a promise not to launch operations against them. This humiliating defeat was projected by PA as a victory, claiming that 'high value targets', including Al-Qaeda's number 2, Ayman al Zawahiri, were either captured, pinned down or killed. At least 60 ranks of PA were killed in this operation, after which its units amounting to a few thousands of soldiers were moved from the troubled Azam Warsak area to a safer location near Wana, the regional capital of Waziristan. If someone like Nawab Bugti could be located and killed, there must be some compelling reasons for bin Laden being alive to celebrate the fifth year of 9/11.

Some interesting inputs were provided in "Pakistanisation of Al-Qaeda" by Khaled Ahmed, published in The Friday Times, December 03-09, 2004: 'Although few in Pakistan believe the official erosion of the Wana Operation, external observers merely see in it the confirmation of what they had known earlier. The adoption of Al-Qaeda by a vast number of people in Pakistan, including the MMA government of the NWFP whose ministers at times swear by the Taliban brand of Islam, cannot be ignored. Senators and MNAs from the Tribal Areas pretend to be on the side of the government and pose as mediators but are clearly loyal in to the worldview of Al-Qaeda; and some of them have benefited financially from this loyalty.

One MNA Shah Abdul Aziz has appeared on a private channel and has admitted to having nursed Abdullah Mehsud—the Guantanamo Bay ex-inmate who abducted the Chinese engineers from the Gomalzam Dam in South Waziristan—when the two were in the tutelage of Mufti Shamzai of Banuri Masjid in Karachi. It was very clear that the loyalty of MNA Shah Abdul Aziz was more to the cause of Al-Qaeda than to Pakistan..... Mariam Abou Zahab is a well-known French scholar who has studied the sectarian scene in Pakistan and written about it, including one path-breaking study of the city of Jhang, where Deobandi Islam gave birth to Sipah Sahaba.

Her latest book with Olivier Roy has one chapter titled The Pakistanisation of Al-Qaeda which tells us that after the fall of the Taliban in 2002 militants regrouped in Karachi with the help of a still un-purged ISI.... Al-Qaeda first fled to South Waziristan. It was later deployed to other areas in Azad Kashmir and Karachi. The authors are of the view that this deployment could not have been possible without collaboration from the ISI...'

Pervez Musharraf's promise of no group being allowed to use Pakistan as a springboard for attacks on other countries is utterly meaningless, as India is only too well aware of. Anyway, five years later, terrorism thrives, just as its organisers do. Need we say more?

2007

June: Speaking to al Jazeera, a high ranking Taliban leader Mullah Bakht Mohammed stated that "Sheikh Osama bin Laden is alive and active. He's carrying out his duties. The latest proof that he is alive is that he sent me a letter of condolences after the martyrdom of my brother. He advised me to follow my brother's path." Mohammed's brother Dadullah had led military operations for the Taliban until his death in May 2007. Mohammed stated that "Sheikh Osama prefers not to be seen or meet anyone because if he makes himself available to the media maybe he will be facing danger."

It is seen that no new video footage of Osama bin Laden has surfaced in any of the Al-Qaeda videos which have been released from 2007 onwards. This fact is reflected in the details of video and audio tapes that have been tabulated in the Appendix I.

In December 2007, Taliban announced that Bakht has been replaced as military commander due to insubordination. He will continue fighting for the Taliban, however, was injured and captured by Pakistani forces near the Pakistan–Afghanistan border in February 2008.[8]

September 7: Former counter-terrorism official Richard A. Clarke speculated that bin Laden's "phony looking beard" in a recent videotaped message may mean his original beard has been shaved to help him blend into different Muslim communities. Clarke stated to ABC News that beards would stand out in Southeast Asia, the Philippines, or Indonesia, and noted that "No one's thought he was there, but that is an environment where most men, Muslim men don't have beards."

2008

July 12: Pakistani Interior Minister Rehman Malik, speaking in opposition to drone attacks in Pakistan, claimed to the British *Sunday Times* that "If Osama was in Pakistan we would know, with all the thousands of troops we have sent into the tribal areas in recent months. If he and all these four or five top people were in our area they would have been caught, the way we are searching."Malik claimed that drone strikes in Pakistan were a waste of time," stating that "according to our information Osama is in Afghanistan, probably Kunar."

November 2: The arrest of Mansoor Dadullah, brother of slain Taliban military commander Mullah Dadullah, was a boost for the U.S.-backed campaign against the Taliban and Al-Qaida, though it also demonstrated that militant chiefs operate inside Pakistan despite its deployment of 100,000 troops along the border. It followed a January 29 U.S. missile strike on a militant hideout in the northwestern tribal belt that killed Abu Laith al-Libi, a top Al-Qaeda commander in Afghanistan.

Mansoor Dadullah was caught in the southwestern province of Baluchistan, but there was some confusion over exactly how and where. The Pakistani army said Dadullah was wounded along with five militant associates in a firefight with security forces near a village in Qila Saifullah district after they sneaked across the border from Afghanistan. But local intelligence officials placed the clash in neighbouring Zhob district, describing it as a raid launched by security forces against the militants hiding at a religious seminary.

Maj. Gen. Athar Abbas, the army spokesman, denied initial reports that Dadullah had died. "Dadullah was arrested alive, but he is critically wounded," Abbas said. The intelligence officials, who spoke on condition of anonymity because they were not authorized to speak to journalists, said all the suspects were moved by helicopter from Zhob. It was not clear where they were taken or whether Dadullah would be handed over to Afghan authorities.[9]

November: CIA Director Michael Hayden, in a speech to the Atlantic Council, states that bin Laden is probably hiding in the tribal area of northwest Pakistan and that his capture remains a top U.S. priority. Hayden states that bin Laden is "putting a lot of energy into his own survival, a lot of energy into his own security. In fact, he appears to be largely isolated from the day-to-day operations of the organization he nominally heads."

2009

February 17: A research team led by Thomas W. Gillespie and John A. Agnew of UCLA publish a report in which they use satellite-aided geographical analysis to pinpoint three compounds in Parachinar as likely hideouts of bin Laden.

March: The *New York Daily News* reported that the hunt for bin Laden had centered in the Chitral District of Pakistan, including the Kalam Valley. According to the report, author Rohan Gunaratna states that captured Al-Qaeda leaders have confirmed that Chitral is where bin Laden is hiding.

April 27: According to the Irish Times, Pakistan's president, Asif Ali Zardari announced that the whereabouts of Al-Qaeda leader Osama bin Laden remained a mystery, and there was a suspicion that he could be dead after Pakistani intelligence and officials could find "no trace" of the Al-Qaeda chief.

November 29: News report states bin Laden is living in Pakistan and Gordon Brown orders Pakistan to do more to break Al-Qaeda and find Osama bin Laden.

December 4: BBC reports of informant having knowledge of bin Laden in Ghazni, south east Afghanistan in early 2009. Ghazni is a Taliban stronghold and many areas do not permit coalition forces. The detainee was involved in kidnappings and fundraising operations for Taliban operations in Afghanistan and Pakistan. Former CIA analyst Bruce Riedel is quoted as saying "The entire Western intelligence community, CIA and FBI, have been looking for Osama bin Laden for the last seven years and haven't come upon a source of information like this."

2010

Nasser al-Bahri, a bodyguard for bin Laden in the late 1990s, writes a book, published in French as *Dans l'ombre de Ben Laden* (In the Shadow of Bin Laden), with French journalist Georges Malbrunot of the newspaper *Le Figaro*. According to al-Bahri, bin Laden is hiding in the regions in Afghanistan or along the border with Pakistan. Malbrunot stated in an interview with Mark Colvin of *PM* that bin Laden is likely "protected by tribes which are very loyal to him. Bin Laden has known these tribes for the last 20 years. He helps them financially and materially in the '80s and these tribes also, I think it's an important factor, are more loyal to the religion than to the typical tribal character, which means that it's not very easy to bribe them." Malbrunot noted, "He's protected by perhaps, he kept three or four people around him from al-Qaeda, and he can move with the protection of the tribal leaders and tribal connections in this region along the Pakistan, the Waziristan."

Feathered Cocaine, a documentary by Icelandic filmmakers Om Marino Arnarson and Thorkell S. Hardarson dealing with the global falcon trade and featuring falconer Alan Parrot, claims that bin Laden, an avid falcon hunter, "has been taking part in the sport relatively freely" in Tehran in Iran since 2003.

June 7: The Israeli-based intelligence news service DEBKA reports that bin Laden and top lieutenants have been living in the remote mountainous town of Sabzevar in northeastern Iran for the past five years, and that Turkish intelligence officials were aware of it.

June 27: CIA Director Leon Panetta, speaking on ABC News' *This Week*, stated that last time the CIA had "precise information" on bin Laden was "the early 2000s." Panetta states, "He is, as is obvious, in very deep hiding. He's in an area of the tribal areas of Pakistan that is very difficult. The terrain is probably the most difficult in the world...All I can tell you is it's in the tribal areas...we know that he's located in that vicinity." Panetta states that "If we keep that pressure on, we think ultimately we can flush out bin Laden and Zawahiri and get after them."

October 18: A senior NATO official tells CNN about claims that bin Laden is alive and well, living comfortably in a house in the north-west of Pakistan and being protected by local people and elements of Pakistani intelligence. Stating that "Nobody in al-Qaeda is living in a cave," the official stated the bin Laden was likely to have moved around in recent years in areas from the mountainous Chitral region in the far northwest, near the Chinese border, to the Kurram Valley bordering Tora Bora in Afghanistan. The official stated that Ayman al-Zawahiri is believed to be hiding close to bin Laden in houses in northwest Pakistan, but are not together. Another U.S. official stated that bin Laden and Zawahiri are "somewhere in the tribal areas of Pakistan near the Afghanistan border," but that their exact locations are unknown: "If we knew where he was—in a house, an apartment, a villa or an underground cave or bunker—we would have gotten him; we can't rule out he may be in a cave one day and a house in a city on another."

October 28: An audio recording of bin Laden threatening France over their involvement in Afghanistan is pronounced genuine by the French Foreign Ministry.

2011

May 1 2011: President Barack Obama, addressed the nation at 11:35 pm EST., that Osama bin Laden had been killed in Abbottabad in a U.S. operation. The compound is located at 34°10′9?N 73°14′33?E.

2012

Of the three widows that Osama bin Laden left behind after Abbottabad the older two namely Kharia Hussain Sabir and SIham Sharif have refused to cooperate with the investigators. However the youngest bride that bin Laden took in July 2000, has given much information that helps shed light on the head of the family's wanderings in the years that the west hunted for for him. The information contained in a police report has hr words paraphrased by a police officer. While there is no detail about the Pakistanis who helped the bin Laden family in their efforts to avoid being caught by their pursuers, there is a lot of information that clears up the frustration that some western intelligence agencies may have felt in the decade long pursuit.

Amal Ahmad Abdul Fateh was only 18 years old when she flew to Karachi to "marry a mujahid "as per her own choice. She then crossed into Afghanistan to join her future husband and two other wives at a farm outside Kandahar. She lived there till the 9/11 attacks after which the family had to scatter. The family headed in different directions for safety reasons. Amal then returned to Karachi with her new born daughter Safia. Over the next nine months she changed houses seven times with the intervention of a Pakistani family and bin Laden's elder son, Saad.

In the latter half of 2002 she went to Peshawar where she was reunited with her husband.[10]

Bin Laden then took his family into the rural mountain areas of northwest Pakistan. As per Amal the family stayed in the Shangla district in Swat in two different houses for eight to nine months. In 2003 the family moved to a small town near Islamabad called Haripur. They stayed in Haripur in a rented house for nearly two years. Haripur is a city in Haripur District in the Hazara Division of Hazara, some 65 km (40 mi) north of Islamabad and 35 km (22 mi) south of Abbottabad, in a hilly plain area at an altitude of 520 m (1,706 ft). The city is situated on the Karakoram Highway (N35).

It was here that Amal gave birth to her daughter Aasia in 2003 and her son Ibrahim in 2004. The children were both born in a government hospital in the city as per Amal. It was in mid 2005 that the bin Laden family finally moved to Abbottabad to live in the walled compound where Osama bin Laden was eventually traced and killed by the Americans.

WHY WAS KILLING OSAMA BIN LADEN SO IMPORTANT?

Al-Qaeda is not the formal organization that the west thinks it to be. It is quite literally "the base" from which many terrorist organizations worldwide seem to dip into for resources, training and support. This availability was subject to finances that were controlled by Osama bin Laden. His personal fortune was used as a piggy bank for a number of dissatisfied Muslim groups that decided to take up arms against their current regimes.

By no means was his money the only money that was available to the terrorist groups. The Taliban has long grown poppy as a cash crop to prop up its funds. Local farmers in Afghanistan are often persuaded to grow poppy with promises of protection and a share of the profits. Helmand Province in Afghanistan is not just the poppy growing capital of the nation, but of the world. Even as the government tries to battle the southern opium belt the local people themselves are happy to propagate it as it leads to better income for their families.

Daoud Ahmadi, the spokesman for the governor in the Helmand Province said that "This year (2012) there is more poppy cultivation in Helmand, especially in places where people have confiscated the government lands and in places that were desert." The beautiful red fields in full bloom do not convey the horror that the money gained from their trade can generate in the hands of a terrorist.[11]

While the illegal activities practiced by the terrorists did bring in some funds, it was nowhere near the level required for armed retaliation. This is why bin Laden could develop a base in Afghanistan helping the Taliban.

He literally paid his way into this exclusive club where, by throwing around his money he could play at being head honcho. This is the primary reason he became the face of Al-Qaeda and public enemy number one for America.

NOTES

[1] S. Scott, "Senate Report Explores 2001 Escape by bin Laden From Afghan Mountains," *The New York Times*, January 19, 2011. A version of this article appeared in print on November 29, 2009, on page A20 of the New York edition.

[2] "Bin Laden deputy's 'narrow escapes' in Pakistan," *The Independent*, December 1, 2010, http://www.independent.co.uk/news/world/asia/bin-laden-deputys-narrow-escapes-in-pakistan-2147913.html (Accessed December 15, 2011).

[3] "Bin Laden is Alive and Well –Taliban Chief" at http://www.chinadaily.com.cn/english/doc/2005-06/15/content_451793.htm (Accessed December 15, 2011).

[4] M. Mazzetti, J. Perlez, E. Schmitt and A.W. Lehren, "Pakistan Aids Insurgency in Afghanistan, Reports Assert" at http://www.nytimes.com/2010/07/26/world/asia/26isi.html (Accessed December 15, 2011).

[5] D. White,"Senator Harry Reid Told Osama bin Laden Killed in Pakistan Earthquake" at http://usliberals.about.com/b/2005/11/25/senator-harry-reid-told-osama-bin-laden-killed-in-pakistan-earthquake.htm (Accessed December 15, 2011).

[6] M. Ladeen, "Bin Laden Dead...Again?" at http://www.nationalreview.com/corner/129075/bin-laden-dead-again/michael-ledeen (Accessed December 15, 2011).

[7] B. Roggio, "Fighting in Uruzgan; Osama bin Laden sighting in Pakistan" at http://www.longwarjournal.org/archives/2006/05/fighting_in_uruzgan.php (Accessed December 15, 2011).

[8] 2007, "Taliban Leader Says Bin Laden Is Alive and Recently Sent Letter" at http://www.historycommons.org/context.jsp?item=a060507bakhtbinladen#a060507bakhtbinladen (Accessed December 15, 2011).

[9] M. Pennington, "Senior Taliban Figure Caught in Pakistan" at http://www.usatoday.com/news/world/2008-02-11-604457253_x.htm (Accessed December 15, 2011).

[10] Declan Walsh, *The Asian Age*, 31 March 2012, "On the run, Laden had 4 kids, 5 houses"

[11] Taimoor Shah and Alissa J. Rubin, *The Asian Age*, 13 April 2012, "Poppy war, Taliban aim to protect a cash crop. "

CHAPTER 5

Tenth Life

EXECUTION OF THE OPERATION

The operation to bring down bin Laden was carried out by approximately two dozen heliborne United States Navy SEALs from the Red Squadron of the Joint Special Operations Command's United States Naval Special Warfare Development Group (DEVGRU). For legal reasons (namely that the U.S. was not at war with Pakistan), the military personnel assigned to the mission were temporarily transferred to the control of the civilian Central Intelligence Agency.[1] The DEVGRU SEALs operated in two teams and were reportedly equipped with Heckler & Koch 416 carbine military assault rifles (with attached suppressors), night-vision goggles, body armour and handguns.

According to *The New York Times*, a total of "79 commandos and a dog" were involved in the raid.[2] The military working dog[3] was a Belgian Malinois named Cairo. According to one report, the dog was tasked with tracking "anyone who tried to escape and to alert SEALs to any approaching Pakistani security forces". The dog was to be used to help deter any Pakistani ground response to the raid and to help look for any hidden rooms or hidden doors in the compound. Additional personnel on the mission included a language translator, the dog handler, helicopter pilots, "tactical signals, intelligence collectors, and navigators using highly classified hyperspectral imagers".[4]

The SEALs flew into Pakistan from a staging base in the city of Jalalabad in eastern Afghanistan after originating at Bagram Air Base in northeastern Afghanistan. The 160th Special Operations Aviation Regiment (SOAR), an airborne US Army Special Operations Command unit known as the "Night Stalkers", provided the two modified Black Hawk helicopters that were used for the raid itself, as well as the much larger Chinook heavy-lift helicopters that were employed as backups.

The Black Hawks appear to have been never-before-publicly-seen "stealth" versions of the helicopter that fly more quietly while being harder to detect on radar than conventional models; due to the weight of the extra stealth equipment on the Black Hawks, cargo was "calculated to the ounce, with the weather factored in."

The Chinooks kept on standby were on the ground "in a deserted area roughly two-thirds of the way" between Jalalabad and Abbottabad, with two additional SEAL teams consisting of approximately 24 DEVGRU operators[5] and Army Rangers for a backup "quick reaction force" (QRF). The Chinooks were equipped with M134 Miniguns and extra fuel for the Black Hawks. Their mission was to interdict any Pakistani military attempts to interfere with the raid. Other Chinooks, holding 25 more SEALs from DEVGRU, were stationed just across the border in Afghanistan in case reinforcements were needed during the raid.[6]

The 160th SOAR helicopters were supported by multiple other aircraft, including fixed-wing fighter jets and drones.[7] According to CNN, "the Air Force had a full team of combat search-and-rescue helicopters available".[7]

The raid was scheduled for a time with little moonlight so the helicopters could enter Pakistan "low to the ground and undetected". The helicopters used hilly terrain and nap-of-the-earth techniques to reach the compound without appearing on radar and alerting the Pakistani military. The flight from Jalalabad to Abbottabad took about 90 minutes.[6]

According to the mission plan, the first helicopter would hover over the compound's yard while its full team of SEALs fast-roped to the ground. At the same time, the second helicopter would fly to the northeast corner of the compound and deploy the translator, the dog, and four SEALs to secure the perimeter. The second helicopter would then hover over the house and the team leader and six SEALs would fast-rope onto the roof. The team in the courtyard was to enter the house from the ground floor.

As they hovered above the target, however, the first helicopter experienced a hazardous airflow condition known as a vortex ring state. This was aggravated by higher than expected air temperature ("a so-called 'hot and high' environment") and the high compound walls, which stopped the rotor downwash from diffusing. The helicopter's tail grazed one of the compound's walls, damaging its tail rotor, and the helicopter rolled onto its side. The pilot quickly buried the aircraft's nose to keep it from tipping over. None of the SEALs, crew and pilots on the helicopter were seriously injured in the soft crash landing, which ended with it pitched at a forty-five-degree angle resting against the wall. The other helicopter then landed outside the compound and the SEALs scaled the walls to get inside. The SEALs advanced into the house, breaching walls and doors with explosives.

The raiding party entered the *haveli* by blasting their way into the bedroom (through a hole created by the blast) where Osama bin Laden was found and he was shot in the head and chest. BBC news reports also indicate that three men, his courier, younger brother and a son with him in the room were also killed, but not his wife; his wife was reported to have been injured in the shooting.

The extraordinary security measures, both physical and operational, indicated a well-planned hideout. Apart from sectioning of the mansion with high raised walls of varying heights, the layout included a wall on the terrace of the third floor which point to a custom-built structure.

The U.S. National Counterterrorism Center, using drone-derived intelligence, developed "what amounted to a detailed 'map' of the bin Laden compound and its occupants and their patterns of living and working." This map was used to create a model of the compound for practice runs.

CIA director Leon Panetta issued a memo that also credited the National Security Agency and National Geospatial-Intelligence Agency for contributing to the intelligence-gathering that made the raid possible. The *National Journal* reported that "NSA figured out, somehow, that there was no telephone or Internet service in the compound"; although a satellite dish is plainly visible on a building on the complex. Its residents burned their trash, unlike their neighbors, who simply set it out for collection.

Evidence seized from the compound is said to include 10 cell phones, 5 to 10 computers, 12 hard drives, at least 100 "computer disks" (including thumb drives and DVDs), handwritten notes, documents, weapons and "an assortment of personal items." A special CIA team has been tasked with combing through the digital material and documents removed from the bin laden compound. The material is being stored at the FBI Laboratory in Quantico, Virginia, where forensic experts will analyze fingerprints, DNA and other trace left on the material.

ARCHITECTURE OF THE BIN LADEN HIDEOUT

In the urban setting, the architecture of the bin Laden hideout has been called by an architect as "surprisingly permanent—and surprisingly urban" and "sure to join Saddam Hussein's last known address among the most notorious examples of hideout architecture in recent memory". The compound was fortified with many safeguard features which would confuse would-be invaders, and US officials described the compound as "extraordinarily unique". Constructed between 2003 and 2005, the three-story structure is located on a dirt road 2.5 miles (4.0 km) northeast of the city center of Abbottâbad. While the compound was assessed by US officials at a value of US$1 million, local real-estate agents assess the property value at US$250,000. Intelligence reports have indicated that bin Laden may have moved into the complex on January 6, 2006.

The CIA used surveillance photos and intelligence reports to determine the identities of the inhabitants of the Abbottabad compound to which the courier was travelling. In September 2010, the CIA concluded that the compound was "custom-built to hide someone of significance," and that bin Laden's residence there was very likely. Officials surmised that he was living there with his youngest wife.

Google Earth maps show that the compound was not present in 2001, but did exist on images taken in 2005. Built in 2004, the three-story compound was located "at the end of a narrow dirt road", 2.5 miles (4 km) northeast of the city center of Abbottabad. Abbottabad is about 100 miles (160 km) from the Afghanistan border on the far eastern side of Pakistan (about 20 miles [32 km] from India). The compound is 0.8 miles (1.3 km) southwest of the Pakistan Military Academy (PMA), a prominent military academy that has been compared to Sandhurst in Britain and West Point in the United States. On a plot of land eight times larger than those of nearby houses, it was surrounded by 12-to-18-feet high (3.7–5.5 m) concrete walls topped with barbed wire. There were two security gates, and the third-floor balcony had a 7-feet-high (2.1 m) privacy wall (which could easily hide a 6 ft 4 in [1.93 m] bin Laden).

There was no Internet or telephone service connected to the compound. Its residents burned their trash, rather than setting it out for collection. Local residents called the building the *Waziristan Haveli* (*haveli* is a term used in India and Pakistan that roughly translates to *mansion*).

Security cameras were found installed and aerial photographs show several satellite dishes. There were two security gates and the third-floor balcony had a 7-foot (2.1 m) privacy wall. The compound measured 38,000

Abbottabad Compound, 2005

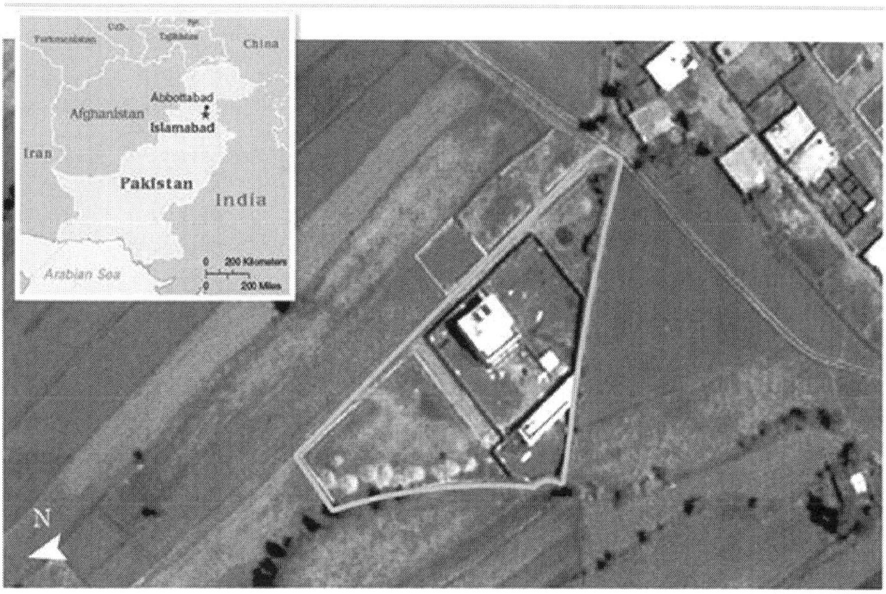

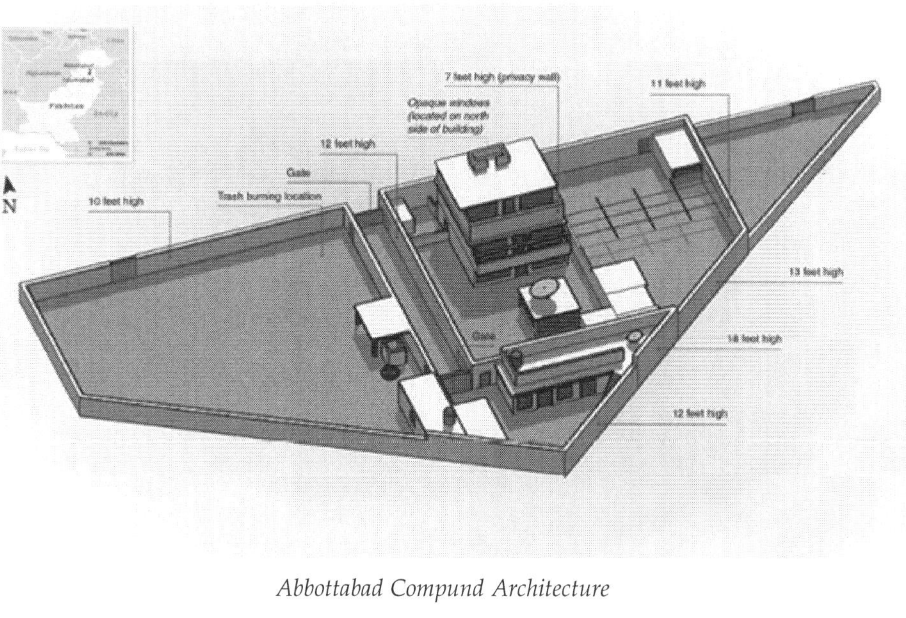

Abbottabad Compund Architecture

square feet in size, and had very few windows. The mansion was known as *Waziristan Haveli* by the local residents, and owned by a transporter from Waziristan; bin Laden previously spent time in the Waziristan area of Pakistan. One of the main builders of the compound, Gul Mohammed, was instructed to construct the 18ft high perimeter fence and then to build another wall 7ft tall around one of the dwellings. He was suspicious due to the activities of his men and when requested to build huge-fort like walls was curious and was told it was none of his business. According to Mohammed, one or two men came to supervise his work and that they were not restrictive with their money. He was to refer to the main occupant of the household as "The Master", even though he never met him. The compound had an adjacent grazing area which hosted cows and a buffalo as well as a deep water well, possibly allowing it a water supply separate from the local municipality. There was a small garden on the north side of the house that included poplar trees. Cabbages, potatoes and marijuana were found growing on the compound grounds.

The CIA established a safe house in Abbottabad from which a team observed the compound over a number of months. The CIA team used informants and other techniques to gather intelligence on the compound. The safe house was abandoned immediately after bin Laden's death.

The hideout, now under the security control of the Pakistan Police, indicates highly fortified compound walls made of concrete blocks with three gates, zoning the building from the large courtyard and a garden planted with immature fruit trees in front of a collapsed wall. The remains of the Navy SEALs' helicopter that crashed during the U.S. operation were later removed from the site by a tractor. Police have allowed reporters and locals to approach the wall of the hideaway. The doors are lodged in place, but police did not exert themselves to open them.

LOCAL RESIDENTS AND THEIR INTERACTION

Locals have disclosed details about their interactions with the residents of the compound to an AP journalist in Pakistan. A woman who distributed polio vaccine to the compound said she saw expensive SUVs parked inside. The men received the vaccine and instructed her to leave. A woman in her seventies said that in rainy weather one of the men from the hideaway gave her a ride to the market. Her grandchildren had played with the children living in the house, and received rabbits as presents. One farmer said, "People were skeptical in this neighbourhood about this place and these guys. They used to gossip, say they were smugglers or drug dealers. People would complain that even with such a big house they didn't invite the poor or distribute charity". Present at some neighbourhood funerals, two men from the compound were "tall, fair skinned and bearded" and self-identified as cousins from elsewhere in the region. If a child's cricket ball went over the fence, the men in the compound did not return that ball. Instead they paid the child 100-150 Pakistani Rupees (about US$2-3), many times the value of the ball.

LOCATING BIN LADEN

Identity of his courier

Identification of Al-Qaeda couriers was an early priority for interrogators at CIA black sites and Guantanamo Bay detention camp, as bin Laden was believed to have concealed his whereabouts from Al-Qaeda foot soldiers or top commanders, communicating instead through such couriers.

By 2002 interrogators had heard uncorroborated claims about an Al-Qaeda courier with the nom de guerre (or "pseudonym of war") Abu Ahmed al-Kuwaiti (sometimes referred to as Sheikh Abu Ahmed, from Kuwait).[17] In 2003 Khalid Sheik Mohammed, the alleged operational chief of Al-Qaeda, revealed under interrogation that he was acquainted with al-Kuwaiti but that he was not active in Al-Qaeda.

In 2004 a prisoner named Hassan Ghul told interrogators that al-Kuwaiti was close to bin Laden as well as Khalid Sheik Mohammed and Mohammed's successor Abu Faraj al-Libi. Ghul further revealed that al-Kuwaiti had not been seen in some time, a fact which led U.S. officials to suspect he was travelling with bin Laden. When confronted with Ghul's account, Khalid Sheik Mohammed maintained his original story. Abu Faraj al-Libi was captured in 2005 and transferred to Guantánamo in September 2006. He told CIA interrogators that bin Laden's courier was a man named Maulawi Abd al-Khaliq Jan and denied knowing al-Kuwaiti. Because both Mohammed and al-Libi had minimised al-Kuwaiti's importance, officials speculated that he was part of bin Laden's inner circle.

In 2007 officials learned al-Kuwaiti's real name, though they will not disclose the name nor how they learned it. Since the name Maulawi Abd al-Khaliq Jan appears in the JTF-GTMO detainee assessment for Abu Faraj al-Libi released by WikiLeaks on April 24, 2011, there was speculation that the U.S. assault on the Abbottabad compound was expedited as a precaution. The CIA never found anyone named Maulawi Jan and concluded that al-Libi made the name up. A 2010 wiretap of another suspect picked up a conversation with al-Kuwaiti. CIA officials located al-Kuwaiti in August 2010 and followed him back to bin Laden's Abbottabad compound. The courier and a relative (who was either a brother or a cousin) were killed in the May 2, 2011 raid. Afterwards some locals identified the men as Pashtuns named Arshad and Tareq Khan. Arshad Khan was carrying an old, non-computerised Pakistani identification card which said he was from Khat Kuruna, a village near Charsadda in northwestern Pakistan. Pakistani officials have found no record of an Arshad Khan in that area and suspect the men were living under false identities.

Approximately 19 persons are accounted for as residents in the compound at the time of the raid:

1. Killed in action (5), in order
    - Abu Ahmed al-Kuwaiti, courier, killed while firing a weapon
    - Adult female, possibly wife of courier, unarmed
    - Adult male, possibly cousin of courier, unarmed
    - Hamza or Khalid bin Laden, son of Osama, unarmed
    - Osama bin Laden, unarmed
2. Wounded in action
    - Amal Ahmed Abdul Fatah, bin Laden's fifth wife, unarmed
    - Adult female, unarmed
3. Possibly captured by U.S. military
    - Adult male
4. Others present at the time of the raid but left behind alive and not wounded
    - 12-year-old female, bin Laden's daughter Safia
    - 8 other children ranging in age from 2 to 12 years old
    - Two adult females, possibly wives of bin Laden

ROLE OF PAKISTAN

Pakistan's role in the operation was criticized by many people around the world. Pakistani military and intelligence were suspected outright for sheltering Osama bin Laden, before U.S. forces hounded and traced him down in Abbottabad. Pakistan defended its role and stated that it had no prior information that bin Laden was in Abbottabad.[1]

A fact that is difficult to accept given the location of the hideout and the ease with which it was constructed in the country. Perhaps the right hand of the government really did not know what the left hand was doing, but it is inconceivable that no one in Pakistan knew of Osama bin Laden's hidey hole in Abbottabad.

Connections with Abbottabad

There have been a variety of connections between Abbottabad, Al-Qaeda and Osama bin Laden leading up to bin Laden's death in Abbottabad. On July 21, 2001, about a month and a half before the September 11, 2001, attacks upon the United States by Al-Qaeda, Afghanistan's Taliban ambassador to Pakistan, Mullah Abdul Salam Zaeef, categorically stated at a three-day training convention in Abbottabad that "the Taliban would never hand over Osama bin Laden to the Americans for any so-called trial as it would be tantamount to acceding that the Muslims have no credible system of Justice in Islam."

In the days following the September 11th attacks, U.S. Marine lieutenant colonel Asad Khan, who was born in Abbottabad and whose family founded the country's first commercial poultry farm in Abbottabad in 1947, became one of a handful of Afghan and Pakistani Americans who contributed to U.S. intelligence operations by working the front lines as interpreter, interrogator and liaison officer. It is ironic that it was in the town of his ancestors that the Americans eventually did find bin Laden.

On September 28, 2001, India's external intelligence agency, known as the Research and Analysis Wing, provided the United States with a list of 71 Al-Qaeda training camps spread across Pakistan proper, at locations as diverse as Abbottabad, Peshawar, Quetta and Warsak. In July 2002, *The Christian Science Monitor* published the results of a week-long investigation, which provided evidence that "Al-Qaeda and an array of militant affiliate groups" were operating staff offices near the Karakoram Highway—from Abbottabad along the western perimeter of Kashmir—with the tacit approval of Pakistani intelligence.

In June 2004, Pakistani intelligence agents killed one Al-Qaeda suspect as three others fled in a car in Abbottabad as part of a major Pakistani operation to "flush out Al-Qaeda suspects and their local supporters from hideouts in a remote region near Afghanistan" that left 72 people dead, including 55 terrorists.[37] In response to the October 2005 Kashmir earthquake and in a "desire to bolster Pakistani President Pervez Musharraf when his help was badly needed in hunting down Osama bin Laden and repressing Islamic radicals," the United States provided an "initial contribution" of $50 million to Pakistan that paid for relief efforts at locations such as Abbottabad's Ayub Medical Complex, which received an estimated 1,000 patients directly after the earthquake and is located 2 miles (3.2 kilometers) from Osama bin Laden's hideout compound.[38]

In June 2008, during an interview of Asadullah Jan, a former Guantanamo Bay detention camp detainee, by American journalist Tom

Lasseter, at Jan's home in Abbottabad, Jan revealed that the U.S. Central Intelligence Agency had previously asked him if he was the son of Osama bin Laden. On January 25, 2011, Pakistan authorities arrested one of the most wanted Al-Qaeda-linked Indonesian terror suspects, Umar Patek, in Abbottabad while Patek carried one million US dollars head money, but waited until March 30, 2011, to make Patek's arrest public.

Allegations against Pakistan

Numerous allegations were made that the government of Pakistan shielded bin Laden. Critics cited the very close proximity of bin Laden's heavily fortified compound to the Pakistan Military Academy, which United States chose not to notify Pakistani authorities before the operation, and the double standards of Pakistan regarding the perpetrators of the 2008 Mumbai attacks. U.S. government files leaked by Wikileaks disclosed that American diplomats were told that Pakistani security services were tipping off bin Laden every time U.S. forces approached. Pakistan's Inter-Services Intelligence (ISI) also helped smuggle Al- Qaeda militants into Afghanistan to fight NATO troops. According to the leaked files, in December 2009, the government of Tajikistan had told U.S. officials that many in Pakistan were aware of bin Laden's whereabouts.[8]

In his first interview after the operation, CIA chief Leon Panetta said that the CIA had ruled out involving Pakistan in the operation, fearing that "any effort to work with the Pakistanis could jeopardize the mission. They might alert the targets."[9] However, Secretary of State Hillary Rodham Clinton stated that "cooperation with Pakistan helped lead us to bin Laden and the compound in which he was hiding". Obama echoed her sentiments.

U.S. Senator Joe Lieberman, chairman of the Senate Homeland Security Committee, said "This is going to be a time of real pressure on Pakistan to basically prove to us that they didn't know that bin Laden was there". John O. Brennan, Obama's chief counter-terrorism advisor, said that it was inconceivable that bin Laden did not have support from within Pakistan. He further stated "People have been referring to this as hiding in plain sight. We are looking at how he was able to hide out there for so long."[10]

Senator Dianne Feinstein said that "it's hard for me to understand how the Pakistanis ... would not know what was going on inside the compound", and that top Pakistan officials may be "walking both sides of the street." Senator Lindsey Graham questioned, "How could [bin Laden] be in such a compound without being noticed?" raising suspicions that Pakistan was either uncommitted in the fight against Islamist militants or was actively sheltering them while pledging to fight them. A Pakistani intelligence official said that they had passed on raw phone tap data to U.S. that led to the operation, but had failed to analyze this data themselves.

Indian Minister for Home Affairs P. Chidambaram said that bin Laden hiding "deep inside" Pakistan was a matter of grave concern for India, and showed that "many of the perpetrators of the Mumbai terror attacks, including the controllers and the handlers of the terrorists who actually carried out the attack, continue to be sheltered in Pakistan". He called on Pakistan to arrest them.

Pakistani-born British MP Khalid Mahmood stated that he was "flabbergasted and shocked" after he learned that bin Laden was living in a city with thousands of Pakistani troops, reviving questions about alleged links between Al-Qaeda and elements in Pakistan's security forces.[11]

Gulf News reported that the compound where bin Laden was killed had previously been used as a safe house by Pakistan's Inter-Services Intelligence (ISI), but was no longer being used for this purpose. *The Globe and Mail* reported local police saying that the compound belonged to Hizbul Mujahideen, a militant group supported by ISI that is fighting Indian forces in Kashmir.

Response from Pakistan

According to a Pakistani intelligence official, raw phone-tap data had been transferred to the United States without being analyzed by Pakistan. While the U.S. "was concentrating on this" information since September 2010, information regarding bin Laden and the compound's inhabitants had "slipped from" Pakistan's "radar" over the months. Bin Laden left "an invisible footprint" and he had not been contacting other militant networks. It was noted that much focus had been placed on a courier entering and leaving the compound. The transfer of intelligence to the U.S. was a regular occurrence according to the official, who also stated regarding the raid that "I think they came in undetected and went out the same day", and Pakistan did not believe that U.S. personnel were present in the area before the special operation occurred.[12]

According to the Pakistani high commissioner to the United Kingdom, Wajid Shamsul Hasan, Pakistan had prior knowledge that an operation would happen. Pakistan was "in the know of certain things" and "what happened happened with our consent. Americans got to know him—where he was first—and that's why they struck it and struck it precisely." Husain Haqqani, Pakistani ambassador to the U.S., had said 'that Pakistan would have pursued bin Laden had the intelligence of his location existed with them and Pakistan was "very glad that our American partners did. They had superior intelligence, superior technology, and we are grateful to them."

Another Pakistani official stated that Pakistan "assisted only in terms of authorisation of the helicopter flights in our airspace" and the operation was conducted by the United States. He also said that "in any event, we did not want anything to do with such an operation in case something went wrong."

The mixed reactions coming from various Pakistani citizens in different fields of life accurately reflect the confusion over the issue that exists. Did Pakistan really not know that the compound in Abbottabad was the final hiding place of Osama bin Laden or did they know and not inform their American allies? The question will continue to plague us as neither side will ever admit to the whole truth. However it is very interesting to read murdered Pakistani journalist Syed Saleem Shahzad's take on the event.

AL-QAEDA HAD WARNED OF PAKISTAN STRIKE

By Syed Saleem Shahzad [13]

ISLAMABAD - Al-Qaeda carried out the brazen attack on NS Mehran naval air station in Karachi on May 22 after talks failed between the navy and al-Qaeda over the release of naval officials arrested on suspicion of al-Qaeda links, an Asia Times Online investigation reveals.

Pakistani security forces battled for 15 hours to clear the naval base after it had been stormed by a handful of well-armed militants.

At least 10 people were killed and two United States-made P3-C Orion surveillance and anti-submarine aircraft worth US$36 million each were destroyed before some of the attackers escaped through a cordon of thousands of armed forces.

An official statement placed the number of militants at six, with four killed and two escaping. Unofficial sources, though, claim there were 10 militants with six getting free. Asia Times Online contacts confirm that the attackers were from Ilyas Kashmiri's 313 Brigade, the operational arm of al-Qaeda.

Three attacks on navy buses in which at least nine people were killed last month were warning shots for navy officials to accept al-Qaeda's demands over the detained suspects.

The May 2 killing in Pakistan of Osama bin Laden spurred al-Qaeda groups into developing a consensus for the attack in Karachi, in part as revenge for the death of their leader and also to deal a blow to Pakistan's surveillance capacity against the Indian navy.

The deeper underlying motive, though, was a reaction to massive internal crackdowns on al-Qaeda affiliates within the navy.

VOLCANO OF MILITANCY

Several weeks ago, naval intelligence traced an al-Qaeda cell operating inside several navy bases in Karachi, the country's largest city and key port.

"Islamic sentiments are common in the armed forces," a senior navy official told Asia Times Online on the condition of anonymity as he is not authorised to speak to the media.

"We never felt threatened by that. All armed forces around the world, whether American, British or Indian, take some inspiration from religion to motivate their cadre against the enemy. Pakistan came into existence on the two-nation theory that Hindus and Muslims are two separate nations and therefore no one can separate Islam and Islamic sentiment from the armed forces of Pakistan," the official said.

"Nonetheless, we observed an uneasy grouping on different naval bases in Karachi. While nobody can obstruct armed forces personnel for rendering religious rituals or studying Islam, the grouping [we observed] was against the discipline of the armed forces. That was the beginning of an intelligence operation in the navy to check for unscrupulous activities."

The official explained the grouping was against the leadership of the armed forces and opposed to its nexus with the United States against Islamic militancy. When some messages were intercepted hinting at attacks on visiting American officials, intelligence had good reason to take action and after careful evaluation at least 10 people - mostly from the lower cadre - were arrested in a series of operations.

"That was the beginning of huge trouble," the official said.

Those arrested were held in a naval intelligence office behind the chief minister's residence in Karachi, but before proper interrogation could begin, the in-charge of the investigation received direct threats from militants who made it clear they knew where the men were being detained.

The detainees were promptly moved to a safer location, but the threats continued. Officials involved in the case believe the militants feared interrogation would lead to the arrest of more of their loyalists in the navy. The militants therefore made it clear that if those detained were not released, naval installations would be attacked.

It was clear the militants were receiving good inside information as they always knew where the suspects were being detained, indicating sizeable al-Qaeda infiltration within the navy's ranks. A senior-level naval conference was called at which an intelligence official insisted that the matter be handled with great care, otherwise the consequences could be disastrous. Everybody present agreed, and it was decided to open a line of communication with al-Qaeda.

Abdul Samad Mansoori, a former student union activist and now part of 313 brigade, who originally hailed from Karachi but now lives in the North Waziristan tribal area was approached and talks begun. Al-Qaeda demanded the immediate release of the officials without further interrogation. This was rejected.

The detainees were allowed to speak to their families and were well treated, but officials were desperate to interrogate them fully to get an idea of the strength of al-Qaeda's penetration. The militants were told that once interrogation was completed, the men would be discharged from the service and freed. Al-Qaeda rejected these terms and expressed its displeasure with the attacks on the navy buses in April.

These incidents pointed to more than the one al-Qaeda cell intelligence had tracked in the navy. The fear now was that if the problem was not addressed, North Atlantic Treaty Organization (NATO) supply lines could face a new threat. NATO convoys are routinely attacked once they begin the journey from Karachi to Afghanistan; now they could be at risk in Karachi port. Americans who often visit naval facilities in the city would also be in danger.

Therefore, another crackdown was conducted and more people were arrested. Those seized had different ethnic backgrounds. One naval commando came from South Waziristan's Mehsud tribe and was believed to have received direct instructions from Hakeemullah Mehsud, the chief of the Tehrik-e-Taliban Pakistan (Pakistan Taliban). Others were from Punjab province and Karachi, the capital of Sindh province.

After Bin Laden was killed by American Navy Seals in Abbottabad, 60 kilometers north of Islamabad, militants decided the time was ripe for major action. Within a week, insiders at PNS Mehran provided maps, pictures of different exit and entry routes taken in daylight and at night, the location of hangers and details of likely reaction from external security forces.

As a result, the militants were able to enter the heavily guarded facility where one group targeted the aircraft, a second group took on the first strike force and a third finally escaped with the others providing covering fire. Those who stayed behind were killed.

Syed Saleem Shahzad *was Asia Times Online's Pakistan Bureau Chief and author of Inside al-Qaeda and the Taliban: Beyond Bin Laden and 9/11* published by Pluto Press, UK.

NOTES

[1] K. Dozier and R. Burns (2011), "Raid Raises Question: Who's Soldier, Who's Spy?" at http://abcnews.go.com/US/wireStory?id=13532735#.Tyj00YGHrEE (Accessed February 1, 2012).

[2] S.L. Myers, and E. Bumiller (2011), "Obama Calls World 'Safer' After Pakistan Raid," at http://www.nytimes.com/2011/05/03/world/asia/osama-bin-laden-dead.html (Accessed February 1, 2012.

[3] J. Viegas (2011), "A U.S. Navy Seals' Secret Weapon: Elite Dog Team," at http://news.discovery.com/animals/a-us-navy-seals-secret-weapon-elite-dog-team-110503.html (Accessed February 1, 2012).

[4] A. Marc (2011), "The Secret Team That Killed bin Laden," at http://nationaljournal.com/whitehouse/the-secret-team-that-killed-bin-laden-20110502 (Accessed February 1, 2012).

[5] D. Kimberly (2011), "Bin Laden raiders knew mission a one-shot deal," at http://www.suntimes.com/news/nation/5425816-418/sources-bin-laden-raiders-knew-mission-a-one-shot-deal.html (Accessed February 1, 2012).

[6] N. Schmidle (2011), "Getting Bin Laden," at http://www.newyorker.com/reporting/2011/08/08/110808fa_fact_schmidle?currentPage=all (Accessed February 1, 2012).

[7] C. Drew (2011), "Attack on Bin Laden Used Stealthy Helicopter That Had Been a Secret," at http://www.nytimes.com/2011/05/06/world/asia/06helicopter.html (Accessed February 1, 2012).

[8] T. Ross (2011), "Osama bin Laden 'protected' by Pakistani security," at http://www.telegraph.co.uk/news/worldnews/asia/pakistan/8488236/WikiLeaks-Osama-bin-Laden-protected-by-Pakistani-security.html (Accessed February 1, 2012).

[9] M. Calabresi (2011), "CIA Chief: Pakistan Would Have Jeopardized bin Laden Operation," at http://swampland.time.com/2011/05/03/cia-chief-breaks-silence-u-s-ruled-out-involving-pakistan-in-bin-laden-raid-early-on/ (Accessed February 1, 2012).

[10] E. MacAskill and D. Walsh (2011), "Osama bin Laden: Dead, but how did he hide so long?" at http://www.guardian.co.uk/world/2011/may/02/osama-bin-laden-pakistan-awkward-questions (Accessed February 1, 2012).

[11] A. Woodcock (2011), "MP 'shocked' at bin Laden Pakistan discovery," at http://www.independent.co.uk/news/world/asia/mp-shocked-at-bin-laden-pakistan-discovery-2277941.html (Accessed February 1, 2012).

[12] N.P. Walsh (2011), "Official: Pakistan had but didn't probe data that helped make raid," at http://edition.cnn.com/2011/WORLD/asiapcf/05/02/bin.laden.pakistan.role/ (Accessed February 1, 2012).

[13] Syed Saleem Shahzad, "Al-Qaeda had warned of Pakistan strike," at http://www.atimes.com/atimes/South_Asia/ME27Df06.html (Accessed February 1, 2012).

CHAPTER 6

Aftermath in Pakistan

IMMEDIATE PHYSICAL REPERCUSSIONS

Is there any connection between and timing to the various installments of Wiki Leaks, the Jasmine Revolution and obliteration of Osama bin Laden by American Special Forces?

This is one question among many others emerging since the plethora of news reports began gushing or trickling in and are expected to continue for some more time. And it will be necessary to sift the wheat from the chaff in news and views, as some are bound to be very tall claims.[1]

It remains to be seen to what extent some hitherto hidden facts which are surfacing and more lies that are getting exposed will alter politico-military equations, as already some expected and unprecedented reactions and developments occur in US, Pakistan, Afghanistan and India.

MJ Akbar said that "The four American helicopters which went for the final kill in the long hunt for Osama bin Laden achieved their primary purpose. The world is now busy sifting through the ruins of their second hit. For in the process they also crippled the credibility of Pakistan's most powerful institution, its Army, often described by its apologists as critical to national stability and even cohesion. All pretence and pretension is over; a fudge that the killing of Osama was some sort of "joint operation" was thin camouflage that has been torn apart by minimal public scrutiny."

He adds that "If the Pak military did learn what was happening during the 40-odd minutes that ground operations took, there was too much uncertainty and confusion in its chain of command to fashion an adequate, or any, response. Stark fact: the Pakistan Army is impotent before America."

The first massive attack following Pakistani Taliban's threats against Pakistan army's leadership issued shortly after Laden's killing was by two bomb blasts at a training center for Frontier Constabulary (FC) in Charsadda, killing at least 80 and wounding over 120 others. Most of the victims were trainees from the FC training base who were boarding buses near its main gate to return home on leave. Other victims were in a nearby market. Witnesses said many of the casualties occurred in the second blast, after people came to aid those injured in the initial explosion. At least one of the bombs contained ball bearings and nails to increase the damage. Shortly after the bombing, a Pakistani Taliban spokesman called news agencies claiming responsibility and said the strike was a response to Laden's killing.

James Farwell, author of The Pakistan Cauldron (Pentagon Press), is a political consultant who advises the US Department of Defence on information strategy, information operations, strategic communication and cyber war strategy. As per Farwell in an interaction with the author of this book, "The attack humiliated the Pakistani military. The military gets about 25% of the budget (estimates vary and transparency is not a quality the military is known for). It commands that on the theory that it protects Pakistani sovereignty from foreign attack. Mostly that means India, but it embraces every other threat. The undetected attack demonstrated limits of Pakistani military capability. That affronted military pride and undercut its credibility. Army Chief of Staff Kayani is generally skeptical of the U.S. The raid, which caught him by surprise—he was up, working in his office at 2:00 a.m. when it occurred—angered him."

Farwell said that "Pakistanis felt that they were put into an untenable position. If they knew bin Laden was in Abbottabad, they were complicit. If not, they were ignorant. They are a proud people and their pride was deeply affronted. Of course from a US viewpoint, we summarized the attack in two words: "Mission Accomplished." Given the tendency of conspiracy theories that run wild in Pakistan it was also believed that the strike on Abbottabad was a dress rehearsal for a future raid to confiscate Pakistan's nuclear inventory.

Stung by criticism and being the butt of jokes online, like never before in Pakistan's history, its army caught with its pants down, resorted to the most ironic of histrionics. Admitting intelligence failure, Inter Services Intelligence (ISI) Director General Lieutenant-General Ahmed Shuja Pasha sought an apology from the nation and offered to resign if the parliament so demanded. Of course it did not. "The failure was not intentional but I admit that it was a mistake," the ISI Chief said during the in-camera joint sitting of the Parliament that was briefed by security and intelligence officials. "Who cares!!...another chamcha (spoon-implying a sycophant) will come in his place... the whole system is rotten to the core....", wrote a blogger.

Senior Pakistani Journalist Mohammad Shehzad, known for being blunt, wrote: "By carrying out an operation in Abbottabad near Pakistan Military Academy and killing Osama, the US has got a certificate that unfortunately endorses Pakistan as the safest haven for terrorists. No apology or excuse can make the world change its opinion about us. However, had the army chief Kiyani or the ISI chief Pasha would have tendered their resignations accepting their incompetence; the world opinion could have been changed in our favor – positively to some extent. Ironically, no system of accountability exists in Pakistan and people in power are conscience-less."

Out of the material allegedly found during the raid on Laden's lair in Pakistan's Abbottabad cantonment being referred to as a 'treasure trove' including hard drives, disk drives, thumb drives, flash drives, recording devices, videos and a journal, the US is reported to have released five videos. While it may well be a treasure trove, it remains to be seen how the US manages whatever operationally valuable information it finds related to Al-Qaeda's plans in/for Afghanistan, Pakistan and other countries-particularly US.

News reports say that Laden was well in touch with his operational commanders and that he had planned for widely dispersed attacks on soft and populous targets like railways and infrastructure. The raid yielded 2.7 terabytes of data described as the "largest collection of senior terrorist materials ever collected." That was not all. Also recovered was a fairly extensive stash of modern, electronically recorded video porn, which some Indian TV news networks went to town with.

TURMOIL INSIDE PAKISTAN

Hailing Laden as a holy warrior and congratulating the Muslim ummah (brotherhood) on his martyrdom, Al-Qaeda said it will soon release an audio tape made by its leader a week before he died, vowing not to deviate from the path of armed struggle and stated, "We call upon our Muslim people in Pakistan, on whose land Sheikh Osama was killed, to rise up and revolt to cleanse this shame that has been attached to them by a clique of traitors and thieves ... and in general to cleanse their country from the filth of the Americans who spread corruption in it."

An Abbottabad datelined report published in The Asian Age informed about a madrassa close to Laden's hideout where young Pakistani students who considered him to be a religious hero, were furious over his death. With sentiments like "There are many Osamas in the Muslim world and the US can't defeat his ideology…..I will myself become Osama and revenge his death one day," emanating from madrassas in Pakistan (which mushroomed from 250 in 1947, to not exactly known how many thousands more than 20,000), both Pakistan and US need to be very wary.

Prior to Laden's killing, a very serious problem in Pakistan exposed by the murders of leaders who spoke against the anti-blasphemy law was that no one in the government or the army was prepared to take any action or speak out against it or even publicly extend moral or material support to the victims' families. On the other hand, the murderers were being glorified even after being arrested and tried. Besides, with the process of Islamisation of Pakistan army since the days of the third tin-pot president, General Zia ul Haq having matured and "Zia-bharti" (those recruited during Zia's regime) officers becoming senior generals and equivalents, there seems little chance of initiation of any corrective measures like monitoring of madrassas or assisting US in achieving its other aims.

Leaders like Hafiz Mohammed Saeed have gone about organizing special prayers for Osama bin Laden in several cities and towns of Pakistan since he was killed. Saeed's spokesman Yahya Mujahid quoted him as saying in Lahore that the "great person" of Osama bin Laden would continue to be a source of strength and encouragement for Muslims around the world. Mujahid also quoted Saeed as having said that "Martyrdoms are not losses, but are a matter of pride for Muslims. Osama bin Laden was a great person who awakened the Muslim world, Osama bin Laden has rendered great sacrifices for Islam and Muslims, and these will always be remembered."

In an interview with media, author and historian Webster Griffin Tarpley elaborated on a US ploy to divide Pakistan. He said, "I think they're (relations between US and Pakistan) very bad. They could be going in the direction of open war. The war against Pakistan was basically declared by Obama in his West Point speech in December of 2009….This has now been escalated. We've had the Ray Davis affair. We've had a series of acrimonious exchanges between General Kayani and Admiral Mullen at this Joint Chiefs of Staff". Tarpley claims that the US plan is to fragment Pakistan in four ways, so that there will never be a Pakistan oil pipeline from Iran into China, a big strategic goal of the US. Stating that the

Pakistan Naval Ship Mehran (shore naval base)

Fire fighters at PNS Mehran

breakup of Pakistan is at the top of US' agenda and that it has to be done indirectly because Pakistan has nuclear weapons.

The deadly attack on Karachi's heavily guarded Pakistan Navy shore base PNS Mehran, claimed by Tehreeq-e-Taliban Pakistan to avenge Laden's killing, yet again caught Pakistan military with its pants down. The well-planned attack by a small and specially trained team of six terrorists, executed with sophisticated weapons and well focused in killing ten Pakistan Navy personnel, injuring many more and destroying two prized PC-3 Orion 'spy' aircraft and more, should ring a sharp alert for Pakistan of course, but also for India, US and other coalition countries.

While this is not the first attack by Pakistani terrorists on Pakistan's top military bases, including the Inter Services Intelligence (ISI) headquarters, PNS Mehran being selected as a target is significant.

If it is true that Mullah Omar, a close associate to Laden, has been killed, soon after and also like the latter, following a decade-long manhunt with the killers not yet identified, it can possibly mean he too was killed by American troops or operatives with or without Pakistan Army being in the loop /supporting such an operation, or by remote-controlled bombing. Even if he has not been killed, the propaganda itself can be considered as very calculated to confuse and confound. And if the news report about Mullah Omar being killed while he was being moved from Quetta to North Waziristan by former ISI chief Lt General Hamid Gul is true, then it only further exposes and humiliates ISI

These two incidents occurring during Lashkar-e-Taiyyaba (LeT) operative Tahawwur Hussain Rana's trial in Chicago for his role in the 26/11 terrorist attacks in Mumbai and his testimony giving more clues confirming earlier suspected links between this Pakistani terrorist group and the ISI, is only going to rile Pakistan Army's leadership further.

This again means that India and the US must be very wary.

Following the long and farcical session in the Pakistan's Parliament post-Op Geronimo and both Kayani and Pasha making uncalled for statements threatening India, Prime Minister Manmohan Singh called a meeting with the Defence Minister, three Armed Forces Chiefs, National Security Adviser and Defence Secretary. At this meeting reportedly, the armed forces' preparedness to meet any security challenge that may be posed by Pakistani terrorist networks in the region and conventional threats from Pakistan's armed forces came up for review. Also discussed was the presence of an almost division strength of Chinese military personnel in Pakistan Occupied Kashmir in the guise of engineering workers and the threat posed by China to the security of Jammu and Kashmir The Indian Prime Minister was briefed on the overall security measures and the general preparedness of the defense forces.

MURDERED JOURNALIST SYED SALEEM SHAHZAD

An earlier development related to Pakistan army's / ISI's terrorist tie-ups is the assassination of Syed Saleem Shahzad, one of Pakistan's best investigative journalists and bureau chief of Asia Times Online, who went missing on May 29 from Islamabad while on his way to a local television channel to participate in a talk show. His body—with his face severely beaten—was found two days later in a canal in Mandi Bahauddin area of Punjab province.

Shahzad's book Inside Al-Qaeda & Taliban - Beyond Bin Laden & 9/11, published in UK and which reached India shortly after, is a damning account of ISI's nefarious connections with terrorist groups as well as many other facts about and cross connections between them.[2]

Shahzad said 26/11 was scripted by ISI, approved by AL-QAEDA commanders and executed by Lashkar-e-Taiba (LeT). From Al-Qaeda the main player was Ilyas Kashmiri and from LeT Haroon Ashik. The common link between Ashik and Kashmiri is that they were both from Pakistan Army, which "has been embedding terror outfits with its own men, especially in the operations and planning department so that there is close co-ordination with what Pakistan Army & ISI demands and its seamless execution by these terror outfits."

The book and Saleem's last article titled published in the publication he worked for, in all likelihood, proved to be his nemesis. An excerpt of this article reads: "Al-Qaeda carried out the brazen attack on PNS Mehran naval air station in Karachi on May 22 after talks failed between the navy and Al-Qaeda over the release of naval officials arrested on suspicion of Al-Qaeda links."

Interior minister Malik, who visited Shahzad's residence to condole his family and condemned his murder, later, while talking to the media, said that Shahzad might have been murdered over personal enmity. Malik also reportedly admitted that journalists in Pakistan are also battling against negative forces like the army and in order to ensure safety of their lives, orders have been passed to allow journalists to carry small arms with them for self-protection.

Nobody has believed Malik's statement that Shahzad had been "murdered over personal enmity". Journalists and human rights activists in Pakistan have said they believed that Shahzad's killing was not militants, but Pakistan's "fearsome spy agencies", the kingpin of which is the ISI. According to Pakistani media, suspicions immediately fell on the ISI, bringing it more bad publicity after the killing of bin Laden by U.S. Special Forces.

The raid, which Pakistan failed to detect or stop, shattered the myth that the agency (ISI) is omnipotent. A former ISI officer is quoted: "The ISI's image had already been tarnished and it is under so much pressure...it's never been as bad as this before." Shahzad was investigating suspected links between the military and Al- Qaeda, a highly sensitive subject at a time when Washington is wondering how bin Laden was able to live for years in a town near Pakistan's capital and about a two hour drive from ISI headquarters. Human Rights Watch is reported to have said that Shahzad, a 40-year-old father of three, had voiced concerns about his safety after receiving threatening telephone calls from the ISI and was under surveillance since 2010.

The third major post-Laden-killing attack was on 01 July 2011, when reportedly three to four hundred heavily armed terrorists besieged a remote Pakistani post on the Afghan border, killing at least one policeman at Shaltalu checkpoint in the remote part of northwestern district Dir, where Pakistan army tried to put down a Taliban takeover two years ago.

With Pakistan's situation being unprecedentedly precarious, it remains to be seen if US will implement the process of thinning out with effect from next year.[3]

Be that as it may, for India, there is little to be satisfied about and much to be very careful along its long International boundary and the Line of Control. Whatever exposures there have been about Pakistan army and ISI, no matter how low their stock is, it has made absolutely no difference to India. While on the ground one long encounter in Jammu and Kashmir, leading to three LET terrorists being killed by Rashtriya Rifles occurred a few days after the attack in Pakistan, Headquarters Northern Command has clearly stated that there were at least seven hundred terrorists waiting to succeed in crossing over to make the summer in the Kashmir Valley and elsewhere in India really hot.

On the post-26/11 or other matters of negotiation too there is nothing at all for India to be elated about. The recently held Siachen talks amounted to naught. No matter how revealing

the disclosures by Daood Gilani alias David Coleman Headley or Tahawwur Hussain Rana may have been during the ongoing trial in

Syed Saleem Shahzad

Syed Saleem Shahzad on the job

Chicago, Pakistan's latest take simply writes them all off by Rehman stating that Gilani/Headley cannot be trusted.

What else can any civilian leader of Pakistan say on this matter after having given Pakistan army and ISI a clean chit during the mockery of the long session in the parliament following the highly successful US Op Geronimo? As things stand, it seems that the best that India can hope for is consolation from further successful strikes by US forces.

As US forces are expected to thin out from Afghanistan, revelations in the assassinated journalist Syed Salim Shahzad's book, *Inside Al-Qaeda and the Taliban* (and Pakistan Army's actions to subjugate Afghanistan) are raising India's anxieties as reflected in think-tanks' discussions.

Syed Saleem Shahzad became the 37th journalist to be killed in Pakistan since the 9/11 attacks, according to the Committee to Protect Journalists. His waterlogged body retrieved from a canal 60 miles from Islamabad, bore 17 lacerated wounds delivered by a blunt instrument, a ruptured liver and two broken ribs.

An investigative journalist contributing to Asia Times Online, who used to write articles exposing the relationship between the militants and the military, Shahzad, had written scathing reports about the infiltration of militants into Pakistan's military.

A New York daily quoted White House officials, who now believe that Pakistan's Inter Services Intelligence (ISI) ordered the killing of Shahzad, confirming the allegation made in media a few weeks ago. Classified intelligence obtained both before Shahzad's disappearance on 29 May and after discovery of his body showed that senior officials of ISI directed the attack in order to silence criticism.

Yet another senior US official was reported to have said that there was enough other intelligence and indicators immediately after Shahzad's death to conclude that the ISI had ordered the killing. "Every indication is that this was a deliberate, targeted killing that was most likely meant to send shock waves through Pakistan's journalist community and civil society," said the official.[4]

The anger over his death followed unprecedented questioning in the media about the professionalism of Pakistan army and the ISI in the aftermath of the US raid that led to the killing of Osama bin Laden.

A report in The New Yorker states that the order to kill Pakistani investigative journalist Saleem Shahzad came from a senior officer on Pakistan army chief General Ashfaq Parvez Kayani's staff. Quoting a Pakistani army officer, *The New Yorker* reported: "According to the

American official, reliable intelligence indicates that the order to kill Shahzad came from a senior officer on General Kayani's staff. The officer made it clear that he was speaking on behalf of Kayani himself."

The report said the presence of Islamists in Pakistan navy, and at Mehran naval base, which was attacked by terrorists, was not a secret among Pakistanis but that Shahzad's article was particularly "incendiary".

May 2011 will go down in Pakistan history as literally a month of mayhem for not only stepped up explosions of gunfire and bombs, but also for exposures of long hidden facts and the shocks they caused to Pakistan's army, its floundering civilian government and mostly to its people. While the killing of the world's worst ever terrorist Osama bin Laden on 2 May, in a surprise-attack by US Special forces in the mansion at Abbottabad exposed yet another major deception of Pakistan army, Syed Saleem Shahzad's book Inside Al-Qaeda and the Taliban: Beyond Bin Laden and 9/11 exposed many more about its various nefarious connections.

The very well planned strike on Pakistan's leading naval base at Karachi, PNS Mehran, two days after Shahzad's article "Al-Qaeda had warned of Pakistani strike" appeared online and after the release of his book already containing many embarrassing exposures of Pakistan's military, may well have egged his killers to expedite his elimination to prevent many more articles elaborating on already exposed linkages.

On May 29, 2011, one week after the release of his book in UK, Shahzad was abducted, days after writing an article suggesting that insiders in the Pakistan navy had colluded with Al-Qaeda in an attack on PNS Mehran. The next day he was brutally murdered and a day later, on May 31, his battered body was recovered from a canal 60 km away from Pakistan's capital Islamabad.

The exposures caused by Osama's killing and attack on PNS Mehran were just precursors to the vast range of wheels within wheels and cross-connections elaborated in Shahzad's book which are of great significance to India, US, Afghanistan and of course Pakistan.

President Barack Obama may well have delivered on his campaign promise to kill Osama bin Laden, but during the decade that he remained on the run, he was not really a functional Al-Qaeda strategist. This book introduces and examines the new generation of Al-Qaeda leaders who have been behind most recent attacks.

EXCERPTS FROM SYED SALEEM SHAHZAD'S BOOK

Shahzad began his narrative by informing that while he had never worked for well-funded international or mainstream media, his functioning as an independent reporter for what he referred to as alternate media, suited his temperament and thus brought him into contact with "those close to the bottom of the ladder", when he met them. Some examples: Mohammad Ilyas Kashmiri, beginning as a Kashmiri terrorist, later commanded his own '313 brigade group', eventually became member of Al-Qaeda's shura (council) and turned out to be a major player in the 26 November 08 attack on Mumbai.

Sirajuddin Haqqani and Qari Ziaur Rehaman, the most dangerous of terrorist commanders in Afghanistan. Of special significance and vital importance to India are Shahzad's meetings with Captain Khurram Askhiq, who had resigned from Pak army's special services group and joined the Taliban and whose "imprint on Al-Qaeda was unmistakeable". While Khurram was killed by the UK army at Helmand, his brother Major Haroon and friend, Major Abdul Rehman (both retired) were the two main planners for Mumbai's 26/11. Also involved in the plot was Kashmiri. It was his idea to expand the ambit of attacks against India, so that India and Pakistan were driven to war, which would bring operations against Al-Qaeda to a grinding halt.

Some revealing excerpts from the book are indeed relevant:

> The Mumbai operation was actually the revival of an old ISI plan. The idea was to deflect the Pakistan Army away from Waziristan and get it to fight India instead. This nearly succeeded: 'Pakistan's militant leaders Mullah Fazlullah and Baitullah Mehsud announced that they would fight alongside Pakistan's armed forces in an India-Pakistan war, and the director general of ISI, Lt Gen Ahmad Shuja Pasha, confirmed this understanding in his briefing to national and foreign correspondents, when he called Fazlullah and Baitullah Mehsud Pakistan's strategic assets' (p. 95).

Al-Qaeda's central hero was Captain Khurram Ashiq of the Pakistan Army who was followed by his brother Major Haroon Askhiq to become Al-Qaeda's hand that wielded the sword: Khurram was an assault commander of the elite anti-terrorist Zarrar Coy from Pakistan's Special Service Group (SSG) in 2001 when he flipped after 9/11. Because of his Salafi background he was shaped into a warrior by Lashkar-e-Tayyaba (LeT). He wrote to Saleem Shahzad about his brother too. 'Major Haroon Ashiq hung up his boots right after 9/11. On his release from service, he joined LeT. One of my unit officers Major Abdul Rahman also followed suit. I joined the outfit soon after, without caring for the consequences' (p. 83).

For Captain Khurram faith came before country. While on a UN mission in Sierra Leone he clearly demonstrated it: 'Khurram built a mosque and a Madrassa in Sierra Leone, despite the opposition of his commander, Brigadier Ahmad Shuja Pasha, later chief of the ISI' (p. 85). Both brothers had joined the LeT, but had soon 'realised that the LET was just an extension of Pakistan's armed forces' (p. 86).

As an Al-Qaeda terrorist, Haroon enjoyed contacts inside the army: 'Haroon developed a silencer for the AK-47. This became an essential component of Al-Qaeda's special guerrilla operations. He then visited China to procure night vision glasses. The biggest task was to clear them through the customs in Pakistan, Haroon called on his friend Captain Farooq, who was (then) President Musharraf's security officer. Farooq went to the airport in the president's official car and received Haroon at the immigration counter. In the presence of Farooq, nobody dared touch Haroon's luggage, and the night vision glasses arrived in Pakistan without any hassle (Farooq was a member of the Hizbut Tahrir, a fact discovered by the military intelligence as late as nine months after his posting as Musharraf's security officer. After being spotted, he was briefly arrested and then retired from the Pakistan Army)' (p. 88).

Al-Qaeda targeted NATO supplies through Haroon in 2008: 'Haroon travelled through North Waziristan to Karachi. When night fell, he stayed in army messes in the countryside. Being an ex-army officer he was allowed that facility. He spoke English and Urdu with an unmistakable military accent' (p. 92).

He took revenge on Major General Ameer Faisal Alavi because the latter had killed a lot of Al-Qaeda men – including Abdur Rehman Kennedy – as leader of a Pakistan Army assault on Angoor Adda in North Waziristan. Haroon ambushed Alavi in Islamabad 'jumping out of his car and killing Alavi with his army revolver' (p. 93).

Haroon believed in the Ghazwa-e-Hind (Battle for India) hadith and thought End of the World was near, and the advent of the Mahdi was at hand with the help of the armies of Khurasan (Afghanistan–Pakistan) (p. 200).

Haroon is now in Adiala jail in Rawalpindi after failing to kidnap an Ahmadi, Sarwar Khan. (The police officer in Adiala jail told Saleem Shahzad he had started admiring his prisoner.) In custody he admitted to killing Major General Alavi and kidnapping Hindu filmmaker Satish Anand with the help of one Major Basit from Karachi. After he discovered that Anand had no money to give he released him on orders from Al-Qaeda's Ilyas Kashmiri 'if he embraced Islam' which Anand immediately did. Later Al-Qaeda decided that to refill its empty coffers it will abduct only non-Muslims, in particular, Ahmadis.

Having read and reviewed books by at least three more bold Pakistani authors, Mohammad Amir Rana (*Gateway to Terrorism*, 2003, and *Seeds of Terrorism*, 2005-New Millennium), Hassan Abbas (*Pakistan's Drift Into Extremism: Allah, The Army and America's War on Terror*, Pentagon Press, 2005) and Amir Mir (*Talibanisation of Pakistan*, Pentagon Press 2009), and having met Abbas some years ago in Delhi, one knows the price such author's have to pay to remain alive. While Abbas moved to the US, Rana and Mir are living very cautiously in Pakistan, another author, Mujahid Hussain (*Punjabi Taliban*, Pentagon Press, 2011—released in India) has recently moved to Belgium.

With his persistence, courage and reputation, Shahzad, as an investigative reporter who worked as Pakistan Bureau Chief of Asia Times Online, had unparalleled access to Al-Qaeda and Taliban commanders, as well as within the ISI. He had been both a hostage and a guest of the Taliban, which gave him a unique insight into the organisation's internal structures. Shahzad's work was praised by US Secretary of State Hillary Clinton for 'bringing to light the troubles extremism poses to Pakistan's stability.'

Syed Saleem Shahzad (1970–2011) is survived by his wife and three children. His book and articles must be translated into other languages and read by all watchers of terrorism the world over. Pentagon Press, the Indian distributor of this book has ordered another consignment after his first one got sold out within weeks.

PAKISTAN'S TROUBLED HISTORY

If the exposures about the duplicity of Pak army/Inter Services Intelligence (ISI) by Wiki Leaks were the first round, exposures following bin Laden's killing were the second major blow to the image and credibility of Pak army, late Syed Saleem Shahzad's book *Inside Al-Qaeda and the Taliban Beyond Bin Laden and 9/11* became the third, and Schofield's book became the fourth and like salt on sore wounds.

Captioned on the cover as *'A Woman's Experience on the Frontline of the War on Terror'*, Carey Schofield', the author of *Inside The Pakistan Army* thanks Generals Parvez Musharraf and Ashfaq Parvez Kayani as well as many other officers and soldiers for all the support and encouragement given to her for the few years that she spent researching for this book. However, her verdict on Pakistan army on the very first page of the book's first chapter titled 'The Question of the Pakistan Army', is bound to have caused much regret to the former and current chiefs of this army mentioned and many others, all the more so because this book got released in India in July 2011, barely two months after Osama bin Laden got killed by American Special Forces in Abbottabad.

And what Schofield has written on the first page is that Pakistan Army has never been entirely trusted by the West, as its role in the "war against terror has been seen to be as ambiguous as it has been central" and mentions some questions, which observers in India, US, Afghanistan, etc., have dwelt on: "Has the Army's notorious ISI continued to support its long term allies amongst the Taliban, with or without the tacit consent of the head of state? Have elements in the Army siphoned off aid given them by the Americans to support the very forces it was supposed to be used to suppress? How strenuous or even sincere has the Army ever been in its attempts to round up Taliban fighters fleeing from NATO forces across its borders? To what extent has every element in the military machine been under the control of the head of the state?"

Pak army has been dogged by these questions. Despite the protestations of successive Army Chiefs, Western officials have continued to brief journalists about the double dealing of Pakistan's Armed forces and the intelligence directorates.

Scofield's conclusions about Pak army are reinforced by Ralph Peters, a retired Army officer, journalist and bestselling author, who worked briefly with the Pakistani military and intelligence leadership during the mid-1990s. An excerpt from his military report, which "Nobody in Washington cared" about, read: "Your tax dollars are being used to help kill and maim our Soldiers, Marines and Navy corpsmen fighting in Afghanistan...Over the past ten years, we've given the Pakistanis—primarily their military—over $20 billion in aid. What did we get in return? Our Pakistani allies hid and protected Osama bin Laden; they increased their support to the Afghan Taliban and its partner, the Haqqani terror network; they sponsored repeated terrorist attacks against India; they provided safe-haven bases on Pakistani soil for terrorists from a "rainbow coalition" of extremist organizations; and all the while they purposely whipped up anti-American hatred among the country's 180-million Muslims. Your tax dollars at work".

Pakistan's first dictator President, General Ayub Khan's bloodless coup was justified by citing that, given the years of chaos and corruption, the Army promised a 'sound, solid and strong nation.' He began by delivering growth and increased prosperity, helped by considerable economic assistance from the USA and Great Britain following two beneficial defence treaties. In 1961 he initiated the process of creating a new capital, from Karachi, which was too far away from Army General Headquarters in Rawalpindi, to the new city of Islamabad, just ten miles away.

Zulfiqar Ali Bhutto, Ayub Khan's Foreign Minister and rabidly anti-Indian, encouraged him to adopt an aggressive policy. Following moves by the US to supply arms to India during its 1962 war with China, Bhutto also instigated a change in foreign policy which until then had been almost entirely pro-Western/US, to building diplomatic ties with China to strengthen Pakistan's position. In 1963 this policy shift culminated in the Sino-Pakistan Agreement, by which China ceded approximately 750 square miles of land to Pakistan, which acknowledged the sovereignty of China over large parts of Pakistan Occupied northern Kashmir. The pact is still not recognised by India, which disputes the legality of negotiating sovereignty over the disputed lands.

Bharat—Sanskrit for India—is the ever present threat that Pak army officers and men are indoctrinated to perceive and speculate endlessly, on Indian intensions and capabilities, of how it opposed partition and—as Pakistanis constantly recall—'snatched Kashmir against the will of the people'. In the 1965 war (launched by Pakistan) over Jammu and Kashmir, the Indian Army reached the outskirts of Lahore.

In 1971 India supported Bengali separatists (which Schofield does not mention, as a result of political suppression by West Pakistan government and oppression Pakistan's Punjabi-dominated army) and contributed to the breakup of the country. Quite apart from its military aggression, Pakistanis point out the Indian national anthem itself refers possessively to Sindh in its second line: 'Thy name rouses the hearts of the Punjab, Sindh, Gujrat and Maratha.' The words of the anthem were written by Rabindranath Tagore in 1911.

In its early years the Pak armed forces' officer cadre comprised mainly sons of landed families and successful professionals, with almost all prominent families having someone in the Army. General Ziaul Haq's planned Islamisation of the army changed that trend resulting in young men conscious about following the Islamic religious regimen and also from less affluent backgrounds entering Pakistan's Military Academy.

Zulfiqar Ali Bhutto

Genral Ayub Khan

General Ziaul Haq

General Parvez Musharraf

Having lost out to India in three conventional wars since 1947—the third of which severed off Erstwhile East Pakistan—this Islamisation was part of Haq's larger plan of launching a much cheaper form of proxy war by export of terrorism to India.

Schofield makes one technical error by stating that President Parvez Musharraf awarded the Sitara-e-Pakistan posthumously in 1994 to William Brown (for raising the flag of Pakistan in Gilgit in 1947—considered an act of high treason against his own King-Emperor). This cannot be so, as in 1994 Musharraf was neither chief nor president, but a Lt Gen heading military operations.

Barring this error, the author, despite praise for Pak army based obviously on official briefings, has written about its inner politics and intrigues and quoted senior officers who criticised it for lack of professionalism, which has plagued it ever since it got transformed from part of undivided Indian Army to the army of the newly formed Islamic Republic of Pakistan. One of them states "recurrent confrontation and collusion with politicians had blackened the army's reputation and had, arguably, hampered its military effectiveness" and that interventions of elected governments "distracted the army from its real job and damaged its image domestically. Civilian resentment at the scale of resources apparently devoured by the military was disturbing to younger officers and to soldiers."

The exposures of long hidden connections and ensuing violence following May 2, 2011 sent shock waves to Pakistan's floundering civilian government and its people, the relations of both Pak army and ISI with the civilian government and the US plunged to an all-time low. Even within Pak army there was seething anger in its ranks as brought out by retired and serving officers interviewed by The Associated Press (AP), which quoted retired Lt. Gen. Talat Masood saying that while the army is Pakistan's strongest institution, and army chief General Ashfaq Parvez Kayani is the nation's most powerful leader, he "has to be very careful".

Like others interviewed, he doubted that Kayani's subordinates would try to unseat him in an intra-army coup, but he noted occasions in the past when disgruntled officers were found to be plotting against their chief. "These rumblings generally occurred after the army suffered an embarrassing defeat, most notably Pakistan's 1971 loss of East Pakistan, now Bangladesh, when India took 90,000 Pakistani prisoners of war who weren't released for a year. Last month's raid on the al-Qaida leader's Abbottabad compound resurrected public comparisons to that Bangladesh debacle", the AP report stated.

US and Pakistan relations have hit an all time low with this incident and the following November 26, 2011 NATO air-strike that killed two dozen Pakistanis. As per James Farwell "The cumulative impact has been to further polarize relations between the two countries, despite efforts by the two militaries to work out some kind of balance. There appears to be some understanding that Pakistan will receive notice of new drone attacks. These have caused a huge backlash in Pakistan against the US. Pakistanis see the attacks as an abuse of their sovereignty and the cause of avoidable civilian deaths. The US views the attacks as necessary to kill Al-Qaeda leaders. Undeniably they have achieved that. The number of civilians killed is disputed. The Taliban has clearly "spun" the attacks to argue that many civilians were killed or wounded but one needs to be cautious in judging such reports. What is clear is that Pakistanis nationally very much oppose the attacks. One irony is that those who lives closest to the Taliban seem less opposed. Those who bear witness to Taliban brutality see the Taliban as extremist, violent terrorists."

MEMOGATE

Meanwhile, another explosive development, which had allegedly begun brewing behind the scenes a day after bin Laden's killing, erupted in October as *"Memogate"*.

Mansur Ijaz, an extremely wealthy Pakistani businessman in US, published an article in the Financial Times alleging that Pakistan's civilian government had asked him to deliver a secret memorandum to the Pentagon seeking US assistance in preventing Pakistan army and ISI. He later claimed that then Pakistan Ambassador to the US, Hussain Haqqani, contacted him the day after bin Laden's killing to ask for his help in conveying the memo from Pakistan's President, Asif Ali Zardari to the Pentagon for assistance of the US military to prevent a coup by Pakistan's military.

After the article was published, Mr. Ijaz reportedly met with the Lt Gen Shuja Pasha, in London and gave him the telephonic record of all his communications with Mr Haqqani. Mr. Ijaz said he wrote a memorandum using the material provided by Mr. Haqqani and then sent it to General James Jones, a former US security adviser, who conveyed it to Admiral (recently retired) Mike Mullen, who admitted receiving the memo, but dismissed it. He indicated that the content of the memorandum was published by the media and was freely available. With the memo becoming a serious issue in Pakistan, Mr. Haqqani resigned from his post of Ambassador and the new Ambassador, Ms. Sherry

Mansur Ijaz

Asif Ali Zardari

Rahman, has not yet taken her post in Washington. The Supreme Court of Pakistan is conducting an inquiry into the scandal.

Contents of the confidential memo were published in its entirety on Foreign Policy magazine's website on November 17. The memo, addressed to Admiral Michael Mullen requested the Obama administration to convey a "strong, urgent and direct message to General Kayani and General Pasha" to "end their brinkmanship aimed at bringing down the civilian apparatus" and made certain explicit offers to the United States government in exchange for its support. These included the following quoted directly from the memo:

> "In the event Washington's direct intervention behind the scenes can be secured through your personal communication with Kayani (he will likely listen only to you at this moment) to stand down the Pakistani military-intelligence establishment, the new national security team is prepared, with full backing of the civilian apparatus, to do the following:

1. President of Pakistan will order an independent inquiry into the allegations that Pakistan harbored and offered assistance to UBL (Usama bin Laden-as spelt in FBI's 10 Most Wanted list) and other senior Qaeda operatives. The White House can suggest names of independent investigators to populate the panel, along the lines of the bipartisan 9-11 Commission, for example.
2. The inquiry will be accountable and independent, and result in findings of tangible value to the US government and the American people that identify with exacting detail those elements responsible for harboring and aiding UBL inside and close to the inner ring of influence in Pakistan s Government (civilian, intelligence directorates and military). It is certain that the UBL Commission will result in immediate termination of active service officers in the appropriate government offices and agencies found responsible for complicity in assisting UBL.
3. The new national security team will implement a policy of either handing over those left in the leadership of Al-Qaeda or other affiliated terrorist groups who are still on Pakistani soil, including Ayman Al Zawahiri, Mullah Omar and Sirajuddin Haqqani, or giving US military forces a "green light" to conduct the necessary operations to capture or kill them on Pakistani soil. This "carte blanche" guarantee is not without political risks, but should demonstrate the new group's commitment to rooting out bad elements on our soil. This commitment has the backing of the top

British General Sir Richard Dannatt with General Ashfaq Parvez Kayani, Chief of Pakistan Army

Inter Services Intelligence (ISI) Director General Ahmed Shuja Pasha with General Kayani

echelon on the civilian side of our house, and we will insure necessary collateral support.

4. One of the great fears of the military-intelligence establishment is that with your stealth capabilities to enter and exit Pakistani airspace at will, Pakistan's nuclear assets are now legitimate targets. The new national security team is prepared, with full backing of the Pakistani government—initially civilian but eventually all three power centers —to develop an acceptable framework of discipline for the nuclear program. This effort was begun under the previous military regime, with acceptable results. We are prepared to reactivate those ideas and build on them in a way that brings Pakistan's nuclear assets under a more verifiable, transparent regime.
5. The new national security team will eliminate Section S of the ISI charged with maintaining relations to the Taliban, Haqqani network, etc. This will dramatically improve relations with Afghanistan.
6. We are prepared to cooperate fully under the new national security team's guidance with the Indian government on bringing all perpetrators of Pakistani origin to account for the 2008 Mumbai attacks, whether outside government or inside any part of the government, including its intelligence agencies. This includes handing over those against whom sufficient evidence exists of guilt to the Indian security services."

Could the requests and offers made in this alleged memo be categorized as unprecedented? In the past the US supported Pakistan's civilian leaders, like late Benazir Bhutto, who was facilitated to return to Pakistan and succeeded in becoming the Prime Minister. But one constant till May 2, 2011 was that US always supported Pak army. And no civil government in Pakistan made such bids. OBL's obliteration has set some new precedents.

Gen. Kayani may be seething, but there now seems little possibility of the classic Pak army coup, even though he has appointed a new commander for the coup brigade-111. The same Supreme Court, whose Chief Justice former fourth dictator president Parvez Musharraf intimidated is ironically now supporting a disgraced or discredited army/ vice-versa. And the same Musharraf in exile has decided to remain so, following much bluster about returning to Pakistan to contest elections, because he may face arrest on arrival for being instrumental in liquidating Benazir. The civilian leadership, particularly Prime Minister Yusuf Raza

Pakistan's Foreign Minister Hina Rabbani Khar

Pakistan's Defence Minister Chaudhry Ahmad Mukhtar

Gilani seems to be bearing up not too badly, with his impassioned speech in the Senate getting him many table-thumping cheers from his political colleagues and his appearing to bear up well in the Supreme Court.

Political tumult and trapeze is not new to Pakistan, but this time around the army-civil equation is not quite the same. For the first time political will has overruled the Pakistan Army with the appointment of Lt General Zaheerul Islam as the new ISI chief. Pakistan Prime Minister Yousaf Raza Gilani made the appointment in sharp contrast to the wish of the Pakistani Army that Lt General Ahmed Shuja Pasha be given an extension.[5]

Pakistani political analyst and TV anchor Moeed Pirzada makes an interesting observation: "In this new set-up Pakistan's all-powerful military is not 'the player' but one of the key players along with the government in Islamabad, the government in Punjab, a powerful media, Imran Khan's Pakistan Tehreek-e-Insaf and the Supreme Court. Among these, the Supreme Court is the most misunderstood and underestimated. It is no doubt a political actor with its own mind, but unlike in the past it is no one's handmaiden. It may tactically align itself in different situations to one or the other player, but it is now a player in its own right and has made it abundantly clear to the generals that their intervention will never be legitimized".

James Farwell said that "Another impact of the bin Laden attack has been to weaken the elected civilian government in relation to the military. I do not believe the military wanted to execute another coup. The last thing it desires is responsibility for dealing with Pakistan's corrupt, incompetent civilian government, its economic problems, the consequences of the tragic flooding, a school system that fails, a judicial system that is dysfunctional and riddled with politics and other challenges. The military has the power it wants as to the matters in which it is interested. Still, the PPP, which has forged a decent working relationship with the army, has refused to stand up to the military. Mostly the military would like to get rid of Zardari. It sees Zardari as weak and I suspect it dislikes the aura of corruption that has surrounded his reputation. It bears noting that he has never been convicted of a crime and hotly denies the corruption charges."

Inder Malhotra went so far as to say that America and Pakistan are separated but not divorced. He added that, "Over the years there have been grave crises between the US and Pakistan (America's "most allied ally", in the words of Ayub Khan), but these have been overcome somehow or the other, especially when America needed the rapprochement. Two life-long American experts on South Asia, Teresita and Howard Schaffer (a husband-and-wife team each of whom served as deputy assistant secretary of state for the region), wrote a book on the subject with the eloquent title *Three Marriages, Two Divorces.* Is a third divorce in the offing, or will the two partners prevent it? All things considered, the second alternative seems more likely. America and Pakistan need each other. More than the southern supply route, the US requires Pakistan's cooperation in the endgame in Afghanistan. Pakistan, with its precarious economy, cannot do without American largesse."

While much may have happened in confidence building measures between India and Pakistan in 2011 Pak army's support and export of terrorists to India though well defended by Indian Army and security forces, continues unabated. And whatever may be its political future, Pak army's India policy is not expected to change. So India remains fated to watch warily.

NOTES

[1] Saba Imtiaz, April 26, 2011, The Express Tribune, "WikiLeaks reveals: 'US classified ISI as terror affiliate' " at http://tribune.com.pk/story/156279/wikileaks-us-guantanamo-documents-says-isi-may-have-supported-al-qaeda/ (Accessed March 7, 2012).

[2] Sayed Saleem Shahzad, "Inside Al-Qaeda and the Taliban—Beyond Bin Laden and 9/11", Pluto Press Palgrave Macmillan, 2011, p. 70.

[3] Adrian Croft, Reuters, 29 January 2012, "Britain says Afghan withdrawal must be carefully phased " at http://www.reuters.com/article/2012/01/28/us-afghanistan-britain-idUSTRE80R0JN20120128 (Accessed March 15, 2012)

[4] Jane Perlez, Eric Schmitt, The New York Times, "US believes ISI ordered murder of reporter Saleem Shahzad" at http://www.ndtv.com/article/world/us-believes-isi-ordered-murder-of-reporter-saleem-shahzad-116935&cp (Accessed March 14, 2012).

[5] Shafqat Ali, 10 March 2012, "Gilani appoints new ISI chief" at http://www.asianage.com/international/gilani-appoints-new-isi-chief-747 (Accessed March 20, 2012).

[6] Chandan Singh, Jun 18, 2011, "Pak Army's Old Friend and Terrorist Guest Osama Obliterated by US" at http://www.articlesbase.com/politics-articles/pak-armys-old-friend-and-terrorist-guest-osama-obliterated-by-us-4921724.html (Accessed March 7, 2012).

CHAPTER 7

Changing Equations for U.S., Afghanistan and India

Almost ten years later, the CIA-SEALS team proved that Osama bin Laden was not gifted with a tenth life like the cat with nine. Without doubt, Op Geronimo was most meticulously planned, prepared and implemented. The operation and its success became far more significant, with the target being a very well shielded mansion barely half a kilometer away from the Pakistan Military Academy in Abbottabad cantonment. Because there is no way that Laden could have been where he was found and killed—for even a day or for six or eight years—without the specific approval and support of Pakistan's military and its infamous Inter Services Intelligence (ISI).[1]

Pakistan military's first reaction of believing that this was an attack from India, while nothing short of ludicrous, but not surprising, also meant quite obviously, that it was not within the planning loop of Op Geronimo. And probably just as well, because otherwise, Laden may have lived ten lives and more.[1]

The timing of two reports in the media days before the operation was launched is interesting. One was about leaked documents of Guantanamo Bay stating that the US military classified Pakistan's top spy agency, ISI, as a terrorist support entity in 2007 and used association with it as a justification to detain prisoners there. The other was about a senior Al-Qaeda commander claiming that the terrorist group has hidden a nuclear bomb in Europe which will be detonated to unleash a "nuclear hailstorm", if Laden was ever caught or assassinated.

However, it is the avalanche of news, reactions, speculations, etc., following Laden's killing that need to be analyzed for the old and new lies they expose about Pakistan's military-mullah combo and some of the omissions and commissions of the US and Afghanistan as well as what they indicate about the possible post-Laden developments related to these three countries, Pakistan-sponsored terrorism and its implications for India.

Pakistan's credibility, often questioned by US officials over the last few years, has taken a further hard blow and while its spin doctors are functioning on high rpm, they do not seem to be cutting much ice, what with wide civilian anger and further anti-American sentiment.

CHINESE SUPPORT FOR PAKISTAN

The China factor was further heightened by Pakistan's Prime Minister Yousuf Raza Gilani's official and Pasha's sudden and secret visit to China immediately after Op Geronimo and China stating that the international community "must respect" Pakistan's sovereignty, tacitly confirms reports that it has asked the US not to violate Islamabad's territorial integrity, following the killing of Osama bin Laden.

Asked about reports that China has asked US during its recently concluded strategic dialogue with Washington to respect Pakistan's sovereignty as Islamabad came under heavy pressure after bin Laden's killing, Chinese Foreign Ministry spokesperson, Jiang Yu reportedly told media that "sovereignty and territorial integrity of Pakistan must be respected." Then came the most ironic claim: "We believe that Pakistan has made great contribution to international counter-terrorism efforts, as well as huge sacrifices. The international community should understand and support Pakistan's efforts to restore national stability and develop its economy," she said.

According to Pakistan's state run news agency, Gilani told Pakistan media after his meeting with Chinese Premier Wen Jiabao that "China supported Pakistan's cause on its own." Gilani said the Chinese conveyed a clear message to the US that "there should be no harm to the Pakistani sovereignty and the US should understand and appreciate concerns of Pakistan."

Also, China is reported to have asked the US to "work with Pakistan in improving their bilateral relations in view of the present scenario.... that Pakistan should be helped and its honour should be upheld keeping in view its sacrifices in war on terror." Gilani also quoted Wen as saying that

Chinese Foreign Ministry spokesperson Jiang Yu

President Barack Obama

Pakistan faced challenges in the wake of killing of bin Laden and Chinese leadership was categorical in supporting Pakistan's stance as well as its concerns over national honour and sovereignty.

A Pakistani daily quoted diplomatic sources as saying that China has "warned in unequivocal terms that any attack on Pakistan would be construed as an attack on China", The warning was formally conveyed by the Chinese foreign minister at last week's China-US strategic dialogue and economic talks in Washington, it said. Gilani reiterated Pakistans's support for its policy of 'One China' and said his country fully supports China on the issues of Taiwan and Tibet.

Whereas earlier, the Chinese used to cite these phrases to counter the Indian position in South Asia, it appears now it is the US's turn to face the Chinese music—despite more than $20 billion in aid that the US contributed to Pakistan in the last decade.

Jiang's statement that China 'will unswervingly continue to support Pakistan's efforts to fight terrorism' may also have much to do with the fact that China needs Pakistan's and the Taliban's support to control Uighur protests in the north-western region of Xinjiang.

While Jiang during her briefing skirted questions about Pakistan-China signing new defence agreements, the fact remains that China has provided Pakistan with a very substantial package, which has been enhanced during this visit., Srikanth Kondapalli, Professor in Chinese Studies at JNU, said that the earlier consignment included JF-17 fighters (70 out of 250 already delivered), four F-22 P frigates (three already delivered), six submarines, early warning aircraft and other ground forces equipment. "More such projects have been committed during this visit like the technical support by Chinese scientists at Pakistan's Fatehganj missile production factory."

Some Chinese retired naval officers and others have also demanded recently that China should set up military "facilities" in Pakistan. After the Chinese assistance to the Chashma III and IV nuclear power plants were cleared by the International Atomic Energy Agency in March this year (as a counter to the US-India 123 agreement), and as moves towards the Fissile Material Cut-off Treaty are being made, the news about substantial increases in Pakistan's capability to produce nuclear warheads, is not surprising, according to Kondapalli.

PAKISTAN ARMY AND THE NATO TROOPS

As investigations begin into intelligence failings over Osama bin Laden's whereabouts and Pakistan army facing a rare barrage of criticism, its chief General Ashfaq Kayani, smarting from this embarrassing development, is reported to have demanded for the number of US troops based in Pakistan to be reduced. While it is not known how many US personnel are currently stationed in Pakistan, Kayani wants their numbers kept to a minimum. It remains to be seen how Pakistan will ensure such a move, or whether the US will agree to accede to such a demand by Pakistan. On the other hand the UK is sticking to its schedule of a 2014 pullout from Afghanistan.

While US President Barack Obama has assured that if felt necessary, such an operation may be repeated, Kayani has stated that any similar action violating the sovereignty of Pakistan will warrant a review on the level of military/intelligence cooperation with the United States.

The war against terror that the US has been fighting since 9/11 is certainly not going to end with Laden's elimination. Over these ten years the, US has many more Islamists gunning for it in addition to the surviving players like Mullah Omar in Afghanistan/Pakistan and others elsewhere.

Having been on the run/in hiding for a decade, Laden's exit may only mean a loss of the ideological figurehead, which may affect Al-Qaeda a bit but it is not expected to peter out.[3]

Dr Lal Khan, in his book *The Pakistan's Other Story*, released in October 2009, wrote that to look at the Pakistan Army solely as the instrument of the ruling class would mean ignoring the real contradictions that had developed within it. Top military brass were involved directly in the economy, both the legal and the "black economy", including drug running. The heroin pipeline in the 1980s could not have operated without the knowledge, if not connivance, of officials at the highest level of the army, the government and the CIA. Everyone chose to ignore it for the larger task that was to defeat erstwhile Soviet Union.

Drugs control was on nobody's agenda. In this orgy of destruction and loot, while General Zia ul Haq and his coterie of generals amassed huge amounts of black money, they were not content with the black capital coming from the drugs trade because they had to share this drug money with the different warlords, constantly changing loyalties, and the leaders of different Islamic fundamentalist parties and Islamic mercenary outfits involved in this reactionary insurgency.

Hence, Dr. Khan claims, they also started smuggling the most advanced US weaponry for the jihad through the Pakistani supply lines under the auspices of the sections of the Pakistan Army involved in this CIA-planned operation. "There are reports that there is a burning hatred amongst the ranks of the army against the top brass amassing this mammoth wealth. Their perks, their privileges and their plunder have rekindled class hatred amongst the soldiers towards the officer caste. The lower ranking officers are also in a desperate psychological state. The war being fought for US imperialism has led to a rapid rise in the number of desertions within the army. Morale is very low and it is not an accident that the Pakistani military outfits are losing their battles in the tribal areas. It is for these reasons that General Kayani has given wage rises and other privileges to the lower ranks and soldiers. They are rapidly withdrawing army officers from civilian posts where a lot of them had been deployed during the Musharraf regime," Dr. Khan wrote.

According to Ashley Tellis, the daring raid that killed Osama bin Laden marked a turning point not only in U.S-Pakistan ties but also in power relations within Pakistan. Most observers have focused on the first, but have failed to understand how worsening civil-military relations in Pakistan have contributed to the recent meltdown between Washington and Islamabad. "The shock that the United States could discover Bin Laden from thousands of miles away in a cantonment town, when he was overlooked by the military and its powerful intelligence services, confronted the Pakistani public with one of two possibilities: either their army was malicious, harboring an enemy whose allies were ravaging Pakistan every day, or it was incompetent, incapable of its discharging its principal task of protecting the nation.

In either case, the Bin Laden affair raised the fundamental question of why such a military was offered preferential access to the public trough given its debilitating failures. The ease with which homegrown insurgents were able to attack a major Pakistani naval base, even as the intelligence services, for all their fecklessness, were widely suspected of torturing and killing a prominent Pakistani journalist who had uncovered connections between the deep state and extremists, filled the Pakistani populace with dismay and revulsion…Not since the disastrous Kargil war of 1999 has the army's reputation fallen so low. In a praetorian state, a loss of credibility is a threat to survival—and, hence, the Pakistani army struck back resolutely and early," stated Tellis.

In June 2011, Pakistan army launched a series of missile and artillery attacks on Kunar and Nangarhar provinces in eastern Afghanistan, killing dozens of civilians. The missile attacks were accompanied by raids by the Pakistani Taliban, which is backed by the Pakistan army. On July 2, 2011,

Defence Minister Abdul Rahim Wardak said in Afghan parliament that two Pakistani helicopters entered the Afghan territory. On July 5, 2011, Afghan border police commander Aminullah Amarkhel reported that hundreds of fighters from the Pakistani Taliban crossed the border into Afghanistan's Nuristan province, where they attacked police outposts and torched homes.

The Afghan foreign ministry expressed concern, warning Pakistan that "the continuation of such incidents could adversely affect the spirit of improving the trust and cooperation between the Islamic Republic of Afghanistan and the Islamic Republic of Pakistan." Afghan lawmakers strongly condemned the Pakistani missile attacks, describing them as an "invasion" and as a reflection of Pakistan's "dishonesty" in its bilateral talks with the Afghan government, meant to strengthen the Afghanistan peace process. Criticising the Karzai government for its silence over the missile attacks, Afghan lawmaker Farhad Azimi is reported to have said: "I want to ask government officials as to why they call Pakistan a friend when it fires missiles into Afghanistan."

Afghanistan's intelligence service National Directorate of Security (NDS), accused the Pakistan military of being behind the missile attacks. NDS Spokesman Lotfullah Mashal told reporters that Pakistan has long been operating in secret to destabilise Afghanistan by backing the Taliban in the Pakistani tribal regions, "but this time the Pakistani Army is taking its [military] intervention further, through heavily shelling Afghanistan in [broad] daylight."

Afghan President Hamid Karzai referred to the attacks for the first time only on June 26, slamming Pakistan for firing 470 missiles into Afghanistan's eastern provinces. A July 4, 2011 resolution of the Afghan parliament, which urged the UN Security Council and the Organization of Islamic Conference (OIC) to mount diplomatic pressure on Pakistan, described the Pakistani attacks in Kunar, Nangarhar, Khost and Paktia provinces as an "act of invasion" by Pakistan.

Responding to the accusations, the Pakistani army denied targeting Afghanistan. Army spokesman Maj.-Gen. Athar Abbas said: "Rounds were fired for engaging the fleeing militants and there is a possibility that some may have accidentally gone across the border."

The June 2011 attacks were not Pakistan's first use of force against Afghanistan this year. In early February, Pakistani planes bombarded Afghan Border Police posts and civilians' homes in Afghanistan's Nangarhar and Khost provinces.

Pakistan's military campaign to control Afghanistan has been accompanied by the expulsion of U.S. and British military and intelligence officials from Pakistan. According to an April 21 report in the Pakistani media, some 500 CIA personnel were told to leave Pakistan in the beginning of this year. In late June, Pakistani Defense Minister Chaudhry Ahmed Mukhtar revealed that Pakistan has asked the CIA to leave the Shamsi airbase in Pakistan's Baluchistan province, from which drones are dispatched to monitor and attack the Taliban safe havens in the Pakistani tribal region. In addition, 18 British military trainers have been told to leave.

On April 16, 2011, the entire top Pakistani leadership (except for President Asif Zardari) descended on Kabul for bilateral talks with the Afghan leaders. According to reports in the Afghan media, Pakistani Prime Minister Yousuf Raza Gilani presented Karzai with a set of written demands: Afghanistan must sever its relationship with the U.S. and forge ties with China; keep Pakistan informed on the training and number of the Afghan security forces; appoint Pakistani officials to Afghan government institutions; and clarify Pakistan's share in Afghan mining and development projects; in addition, future Afghan governments must implement Pakistani strategies, and Pakistan must be made aware of any agreement between Afghanistan and its Western allies, including the U.S. and NATO.[4]

Pakistan army's reduction of forces on India's borders notwithstanding, New Delhi must plan for some contingencies and be prepared to go it alone.

INDIA AND AFGHANISTAN

Ten days after Op Geronimo, Indian Prime Minister Dr. Manmohan Singh, who visited Afghanistan after six years, was unprecedentedly honoured by being housed in the King's suite of the majestic King Zahir Shah Palace in Kabul, opened for the first time since 2001. In a clear departure from routine protocol, Kabul appointed two ministers-in-waiting instead of one, i.e., the Defence and Foreign Ministers of Afghanistan, who accompanied Dr. Singh at all events during his two-day visit. In another rare gesture, Dr. Manmohan Singh became the first foreign head of state to address a joint session of Parliament on May 15, 2011.

India assured another $500 million in development assistance to Afghanistan and pledged to stand by the country "through thick and thin". The heightened strategic partnership will include an enhanced role in training Afghanistan's security and police forces in counter-terrorism, regular summit level meetings, more institutionalised and regular dialogues at various levels, and on wide-ranging subjects. Besides, both countries will also enter into a strategic economic partnership, to explore closer integration in the economic field, as well as, greater cooperation in sectors ranging from mining to fuel and energy. "The two countries agreed on the importance of regional projects such as the Turkmenistan-Afghanistan-Pakistan-India gas pipeline, in promoting regional integration," said the joint declaration.

The United States military and NATO has said in a secret report that the Taliban, backed by Pakistan, are set to retake control of Afghanistan after NATO-led forces withdraw, raising the prospect of a major failure of Western policy.

The report also exposed the top Taliban leadership's "manipulation" by Pakistan's Inter-Services Intelligence in a "massive double game", and claims that the Pakistan government remains "intimately" involved with the Afghan-based terror group. The report leaked on a day when Pakistan's foreign minister Hina Rabbani Khar arrived in Kabul on a one-day visit.

In Kabul, a spokesman for the NATO-led International Security Assistance Force, Lt. Col. Jimmie Cummings, confirmed the existence of the document, first reported on Wednesday by the BBC and the London Times.

Many of the report's most serious revelations are on the scale of support to the Taliban provided by Pakistan and the influence that the ISI has on it. "The government of Pakistan remains intimately involved with the Taliban," London's Daily Telegraph quoted the report as saying.

The BBC said the report, based on material from 27,000 interrogations with over 4,000 captured Taliban, Al-Qaeda and other foreign fighters, fully exposes the extent of the relationship between the ISI and the Taliban.

In Kabul, Ms Hina Rabbani Khar was dismissive. "We can disregard this as a potentially strategic leak... This is old wine in an even older bottle."

The Pakistan foreign office called it "frivolous", and its spokesman Abdul Basit said in Islamabad: "We are committed to non-interference in Afghanistan." The report claims that Pakistan is aware of the locations of senior Taliban representatives. "Senior Taliban representatives, such as Nasiruddin Haqqani, maintain residences in the immediate vicinity of the ISI headquarters in Islamabad."

Afghan President Hamid Karzai with Indian Prime Minister Dr. Manmohan Singh

President Karzai with NATO Secretary General Anders Fogh Rasmussen

Proverbially, the summer of 2011 following May 2, proved to be quite blistering for Pak army, not only for its fall from grace with the US, but also in the eyes of Pakistan's public. Many events of this year have taken a heavy toll on the morale of Pak army's rank and file. And as the year ended, the Memogate crisis widened the Pakistan's civil-military trust deficit, despite army chief Gen Ashfaq P Kayani's assurances of the army not taking over yet again.

Ever since Pakistan army's duplicitous post-9/11 u-turn of hunting with the hounds and running with the hare, while the US giving it the status of 'frontline ally in the war against terror', kept giving it arms and monetary aid, this writer often asked how long this flawed equation could continue. Most of the arms Pakistan received from the US were not applicable for counter-terrorism operations and got added to Pak army's arsenal meant for use against India. It took ten years and the loss of almost 2,800 coalition casualties for the US to decide upon course-correction vis-à-vis Pak army and Inter Services Intelligence agency. The fissures following the killing of Osama bin Laden in the meticulously planned operation by US Special Forces on May 2, 2011, at Abbottabad, widened over the months, causing serious problems between Pakistan's ever-powerful army and its civilian leadership.

For India, two developments in December 2011 marked a recorded low in the plummeting US-Pak relationship following the killing of Osama bin Laden. The first was the US attack killing 26 Pakistani soldiers on November 26, 2011, exactly three years after ten Pakistani terrorists attacked Mumbai and the second was US announcing a cut in aid to Pakistan almost exactly 40 years after sending its 7th Fleet into Indian waters to support Pakistan, which had provoked the third India-Pakistan War in December 1971. Pakistan waged both the 1965 and 1971wars against India with weapons doled out to it by the US.

Ratcheting up pressure on its "troubled strategic ally," leaders of the US negotiating panel comprising armed services committees from both parties in the House and Senate including Republican Senator John McCain agreed to freeze $ 700 million in US aid to Pakistan until it offers to help in the fight against improvised explosive devices (IEDs) in the region.

IEDs used by terrorists have been the cheapest and most effective weapons against US and coalition troops in Afghanistan as they struggle to fight a resurgent Taliban. Many are made using ammonium nitrate, a common fertilizer shipped across the border from Pakistan to Afghanistan. The freeze on US aid was agreed as part of a defense bill that is expected to be passed this week. "The vast majority of the material used to make improvised explosive devices used against US forces in Afghanistan originates from two fertilizer factories inside Pakistan," McCain said in the Senate recently.

With US $ 20 billion allocated for security and economic aid since 2001, much of it in the form of reimbursements for assistance in fighting militants, Pakistan has been one of the largest recipients of US foreign aid. While the cutback announced is only a small proportion of the $ 20 billion, it may lead to greater cuts as calls in US grow shriller to penalise Islamabad for not only failing to act against militant groups, but worse, helping them.[5]

By July 2011, the strain in US–Pak relations increased after US Chairman, Joint Chiefs of Staff Admiral Mike Mullen reportedly said that Pakistan government had "sanctioned" the kidnap, torture and murder of journalist Saleem Shahzad. Later in September, prior to his retirement, Admiral Mullen, while addressing a US Senate panel, accused Pakistan's Inter Services Intelligence (ISI) of supporting the Jalaluddin Haqqani militant network which attacked the U.S. Embassy in Kabul.

Pakistan was reported to have subsequently arrested military officers suspected of spying for US intelligence agencies and decided to expel more than a 100 US military trainers and tighten the process of granting visas to US military personnel. That move provoked an immediate reaction of slashing US aid, already a subject of heated debate within the US administration since the killing of Osama bin Laden. Expressing increasing frustration with Pakistan's efforts in the war against terror, US lawmakers reportedly made numerous proposals to make US aid to Pakistan conditional on more cooperation in fighting militants such as the Haqqani network, which Washington believes operate out of Pakistan and attacks US troops in Afghanistan.

In July, there were further reactions of bluster and threat by Pakistan. The bluster came after Washington's announcement of suspension of $800 million worth of security aid, when Pakistan's military spokesman Major General Athar Abbas told a foreign news agency: "The army in the past as well as at present has conducted successful military operations using its own resources without any external support whatsoever."

Abbas referred to an extraordinary statement issued by Pak Army Chief General Ashfaq Kayani on June 9 as part of the bin Laden fallout which recommended that U.S. military aid be redirected towards civilians. The suspended aid reportedly included about $300 million to reimburse Pakistan for some of the costs of deploying more than 100,000 soldiers along the Afghan border, Pakistan claims to have deployed 140,000 troops in the northwest, but to do more to crack down on militants, such as the Al-Qaeda-linked Haqqani network, who use its soil to attack within Afghanistan, the army says its troops are too over-stretched. The US also depends on Pakistan as a sea port and land corridor for moving its military supplies in convoys of trucks by road into Afghanistan, which Taliban and other terrorist groups have attacked umpteen times.

The threats came from Pakistan's Defence Minister Chaudhry Ahmad Mukhtar, who piped out that troops would be pulled back from nearly 1,100 check posts set up along the Pakistan–Afghanistan border as his country could not afford to keep forces deployed there following the suspension of US military assistance. Clarifying that $300 million of the suspended aid were specifically meant for troops serving in the troubled tribal region, he further claimed that the proposed US move would sabotage efforts against the Taliban and Al-Qaeda in the region and that if the raids continued there could be cross-border fighting.

Referring to the controversy over Shamsi airbase, reportedly used by US drones, Mukhtar said the US, through the UAE, had been allowed the use of the airbase for "non-lethal weaponry, such as unarmed drones, and as a logistics support site".

"The understanding was that the drones would fly from Shamsi base but only for surveillance...They were not supposed to be lethal and the next thing we knew they were using it for military attacks," he was quoted. While this problem, Mukhtar said, could be resolved if the US and Pakistan came to some "arrangement", he said American military trainers should leave the country because they were seen to be connected with Raymond Davis, a CIA contractor who was arrested earlier this year in Lahore after he shot and killed two armed Pakistani men.

Responding to US' assertion that Al-Qaeda chief Ayman al-Zawahiri was in Pakistan's tribal areas, Mukhtar said that he hoped that the US would not act on its own like the May 2 raid against Osama bin Laden in the garrison city of Abbottabad. "This time round, we hope the Americans will work with the Pakistanis and share their intelligence," he said. However, as per recent reports, Islamabad has closed the border crossings used by US Coalition forces to transfer fuel and other supplies for their troops in Afghanistan.

On December 12, 2011, a senior Pakistani military official was cited by a foreign news agency from Islamabad, stating that Pakistan will shoot down any US drone that intrudes its airspace as per new directives. According to the new Pakistani defence policy, the official was quoted:

"Any object entering into our airspace, including US drones, will be treated as hostile and be shot down." Pakistan Prime Minister Yousuf Raza Gilani was reported to have warned the US and NATO that any future cross-border attack would be met with a "detrimental response". "The democratic government would not allow a similar attack on the country's sovereignty and any attempt in future will definitely meet the detrimental response," he said.

AFGHANISTAN'S CONCERNS

Afghanistan and the US have frequently criticised Pakistan for not doing enough to target sanctuaries on its soil from where terrorists regularly launch attacks against NATO troops in Afghanistan. The Afghan government has also accused Pakistan of firing hundreds of rockets into Kunar over the past few months and killing at least 40 people, an allegation denied by Pakistan.

Since 2004, US drones are estimated to have carried out more than 300 attacks inside Pakistan. On 28 November Maj Gen Abbas had reiterated that no shots were fired from the two posts in Pakistan's Mohmand Tribal Agency, that are situated 330 yards behind a mountain ridge, beyond which are Afghanistan's Nangarhar and Kunar provinces. Pakistan does not believe NATO troops could have mistaken the posts as Taliban militant bases. "We are not saying that this was a deliberate attack. But we are not ruling out such a possibility."

According to retired Air Marshal Ayaz A Khan, "Pakistan's strong response by shutting down NATO supply routes, and resolve to reduce military, intelligence and diplomatic cooperation with the United States would result in complete break in relations between the two countries. Considering Pakistan's economic and geo-strategic situation, this is a bold yet risky decision. Washington knows that US needs Pakistan's cooperation to shut down Taliban safe heavens and bring militant leaders to the conference table. Washington therefore has adopted a conciliatory posture towards Pakistan. President Obama, Secretary Hillary Clinton and Defence Secretary Leo Penata have deeply regretted the NATO attack, but Obama has refused to apologise. White House Press Secretary Jay Carney called the Pakistan Army deaths a "tragedy", reiterating that "the two nations should work cooperatively on our shared goals". Washington's soft pedaling is not enough to curtail Pakistani anger. Any hard posture by Washington will be unwise and against US interests in the region."

While India has welcomed the US decision to withhold or cut military aid to Pakistan by a third, there is nothing for it to feel secure about.

President Obama's belief that the Al-Qaeda in Afghanistan has been substantially weakened and as such, a major troop withdrawal can be done is not shared by Gen David Patraeus, former force commander in Afghanistan, now heading CIA and some others.

Barely a year later he was proved right. The Taliban's coordinated attacks, across various targets in Afghanistan on 16 April 2012 have brought home the fact that it is far from inactive. Those who felt that the NATO forces served as a deterrent to more terrorist activity in the nation have been proved wrong. It was the hope of the western forces that Al-Qaeda and its old associate the Taliban had been at least reduced to dire circumstances if not annihilated. This hope was dashed with what the Taliban spokesperson Zabiullah Mujahid called the "Spring Offensive".

The attacks began at 1.30pm local time and hit 7 sites in all. 20 Taliban fighters in suicide vests with rocket propelled grenades and heavy machine guns targeted dimplomatic installations of US, UK, Germany, Russia, Greece, Turkey and Canada. Mujahid said that "These attacks are the beginning of the spring offensive and that we had planned them for months. We are strong and we can attack anywhere." As per the spokesman it was also a message to those foreign commanders who claimed that the Taliban had lost their momentum.[6]

The Afghan President Hamid Karzai paid tribute to the "bravery and sacrifice of the security forces who quickly and timely reacted to contain the terrorists." He also called the attack a failure of NATO intelligence.

US ambassador to Kabul, Ryan Crocker said that the Taliban did not have the ability to carry out these attacks on their own. He added that they were the work of the Haqqani network, a Pakistan-based militant group allied to the Taliban. Gen John Allen, commander of the Nato-led International Security Assistance Force (Isaf) said "I am enormously proud of how quickly Afghan security forces responded to attacks in Kabul. They were on scene immediately, well-led and well-coordinated. They integrated their efforts, helped protect their fellow citizens and largely kept the insurgents contained."

If this spring offensive by the Taliban gains momentum then the US may well have to rethink on its exit plans. Exit of the bulk of US/other coalition forces from Afghanistan will give terrorists of all hues far greater freedom of movement and action wherever they want to. Whenever that happens, India will have to be all the more guarded not only in Jammu and Kashmir (J&K) and the rest of the country, but for its reconstruction and assistance organisations in Afghanistan.[7]

When the Afghans themselves are unsure of how the NATO withdrawal of troops in 2014 will affect their country, it makes sense for India to watch out. Many business owners in Afghanistan are planning their own exit along with NATO in 2014. Nearly 30,400 Afghans have applied for asylum in industrialized nations in 2011. The extreme anxiety about the future had led some businessmen to stall investment decisions and others are looking for opportunities abroad.

Afghanistan President Hamid Karzai reacted to the situation in March 2012 saying, "Sometimes I hear that some businessmen are fleeing and moving their businesses to outside Afghanistan. Curses be upon such businessmen that made tons of money here and now that the Americans are leaving they flee." It's not just the Afghans who are fleeing, Standard Chartered, which is the only western bank operating in the country is turning over its operations to a local bank and withdrawing due to the deteriorating conditions.

The chief executive of the Afghan chamber of Commerce and industries Mohammad Qurban Haqjo, said that despite the NATO withdrawal being two years away many businesses are questioning the wisdom of continued operations in Afghanistan. He said that the head of one of the country's four big cell phone companies had also told him that he would be taking his investments out of the country after 2014. The foreign investments in the country are at an all time low and there is no manufacturing or technology base that could bring future triumphs.

The common man is responding to the perceived threat by planning his own exit along with NATO troops from the country. A butcher in Kabul, Abdul Wasay Manani is scouting for a new business and home in India in case things fall aprt after the foreign troops leave. The man grew up in the north of Afghanistan and fought in the civil war of the 1990s. He says that he does not have the energy to take the gun again and start fighting. That is why he is looking for a way out to ensure his family's safety.

While New Delhi should brace itself for raising the guard in all states, J&K government must do so all the more and Mr. Omar Abdullah must not make the mistake of removing the Armed Forces Special Powers Act in the near future.

VINDICATION OF INDIA'S STAND

It is indeed a great pity that it took an unprecedented kind of tragedy like 9/11 for the world to realize what India had been crying hoarse for some years. As it emerges from memoirs of past heads of state, officials, or intelligence files, the Twin Towers tragedy was waiting to happen; valuable inputs about the planning of such an attack were available. The irony got compounded further as the war on terrorism launched by US coalition forces progressed in Afghanistan and its effort got dissipated by US–UK forces moving into Iraq to bark up a tree which they knew was the wrong one.

Anyway, all that is history that impacted some of the following events. It will, in all possibility, continue to do so in the future.

While Indian intelligence agencies had accurate inputs of Pakistan's Inter Services Intelligence (ISI) role in the spread of terrorism not only to India but also elsewhere, even after sharing it before and after 9/11, US authorities as well as scholars maintained their policy of treating Pakistan as a 'frontline' state in its war against terrorism, even selecting it as a non-NATO ally. All this despite the ISI-Al-Qaeda- other jihadis combo providing ideology and training to foreign terrorists launching attacks in other countries, including USA.

Shortly after the entry of US coalition forces into Afghanistan, in November 2001, there was a major movement of Al-Qaeda and Taliban into some areas of Pakistan. The first of the rumblings were heard when coalition forces pursuing these elements in Afghanistan felt the need to cross into Pakistan. Some may have been escaping from Afghanistan to Pakistan, but certainly there were, and still are, many others using Pakistan as a launching pad for hit-and-run attacks on the coalition forces.

India, though vindicated again by re-exposure of Pakistan Army's duplicity regarding its strong terrorist connections, may not have much to feel elated about as there may be no progress on proceedings against 26/11 perpetrators like Hafiz Sayeed and his minions. Even if US decides to repeat Abbottabad in other Pakistani locations to nab or eliminate other terrorist leaders, India must not expect any benefit unless it amounts to reigning in Pakistan's military and ISI.

Whatever was reported about Indian Army and Air Force Chiefs comments on the capabilities of India's armed forces, were only their brief responses on persistent querying by quote-seeking media-persons. With India being Pakistan army's compulsive preoccupation and it being over-jittery about Indian Army, Kayani and foreign secretary Salman Basheer could not help what they said.

As for Kashmiri separatist leader and Pakistan's anti-India terrorism supporter 'Amir' SAS Geelani's call for namaz-e-janaza (funeral prayers) for dead bin Laden in Kashmir, failed to whip up the frenzy he expected to provide him political oxygen after being sidelined by the recent electoral turnout. However, Centre and State must be clear that Kayani's recent rhetoric is bound to have fallout of this summer being hotter terror-wise not only on the Line of Control, the Valley and the International Boundary in Jammu and Kashmir but in other States also.

India must treat recent developments as yet another important wake-up call and shake out of its historic soft-state syndrome. Its sheer size, geo-strategic location, history, threats from within and its neighbourhood, necessitate it to develop and steadfastly maintain conventional superiority and deterrence capability beyond its borders, which it has the potential of. Long pending security related reforms, cleansing its body-politic of the scourge of communalism and corruption, expediting necessary arms acquisitions and most important, straightening and strengthening of the political backbone are no longer merely seminar points but very crucial factors for India's well-being.

Pakistan Army's response to New Delhi making public the names of 50 Pakistanis accused of involvement in terrorist activities in India, which include five serving Pakistani Majors, has been a vehement denial that any serving officer, either in the military or the ISI, has been involved in terrorist activities inside India.

This is yet another outright lie, already exposed and known to the US through investigations on Dawood Gilani alias David Coleman Headley and Tahawwur Hussain Rana. This was shortly followed by the disgraced ISI boss Pasha's bluster that any "Abbottabad-like attack by India will invite a 'befitting response' from Pakistan on 'targets in India already identified and rehearsals carried out' ".

While India has tried to increase diplomatic pressure on Pakistan post Laden's killing and though more evidence of ISI's terrorist activities may surface as the trial of these two Lashkar-e-Tayyaba operatives' involvement in 26/11 progresses, Pakistan can be expected to continue stonewalling India's efforts.

Pakistani Interior Minister Rehman Malik's response to India's demand for disclosure of Dawood Ibrahim's whereabouts that he was not in his country is yet another blatant lie, which was countered by Home Secretary G. K. Pillai stating, "If the Minister is so sure that Dawood is not in Pakistan, he should tell us where he is".

While the US-Pakistan relationship has no doubt deteriorated and do so further if US repeats attacks ala Laden against more terrorist bosses,

New Delhi seems destined to plod on against Pakistani lies and watch cautiously, while spending crores on hosting hard-core terrorists like Kasab.

Some vindication of India's stand may be seen in the fact that Hafiz Muhammad Saeed, who was called 'a mainstream political and religious leader' in Pakistan, but has been constantly referred to as one of the architects of the 26/11 Mumbai terror attacks in 2008 by India, has finally been accepted as a terrorist by the US. The US has placed a $ 10 million bounty on his head and declared him a most wanted terrorist in April 2012. The decision was announced by US Undersecretary of State Wendy Sherman on a visit to India.

Hafiz Muhammad Saeed is the founder of the Lashkar-e-Taiyyaba terror outfit which started out as an anti India group raised by the Pakistan Army and the ISI, but has grown in its sphere of influence due to support of the Al-Qaeda. It is now operating on a multinational basis and can pose a major threat to other nations as well, a fact that is recognized by the US by this decision to place its founder on the terrorist leader board. When *Lashkar-e-*Taiba was *banned* in Pakistan on January 12, 2002 the organization renamed itself *Jamaat-ud Dawa* and continued functioning in the guise of a charitable organization.

In true rhetoric fashion Saeed responded to this move with the statement that "The action against me is also an act of terrorism and America is doing it on the behest of India which is making fool out of it," he added that "The movement that we have organised after the formation of Defence of Pakistan Council is becoming very effective and it is impacting parliament's decision about NATO supplies and this factor is disturbing for America and that is why they have announced a bounty on me."[8]

The bounty announced by the US is not restricted to the founder. Another bounty of $2 million has been declared by the US for Saeed's deputy and brother in law, Abdul Rehman Makki. Makki has also been connected with both Lashkar-e-Taiyyaba and its charitable front Jamaat-ud-Dawa. Its founder leaders Saeed and Azzam were close partners with Osama bin Laden in the 1980s. Azzam was the intellectual guru who created the modern Islamic extremist movement. Azam should properly be seen as the "father of the global jihad." Saeed stayed in close contact with bin Laden until his death a year ago, according the material found in the al-Qaeda leader's hideout in Abbottabad. Hafiz Saeed openly mourned bin Laden in a bitter eulogy the Friday after the killing of bin Laden.[9]

The bounty offer on Saeed could complicate the existing US-Pakistan relations at a time when the situation is already volatile. Pakistan's parliament is debating a revised framework for ties with the US following the American air-strikes that killed 24 Pakistani soldiers in November 2011. Islamabad had closed the supply lines to NATO troops in response to the incident. It is the reopening of these supply lines that Hafiz Saeed has organised rallies against.

The situation in Pakistan may have changed and balnce of power may be different, but nothing detracts from its anti – India stand. James Farwell said, "We may see a more realistic mutual appraisal of the self-interests of the US and Pakistan as they deal with Afghanistan. I'm not sure that Pakistan's military/intelligence establishment is united on Afghanistan.

Certainly the ISI has helped to revive and support the Afghan Taliban. Reports suggest that it has worked to keep the Pakistan Taliban in line by suggesting it avoid attacking Pakistanis and instead attack American and NATO forces. ISI's meddlesome role is manifest, I think, in the attacks that terrorist proxies have launched against India. I am astonished by India's restraint in the face of these attacks, although they manifest strong prudence. Not every country would be as measured in its response to similar engagements."

AL-QAEDA AFTER OSAMA

In recent years, it is Ayman al-Zawahiri, who has been more of Al-Qaeda's public face rather than his dead boss, speaking out more often and even writing a book last year on how to overthrow Pakistan. Zawahiri was the target of the joint U.S.-Jordanian operation in December 2009 that ended when an Al-Qaeda double agent blew up the CIA's base camp in Afghanistan, killing more spies than in any disaster since Beirut in 1983.

Then there is reportedly the New Mexico-born Colorado State graduate Anwar al-Awlaki, who seems best poised to lead Al-Qaeda's response to the new Arab world order. His Yemeni cells proved to be lethally creative by designing an underwear bomb for Christmas 2009 and a year later parcel bombs targeting Chicago. Al-Awlaki's English-language online magazine, *Inspire*, was the first Qaeda journal to laud the "tsunami" of change in Arabia and lay out a plan for the group to benefit from it. As such, he may well play a greater ideological role.

Hafiz Mohammad Saeed, founder of Lashkar-e-Taiba (LeT, who abandoned its leadership after India blamed it and another terrorist group for attacking the Indian Parliament in December 2001), was one of the first to take to the streets urging his followers to be "heartened by the death of Osama bin Laden, as his 'martyrdom' would not be in vain"; he had LeT organise special prayers for Laden in several cities and towns, hailing him as a great person who awakened the Muslim world.

Yet another enemy of India, Ilyas Kashmiri, suspected to be involved in the 26/11 terrorist act-of-war at Mumbai and Pakistan Navy's shore base, PNS Mehran at Karachi, reportedly being killed in a drone attack by US forces in the restive South Waziristan tribal region, reveals and confirms wide and complex connections between Pakistan's various jihadi outfits and of course, its infamous Inter Services Intelligence (ISI).

An interesting surprise a day later, however, is the US expressing doubts on Kashmiri being killed in the drone attack because of his body not being recovered. "All ground intelligence shows that he is dead. What I can say is there is a 98 percent chance he is dead," Pakistan's Interior Minister Rehman Malik said in media. "Since we do not have the body. We do not have DNA we need to confirm. This is the substantive evidence we are looking for." is what is reported to have been stated from Washington.

Harkat-ul-Jihad al-Islami's (HUJI) 313 Brigade, which confirmed the "martyrdom of our leader Ilyas Kashmiri in a US drone strike on June 3, 2011 at 11.15 pm...We will take revenge (for the killing of) our leader from the US," through its spokesman Abu Hanzala said in a handwritten fax message sent to Pakistani media groups. And he was reportedly killed along with Taliban commander Amir Hamza and seven/eight others—all of the Pakistani Punjabi Taliban. "I confirm the commander Ilyas Kashmiri was martyred. We have buried his body in Lamand," Sidiqullah, a Taliban commander in South Waziristan told media. Follow this up with reports of Ilyas Kashmiri having been sighted well and alive in March 2012, it is difficult to trust any statement made regarding Kashmiri. Kashmiri being involved with Lashkar-e-Taiyyaba's (LeT) 26/11 attack on India and Al-Qaeda's recent attack on PNS Mehran is ironic.

Hailing from the Kotli / Mirpur District of Azad Kashmir in Pakistan-Occupied Kashmir, former member of the elite Pakistani Special Service Group (which he denied), his link with Al-Qaeda was strong enough for him to be considered as a possible successor to Osama bin Laden. During the 1980s Soviet-Afghan War, on behalf of Pakistan he trained Afghan Mujahideen in mine warfare at Miranshah .

Having lost an eye and an index finger while fighting in Afghanistan,

Hafiz Mohammad Saeed, founder of Lashkar-e-Taiba, arriving for funeral prayers held for Osama bin Laden

Ilyas Kashmiri

he continued his official terrorist work in Kashmir after the war as a member of Harkat-ul-Jihad-al-Islami (HuJI), though disagreements with leader Qari Saifullah Akhtar several years after initially joining in 1991 led Kashmiri to establish his own new unit within HuJI known as the 313 Brigade.

During the mid-1990s Kashmiri and Nasrullah Mansoor Langrial were near Poonch when they were seized by the Indian Army and sent to prison, where he spent the next two years before escaping and returning to Pakistan. Upon his return Kashmiri continued to conduct operations against India, once reportedly being rewarded personally with cash by then Army Chief General Pervez Musharraf for presenting the head of an Indian army soldier to him.

Kashmiri, Mullah Omar and Ayman al-Zawahiri are part of a list of five most wanted terrorists drawn up by the US. If Kashmiri has been killed, barely over a month after Osama bin Laden was killed by US Special Forces in Abbottabad cantonment, and also without participation / involvement of Pakistan army, then it underscores the widening rift between the two and indicates better progress in intelligence gathering and accuracy in striking by US Forces. If Kashmiri was a contender for replacing Laden, then his elimination is also a telling blow to Al-Qaeda.

Rajeh Said wrote in a report in the Asia Pacific Defense Forum in Feb. 2012 about the Al- Qaeda reeling from the numerous deaths of its leaders. With the US in clean up mode a number of senior leaders of Al-Qaeda have been killed, Rajeh Said also mentioned that "Al-Qaeda's latest casualty occurred in Pakistan where Badr Mansour, the leader of al-Qaeda in Pakistan, was killed February 9 near Miranshah, the largest city in North Waziristan. Mansour was believed to have been the leader of al-Qaeda in Pakistan following the reported death of his predecessor, Elias Kashmiri."

As per Rajeh Said, "Various reports indicate that al-Qaeda lost five of its leaders in recent days, one in Pakistan, three in the Philippines, and one in Somalia. It might be too early to assess the impact of these losses on the organization and its branches, but it is clear the strikes have left al-Qaeda reeling and unable to rebuild its depleted ranks."

The Philippine Army launched a strike against a terrorist camp on the island of Jolo, "Of the 15 people who were reportedly killed in the raid, two of them are said to be foreigners belonging to the al-Qaeda-affiliated Jemaah Islamiyah, which is active in Southeast Asia. The two are Zulkifli bin Hir, a Malaysian, who is also known as "Marwan" and Abdullah Ali, a Singaporean, who is also known as "Muawiya." The leader of another al-Qaeda-linked organization was also reportedly killed in the raid. Umbra Jumdail, also known as "Abu Bala" who was one of the founders of the Abu Sayyaf group, was killed."

In Somalia Bilal al-Berjawi, a dual citizen of Lebanon and Britain who was stripped of his British citizenship was killed in South Mogadishu. He was also known as "Abu Hafsa." Rajeh Said's report said that "Al-Berjawi was reported to have been al-Qaeda's second-in-command in Somalia after slain leader Fazul Abdullah Mohammed, who was accused of being involved in the 1998 bombings of U.S. embassies in Kenya and Tanzania. Somali police killed Fazul Abdullah in June 2011. Two other prominent leaders suspected of having links with al-Qaeda, Saleh Ali Saleh al-Nabhan and Adam Hashi Ayro, were killed in 2009 and 2008, respectively".[10]

Even as the old guard of the Al-Qaeda is put out of action by either age or death, a new string of leaders is stepping in to fill in their boots. The booty snatched from the Abbottabad complex has proved that Osama bin Laden was in touch with his top team and the Taliban leader Mullah Omar right till the end. It is also a well documented fact that Mullah Omar has close ties to many other top Al-Qaeda leaders. These leaders of the Al-Qaeda now have the unenviable task of choosing the new regime.

The top Al-Qaeda leadership has chosen Farman Ali Shinwari as the new Al-Qaeda chief for Pakistan. The resident of Landikotal, in the Kyber tribal area of Pakistan, was chosen because of his proven track record and his close association with Badr Mansoor. Four of Farman Shinwari's brothers have also been associated with terrorism in Jammu and Kashmir. Their involvement with the Harkat ul Ansar and other groups is established.

The Al-Qaeda also seems to be looking at bringing in fresh blood for a new age battle . The 30 year old Farman Shinwari is fluent in English and computer literate. He belongs to the Khugakhel sub tribe of the Shinwari tribe. His appointment at the head of the Al-Qaeda network in Pakistan was confirmed by a statement issued by the Dawa Wing of the Al-Qaeda. The statement said that given his knowledge of the Pakistani tribal belt and his affiliation with Badr Mansoor, he was seen as an ideal candidate for the post. Badr Mansoor was killed in a US drone attack in North Waziristan in February 2011.[11]

FUTURE THREAT

America must now focus on LeT, one of the largest and best-funded militant organizations in South Asia, behind the November 2008 terrorist assault on Mumbai, which killed 166 people including Americans and other foreigners. Admiral Robert Willard, heading the United States military's Pacific Command, recently expressed concern over the expanding reach of LeT, saying it was no longer solely focused on India (as per specific design of Pakistan army) or even in South Asia.

LeT, which has links with Al-Qaeda (and even brought its members to pitch in into its anti-India operations), has been in an expansion mode, trying to attract well-educated youngsters into its fold and may well try to fill any gaps of Al-Qaeda created by Laden's death in other countries.

James Farwell feels that "The Pakistan military perceives the strategic situation in Afghanistan more realistically. It recognizes that chaos on its western border poses an undesired challenge. Contrary to what many in the Western media seem to believe, it realizes that Taliban seizure of control in Kabul would pose a threat to Pakistan. The Taliban that was in power during the 1990's was repressive but focused on Afghanistan. Today's Taliban is expansionist and Islamic. It would immediately move to stir up Islamists in Pakistan who desire imposition of sharia law and would support those who seek to depose the secular, elected civilian government. Such efforts would potentially de-stabilize an already fragile Pakistani state. They could lead to the "Talibanization" of the military — a consequence the military will go at some lengths to prevent.

Farwell believes the Pakistan military will work with the US to try and reach an accord in Afghanistan, "It's my belief that the only accord that can work is one worked out by the Afghan parties at interest. It cannot be imposed externally by the US or other foreign players, although an accord would enhance the ability of all countries to achieve regional stability. The accord requires the participation of the Taliban, which, as you know, is largely Pashtun. It requires as well that of other ethnic groups: Tajiks, Uzbeks, Hazara, etc. I think it requires side-lining Karzai. Anything short of such an accord will produce a prolonged, bloody civil war in Afghanistan between these ethnic groups. Conversely, while any accord would be easy, the presence in a reconciled government (whether strong or weak at the center) of the Taliban would address Pakistani fears that a new government leaned too far towards India, while that of the other ethnic groups would check Taliban expansionism."

US must stay the course in Afghanistan to maintain its painstakingly achieved intelligence grid there and in Pakistan and it must target and neutralise more terrorist leaders and modules. US must also ratchet its pressure on Pakistan army and at least stop the supply of arms for supposedly combating terrorists, as all these consignments have only been used to build up its arsenal against India. In October 2009, when President Obama signed a legislation that tripled economic aid to Pakistan, he aimed at shifting the focus of the US partnership with Pakistan from the military to the country's people and civilian/democratic institutions and the Pakistani people.

After four military dictatorships in over six decades of Pakistan's existence and over two decades of Islamist terrorism nurtured by Pakistan army, the US should in its own interest, continue targeting jihadis, who Pakistan army will not or cannot neutralise and actually, do South Asia, the world and India in particular, a great favour. Because US pressing India to continue talks with Pakistan cannot at all be meaningful till Pakistan's military maintains its stranglehold over the civilian political leadership.

An American daily reported that regarding the massive financial and arms aid US has been providing to Pakistan as expenses to fight Al-Qaeda and other terrorists along the Afghanistan border, there is, not surprisingly, a billing dispute, with Washington rejecting over 40 per cent of the claims submitted by Islamabad. Some US officials also fear that some of the aid is being diverted to the border with India, secret diplomatic cables obtained by Wiki Leaks too showed that the US officials were taken aback by Pakistani claims as early as 2006, including a $26 million charge for barbed wire and pickets, and for almost $70 million in radar maintenance, "although there is no enemy air threat related to the war on terror." It remains to be seen, whether US will review its aid policy to Pakistan.[12]

The American view is best summed up by James Farwell, "I would look for the US to reduce military aid to Pakistan. I think that it will promote greater economic ties between Pakistan and India, and that strikes me as prudent. It will provide economic aid for water conservation, schools, etc but only under relatively tight monitoring, to ensure that the money is properly spent. So far Pakistan has received billions in US aid, and has little to show for it. "Addressing the Unified Commanders Conference in South Block, shortly after Dr Manmohan Singh's meeting mentioned, Defence Minister AK Antony saying that ripples of Osama bin Laden's elimination will have wide ranging impact on India's strategic neighbourhood and asked the top brass of the Army, Navy and Air Force to continuously assess the security situation and remain prepared for any eventualities. Describing the US operations in Pakistan as 'a watershed in the global war on terror', he said the event has 'internationally stamped' Pakistan's position as the core of terrorist activities in the region.

Mr. Antony's directive to the Services Chiefs and the various installations he has inaugurated to enhance post 26/11 coastal security, must now get meaningfully backed by political will to ensure that: firstly, all the inter-ministry and inter-departmental integration is implemented with the required notification; secondly, all necessary procurements are in place; and thirdly, that there is no hesitation in giving a befitting response against any terrorist attack, the possibility of which has greatly increased.

Pakistan's military, particularly army chief General Ashfaq Parvez Kayani and ex head of ISI Lt. Gen. Ahmed Shuja Pasha already smarting from the humiliation of the success of US Special Forces Op Geronimo, will no doubt, be very much more so now with the attack on PNS Mehran and Dawood Gilani, alias David Coleman Headley's further disclosures about ISI's direct involvement.

Given Pakistan's collective military psyche on India and Indian Army, its strong connection with/support of LeT and the mood both are in, India must now all the more watch out on its long land borders, coastline and airspace and all states, where LeT already has its moles and sleepers. All western coastal states, particularly those with strategic assets located close to the sea, must have effective surveillance and reaction capability—with not only the military being alert but the civil and coastal police too.[13]

The Afghan nation has become like a chessboard where regional players such as the current President Hamid Karzai, the old guard of the Taliban led by Mullah Omar, the Taliban youth led by Sirajuddin Haqqani, the ISI, the Pakistani politicians, the US and India all must make moves without being sure of the ultimate outcome. With so many variables at play and counter interests warring with each other it is indeed very difficult to figure out just what the endgame will be.

Neena Gopal said that "As the Afghan leader brings in former diplomat Salahuddin Rabbani and keeps the other Afghan elder and his own mentor Sibghatullah Mojaddedi out, Mr Karzai's belief that the Taliban—old guard or new—can be trusted does not resonate fully even within his own circle, made up of former mujahideen, Western educated liberals and other sundry power brokers."

For prolonged peace after the NATO troops move out in 2014, it is desirable for Karzai to make the overtures of friendship to the weakened old guard of the Taliban, who do not have the will for a protracted fight. However he must also be careful of ISI supported Haqani, whose only mission at present is to remove the "Western Puppet" Karzai from his

Mullah Omar, Taliban Leader

Jalaluddin Haqqani

Sirajuddin Haqqani

post. This son of Jalaluddin Haqqani, an old protégé of ex ISI chief Hamid Gul, can defiantly cause trouble on his own. Even if Mullah Omar accepts the easy way into power by befriending Hamid Karzai, there is no guarantee that Haqqini will follow suit.

As Neena Gopal reminds us "Few can forget that it was the Taliban that trussed up and hung a battered President Najibullah from a lamp post, only a stone's throw from the heavily guarded palace complex that Mr Karzai calls home as Soviet forces withdrew in 1996. The parallels when "occupation forces" withdraw in 2014 are not too difficult to draw."

Another factor that India must consider is the hostility that the Taliban owe India by association with the Pakistan Army and ISI. While India would like to gain a foothold in Afghanistan by helping to rebuild the infrastructure in the war worn country, it will have to consider the security of its nationals in what could easily become a very hostile working environment. If a friendly government continues in Afghanistan it would logically follow that access to the vast mineral wealth of Central Asia and the plying of goods along the Grand Trunk road will be available to India.

Unfortunately the political mix in Afghanistan includes enough variables to make it seem that Karzai is not really the friend India can depend on in Kabul. After nine years the man is making statements of handing over the presidential mantel to a successor. While a Tajik strongman like Marshall Fahim, or Atta Mohammed would be welcome as the next President by India, the Taliban would prefer to have a Pashtun face.

Neena Gopal warns that "Pakistan's violent interjection of the Taliban into the Afghan discourse has left India unable to capitalise on the enormous goodwill that exists among Afghans or counter Islamabad as Washington gives Pakistan's interests precedence. India, epitome of soft power, the country that many Afghans look up to as a role model must move its own pawns on the Afghan chessboard."

THE BIN LADEN FAMILY SURVIVORS

By committing Laden's body to the sea, the US may have denied him a grave, with the potential of being developed into a shrine, but the Abbottabad mansion certainly has the potential to be the same. Destroying it may not help unless the Pakistani establishment decides to ensure that Laden will not be deified.

His family still continues to be held in Pakistan and everyday new reports emerge to give credence to the fact that the US may have had help from someone in the bin Laden family to help them achieve their final aim. There have been rumours that Osama's first wife Khairiah Saber and Zawahri were in cahoots to bring about his death.

His youngest bride, Amal, accused Khairiah of betraying Osama bin Laden. She believed that Khairiah, who had initially escaped to Saudi Arabia and then returned to Osama's family fold in Pakistan a couple of years ago, was guilty of betraying the location of their husband to the enemy. The two of them got into a cat fight at the heavily guarded house in Pakistan where they are currently being held. Security guards had to pry them apart and have now been warned against letting the two get together again.[14]

Amal believes that it was a conspiracy between Zawahri and Khairiah that led to the killing of Osama bin Laden. There have also been alleged rumours about the state of mind of bin Laden and some hushed references to a degenerative disease. While it can never be proved if Zawahri did indeed sell out the leader to take his place as the new head of the Al-Qaeda, it is definitely possible that he got tired of being sidelined. Truth is hidden in the many lies that have come forth after the death of Osama bin Laden.

Following the US Seals attack on the Abbottabad house where Osama bin Laden was hiding, it emerged that the man with his wives and children occupied the second and third floors of the house. Three wives and eight children lived along with him in the three storey building. His youngest wife later said that the family had been living in the house for the last five or six years.

The surviving family, consisting of 16 people in all, was held in detention in Pakistan after the decisive attack. The 45 day detention they were sentenced to in the court was punishment for illegal entry into the country. While two of the older wives refused to give any information, Amal Abdulfattah al-Sadah, the youngest wife from Yemen gave away many details of their lives on the run since 9/11. Including the fact that Osama bin Laden managed to sire four children while being on the world's most wanted terrorist list.

Finally, almost a year after the incident, the surviving family members of bin Laden which included three wives, eight daughters and one grandchild, were to be deported from Pakistan in April 2012. The actual deportation is being delayed by all kinds of reasons. The deportation to the countries of origin, Saudi Arabia and Yemen has not been approved by either of the nations as yet. Also the passport of a member of the family,

Osama bin Laden's Wives Held in Pakistan

House in which they are being held under security in Pakistan

brother in law of bin Laden and Amal's brother, is missing. Not to mention the fact that the Saudi government wants the deportation to take place via a third country. They are unwilling to accept the family members directly from Pakistan as per officials at the Interior Ministry.[15]

Once outside Pakistan, bin Laden's relatives could reveal details about how the world's most wanted man was able to hide in U.S. ally Pakistan for years, possibly assisted by elements of the country's powerful military and spy agency. A fact that Pakistani authorities are well aware of; and may be another factor in the delay in deportation. Aamir Khalil, counsel for Bin Laden's family said that "Both the Interior Ministry and Saudi Arabia are still mulling over when to deport several of Osama bin Laden's family members back to their homeland. We are in touch with the embassies of Saudi Arabia and Yemen and officials of the Interior Ministry in Pakistan for the early deportation of Bin Laden's family," Can we expect new details to surface once the bin Laden family physically leaves Pakistan? Only time will tell.

NOTES

[1] Chandan Singh, Jun 18, 2011, "Pak Army's Old Friend and Terrorist Guest Osama Obliterated by US" at http://www.articlesbase.com/politics-articles/pak-armys-old-friend-and-terrorist-guest-osama-obliterated-by-us-4921724.html (Accessed March 7, 2012).

[2] "Pakistan army warns US and India against Abbottabad-type raids" at http://indiatoday.intoday.in/story/pakistan-army-warns-us-and-india/1/137236.html (Accessed March 5, 2012).

[3] Anil Bhat, The Asian Age, "Aftermath of Op Geronimo and Implications for US, Af-Pak and India" at http://www.asianage.com/ideas/us-afpak-india-dynamics-change-after-osama-132 (Accessed March 9, 2012).

[4] Lawrence Bartlett, The Asian Age 2 February 2012, "Nato leak overshadows Af-Pak talks – Sees ISI –Taliban takeover"

[5] "US senators urge 'full review' of Pakistan funding" at http://www.telegraph.co.uk/news/worldnews/asia/pakistan/8937435/US-senators-urge-full-review-of-Pakistan-funding.html (Accessed March 7, 2012).

[6] *Times of India*, 16 April 2012, "Taliban blitz targest embassies in Kabul, govt forces fight back."

[7] Air Commodore KB Menon, Indian Defence Review Vol. 26.3 July - Sept 2011, "Operation Geronimo: Lessons for India" at http://www.indiandefencereview.com/military-and-aerospace/Operation-Geronimo-Lessons-for-India.html

[8] NDTV.com "US bounty is an act of terrorism: Hafiz Saeed" at http://www.ndtv.com/article/india/hafiz-saeed-mocks-10-mn-bounty-says-us-was-nervous-193668&cp (Accessed April 4, 2012).

[9] Bruce Riedel, The Daily Beast, "Hafiz Saeed, Pakistani Extremist With a $10 Million Price on his Head, Is al-Qaeda's Ally" at http://www.thedailybeast.com/articles/2012/04/03/hafiz-saeed-pakistani-extremist-with-a-10-million-price-on-his-head-is-al-qaeda-s-ally.html (Accessed April 5, 2012).

[10] Rajeh Said, Asia Pacific Defense Forum, 16 Feb 2012, "Al-Qaeda reeling from numerous deaths among its leaders"

[11] Rezaul H. Laskar, The Asian Age, 1 May 2012, pg 8 "Farman Shinwari new Pak Qaeda chief"

[12] Shafqat Ali, *The Asian Age*, 27 Feb 2012, pg 8 "Pak razes Osama den in secret op"

[13] Anil Bhat, Himalayan Affairs, 20 Jan 2011 "Downslided US-Pak Relationships will adversely affect India, particularly J&K and Afghanistan" at http://www.himalayanaffairs.org/article.aspx?id=399 (Accessed March 14, 2012).

[14] Graham Smith, Daily Mail, "Osama's feuding wives: How widows of Bin Laden were pulled apart by troops after fight over deadly 'betrayal' of Al-Qaeda leader" at http://www.dailymail.co.uk/news/article-2115326/Osama-Bin-Ladens-feuding-wives-How-widows-fought-betrayal-Al-Qaeda-leader.html#ixzz1pXdwoB52 (Accessed March 19, 2012)

[15] Muhammad Lila, ABS News "Osama bin Laden Wives' Pakistan Deportation Delayed" at http://abcnews.go.com/Blotter/osama-bin-laden-wives-pakistan-deportation-delayed/story?id=16162009 (Accessed 19 April 2012)

APPENDICES

APPENDIX 1

Timeline for Video and Audio Releases from Al-Qaeda (accessed from WikiLeaks)

The interest in videos and audios that Al-Qaeda has released periodically to Qatari TV station al-Jazeera became of international interest after the 9/11 attack on the Twin Towers. Suddenly the world wanted to know what this radical terrorist organization led by a former US trained spy, Osama bin Laden, was saying. It must be admitted that the man knew just how to gain the maximum publicity and impact with each such video that was released following a terrorist attack in some part of the world. Here is a timeline for these audio and video tape releases.

2001

June 19, 2001

A video is released by al-Qaida showing Osama bin Laden and his supporters training at their al-Farouq base in Afghanistan. Their leader, who is already the US's most wanted man for his role in the 1998 east Africa embassy bombings, is filmed kneeling down in flowing white robes and squeezing the trigger of an AK-47.

October 5, 2001

Al-Jazeera shows a video clip of the celebrations when Ayman al-Zawahiri, now Bin Laden's possible successor, brought Egyptian Islamic Jihad into al-Qaida. There is no mention of the 9/11 attack. The footage seems to be older than that.

October 7, 2001

Shortly after the first US missiles hit Kabul, television news channels switch their footage from the shots of tracer fire in the night sky to the figure of Bin Laden, dressed in combat fatigues somewhere in the rocky Afghan wilderness. It is clearly pre-recorded (the daylight gives that away) but the impact is as if he was speaking live as he condemns the hours-old attack as a war on Islam.

Excerpts

"I say these events have split the whole world into two camps: the camp of the faithful and the camp of the infidels," he tells the camera. "Every Muslim should support his religion."

The video also contains his first public response to the September 11 attacks. "America is full of fear from its north to its south, from its west to its east. Thank God for that," he says. "Our nation has been tasting fear, hatred and injustices for years."

October 13, 2001

Al-Jazeera screens a video showing Sulaiman Abu Ghaith, an al-Qaida spokesman, warning that "thousands of Muslim youths" are eager to die.

Excerpts

"The storms will not calm, especially the aircraft storm," he says. "We also say and advise the Muslims in the US and Britain, the children, and those who reject the unjust US policy, not to travel by plane. We also advise them not to live in highrise buildings and towers."

December 13, 2001

The Pentagon releases a video it claims shows Bin Laden discussing the September 11 attacks with guests at an al-Qaida dinner at a house in Kandahar. In one section, he gently smiles and explains how "we calculated in advance the number of casualties from the enemy based on the position of the tower," but the attack surpassed his expectations. Apparently found in late November in an abandoned house in Jalalabad, the video is hailed as conclusive proof that Bin Laden was behind the attacks.

Excerpts

"I was thinking that the fire from the fuel in the plane would melt the iron structure of the building and collapse the area where the plane hit and the floors above it only. That is all we had hoped for."

December 26, 2001

Looking gaunt, tired and as if he has aged a decade in the past two months, Bin Laden appears to take credit for the September 11 attacks. He is shot against a brown blanket, masking any clues that may disclose his location. The video was filmed to mark three months since the "blessed attack" on the US, he says, meaning that he survived the US assault on his bases.

Excerpts

"Our terrorism against the United States is worthy of praise to deter the oppressor so that America stop its support for Israel, which is killing our children," he says.

2002

April 15, 2002

Al-Jazeera shows excerpts from a forthcoming documentary made by a pro-al-Qaida production company featuring previously unseen footage of Bin Laden and al-Zawahiri sat by a stream.

The package also includes what appears to be a video message from Ahmed al-Haznawi, one of the Flight 93 hijackers in a segment called The Wills of the New York and Washington Battle Martyrs. The 22-year-old Saudi pledges to give his life to "martyrdom" and swears to send a "bloodied message" to Americans by attacking them in their "heartland".

June 23, 2002

An audio cassette that purports to be from Abu Ghaith says that Bin Laden is alive and planning fresh attacks. He claims responsibility for the April truck bombing of Africa's oldest synagogue, on the Tunisian island of Djerba, in which 21 people, mostly German tourists, were killed. Doubts about Osama bin Laden's health begin to surface in the light of his kidney problems becoming common knowledge.

August 19, 2002

CNN broadcasts an al-Qaida video showing what appear to be poison gas tests on a dog. Also among the cache of 60 tapes obtained by the station is a video of a 1998 press conference to mark al-Qaida's merger with Egyptian Islamic Jihad where Bin Laden declares a formal jihad against "crusaders and Jews".

September 9, 2002

In its own anniversary contribution to mark a year since the 9/11 attack, the new video is released. A voice attributed to Bin Laden praises the hijackers as "great men who deepened the roots of faith in the hearts of the faithful". The video, screened on al-Jazeera, shows the men in a Kandahar house preparing for the attack. Items on a table included an air chart of the US, and a flight instruction manual.

Excerpts

"As we talk about the conquests of Washington and New York," the voice says, "we talk about those men who changed the course of history and cleaned the records of the nation from the dirt of the treasonous rulers and their followers".

November 12, 2002

Al-Jazeera broadcasts an audiotape purporting to be by Bin Laden in which he praises terrorist attacks in Bali, Moscow and against a French tanker off the coast of Yemen. It links Australia's role in East Timor to the October 2002 Bali nightclub bombings. US intelligence officials confirm it is a recent recording of Bin Laden - which would make it the first definitive evidence in almost a year that he is alive - but doubts later emerge over its authenticity. Swiss scientists claim that they were 95% sure that the recording was a fake.

Excerpts

"They ignored our warning and woke up to the sound of explosions in Bali, but the government pretended they were not the target."

December 8, 2002

An audio recording purporting to be a claim of responsibility for a suicide attack on an Israeli-owned hotel in Kenya is broadcast on al-Jazeera. "The Jewish Crusader coalition will not be safe anywhere from the fighters' attacks," says a speaker claiming to be Abu Ghaith. By now medical issues over Osama bin Laden's health have experts wondering how he can survive on the run.

2003

February 11, 2003

Al-Jazeera broadcasts an audiotape calling on Iraqis to carry out suicide attacks against US forces. Washington says it is evidence of an alliance between al-Qaida and Baghdad. Other sections of the recording say "all socialist regimes are run by unbelievers, including that of Iraq." Bin Laden also offers tips to save and defend Iraq.

April 8, 2003

The Associated Press news agency receives an audio tape calling for Muslims to rise up in Pakistan, Afghanistan, Bahrain, Kuwait and Saudi Arabia, criticising governments in those countries for supporting the US-led Iraq war. So called bin Laden voice urges suicide attacks.

September 10, 2003

Al-Jazeera airs a videotape that seems to show a gaunt Osama bin Laden walking through mountainous terrain with al-Zawahiri. In an audiotape that accompanies the video footage, the two men refer to the second anniversary of the September 11 terrorist attacks. Bin Laden also warns of the "real battle to come."

September 28, 2003

Both al-Jazeera and al-Arabiya broadcast excerpts of an audiotape supposedly by al-Zawahri. He calls on Pakistanis to overthrow their president and accuses the US of trying to abolish Islam. There is no voice of bin Laden on the tape. This again fuels speculation about his health and location as the hunt for the Al-Qaeda Leader continues.

October 18, 2003

Bin Laden releases two audiotapes, a series of videotaped threats and several filmed statements by suicide bombers who died in Riyadh in May 2003. The tapes call for attacks on British and US troops in Iraq and "Christians and Jews ... who occupy Islamic lands". Bin Laden urges for a terror blitz on the troops.

2004

January 4, 2004

An audiotape broadcast on al-Jazeera, claiming to be Bin Laden, calls on Muslims to "continue the jihad to check the conspiracies hatched against the Islamic nation". It criticises the government of Saudi Arabia and other Gulf states for supporting the US, saying that "the occupation of Iraq is the beginning of the full occupation of the other Gulf states". The CIA examines the tape for possible fake voice over.

March 26, 2004

No identification of the speaker is given on the audio tape released. The CIA says a voice on a tape urging Pakistanis to overthrow their government more than likely belongs to Ayman al-Zawahiri, the No 2 figure in al-Qaida. The tape was broadcast on al-Jazeera for seven minutes and featured Zawahiri calling Pakistani president Pervez Musharraf a "traitor" for seeking to "stab the Islamic resistance in Afghanistan in the back".

April 15, 2004

A purported Bin Laden tape is broadcast on al-Arabiya. The speaker offers a truce to European countries that decide not to "interfere" in Muslim countries but rules out any such deal with the US. The tape also vows revenge for the killing of Sheikh Ahmed Yassin, the Hamas spiritual leader, in an Israeli helicopter strike.

Excerpts

"President Bush and leaders in his sphere, big media institutions, and the United Nations ... all of them are a fatal danger to the world, and the Zionist lobby is their most dangerous and difficult member, and we insist, God willing, on continuing to fight them," the speaker says.

May 7, 2004

A recorded message attributed to Bin Laden offers 10kg (22lb) of gold to anyone killing the US administrator in Iraq, Paul Bremer, or the UN secretary general, Kofi Annan. A smaller amount of gold is offered to anyone killing soldiers or civilians from countries that are "possessors of the [UN security council] veto, such as the Americans or Britons." The authenticity of the 20-minute message, which appeared on two Islamist websites, is doubted.

June 12, 2004

Al-Arabiya broadcasts audio tape purportedly from Zawahiri in which he criticises a US plan to reform the Middle East as a ploy and says "change will only come through resistance". With no mention of Osama bin Laden or any specific message from him, the world is again left wondering about if the leader of Al-Qaeda is alive.

September 9, 2004

Zawahiri says the US faces defeat in Iraq and Afghanistan. The videotape is broadcast by al-Jazeera. While the messages contain typical sentiments that the world has come to expect from Al-Qaeda there is no mention of Osama bin Laden. Pakistan bombs possible Al-Qaeda camps.

Excerpts

"The Americans in both countries are between two fires. If they continue they bleed to death and if they withdraw they lose everything."

"Southern and eastern Afghanistan have completely become an open field for the mujahideen. The Americans are hiding in their trenches and refuse to come out to face the mujahideen, as the mujahideen shell them, fire on them and cut roads off around them. Their defence is only to bomb by air."

October 1, 2004

Zawahiri urges Muslims to mount worldwide resistance to "crusader America" and its western allies, in a purported audio recording broadcast by al-Jazeera. He gives a long list of American allies to be targeted, including Britain, Australia, Poland, South Korea and Japan.

The inflammatory appeal coincided with the suicide bombing of a Shia mosque in Pakistan which killed at least 25 people.

Excerpts

"Let us start resisting now ... We can't wait or we will be eaten up, country by country," he says.

"People of knowledge and experience should organise their efforts and form a leadership for the resistance to combat the crusaders."

October 29, 2004

Just days before the US presidential election, a videotape of Bin Laden surfaces, with the al-Qaida leader admitting responsibility for the first time for the September 11 attacks, and threatening new strikes against America. He also suggests that the idea for the September 11 attacks stretched as far back as the Israeli aerial bombardment of tall buildings in Beirut in 1982. The impeccable timing of the video may have contributed in no small measure to the disappointment of the American public with the Bush regime.

Excerpts

"Despite entering the fourth year after September 11, Bush is still deceiving you and hiding the truth from you, and therefore the reasons are still there to repeat what happened," bin Laden says.

November 29, 2004

Zawahiri says al-Qaida will continue to attack the United States until it changes its policies towards the Muslim world. In a videotape broadcast by al-Jazeera, he speaks for "a nation of patience [that] will continue fighting you until the last hour". The recording appeared to have been made before the US presidential election. In one excerpt he says the result is of no interest to al-Qaida.

Excerpts

"Vote for whoever you want, Bush, Kerry or the devil himself. This does not concern us. What concerns us is to purge our land from the aggressors."

He advises the Americans to choose between one of two things: "Either you choose to treat us with respect and based on an exchange of interests ... or we will continue to fight you until you change your policies."

December 16, 2004

An audio tape, purportedly of Osama bin Laden in which he blessed a militant attack on a US consulate in Saudi Arabia on December 6, is posted on an Islamist website. The speaker delivers a lengthy message about the conflict between the rulers and the people of Saudi Arabia. He says that while Saudi leaders blame "holy warriors" for trouble in the kingdom, "the truth is that the whole responsibility falls on the shoulders of the regime." Five staff were killed when Islamist gunmen stormed the US consulate in Jeddah on December 6.

Excerpts

"The sins the regime committed are great ... it practised injustices against the people, violating their rights, humiliating their pride."

2005

August 4, 2005

Zawahiri returns four weeks on from the July 7 London bomb attacks with a videotape broadcast on al-Jazeera threatening "more destruction". He says the attacks (the "volcanoes of wrath", in his words) are the consequence of Britain rejecting the offer of a truce from Bin Laden conditional on the withdrawal of its troops from Iraq. He says the prime minister is to blame.

Excerpts

"Blair's policies will bring more destruction to Britons after the London explosions, God willing."

September 19 / December 7, 2005

Al-Jazeera broadcasts a video from the al-Qaida second-in-command recorded to mark the fourth anniversary of 9/11. The video is broadcast in part in September with previously unaired sections shown in December. The initial reaction to the second screening, which al-Jazeera said was the "latest" video from Zawahiri, is that a section claiming Bin Laden is still "leading the holy war" is an attempt from the al-Qaida inner circle to refute the rumours he was one of the 79,000 who died in the Pakistan earthquake.

It then emerges that the filming predates the earthquake. Sections of the video include calls for jihadists to target oil facilities and references to the Queen as "one of the severest threats to Islam". The old videos that claim that bin Laden is alive immediately has the world suspecting that perhaps the Al-Qaeda leader is no more.

2006

January 19, 2006

A tape purportedly recorded by Bin Laden appears more than a year after the last one. The purpose seems to be merely to reiterate that he is alive and well. The audio recording - part of which is aired on al-Jazeera - warns the US that a fresh wave of terror attacks are in preparation. It also offers a truce to the US if it withdrawals from Afghanistan and Iraq so "we can build".

February 20, 2006

The tape released is on a militant website in Egypt. US intelligence confirms that the speaker is Bin Laden, making it his first message in more than a year. In the tape, which appears to be a complete version of the one first broadcast on al-Jazeera, he vows never to be captured alive and says the US military have become as barbaric as Saddam Hussein.

April 24, 2006

A tape released by the Arabic-language news broadcaster al-Jazeera is the first to refer to the conflict in Sudan's Darfur region and to the Palestinian Authority's new Hamas government. The voice is unauthenticated, but al-Jazeera says it sounds like previous recordings of Bin Laden. On the tape, Muslims are urged to ignore western nations' denials that they are waging a war on Islam.

Excerpts

"The politicians of the west do not want dialogue other than for the sake of dialogue to gain time," the speaker says.

May 24, 2006

A message purported to be from Osama bin Laden claims Zacarias Moussaoui, the only man to be convicted in the US in connection with the 9/11 attacks, had nothing to do with the plot. Moussaoui was sentenced to six consecutive life terms earlier in May for failing to tell the FBI about the plot. The message on the five-minute tape, which was released on an Islamist website, also says none of the detainees at Guantáamo Bay were connected to 9/11. However, it suggests two suspects in detention elsewhere had links to the 2001 attacks on New York and Washington.

Excerpts

"I am the one in charge of the 19 brothers, and I never assigned brother Zacarias to be with them in that mission."

June 30, 2006

An audio message purported to be from Osama bin Laden eulogises Al-Qaeda leader in Iraq Abu Musab al-Zarqawi, who was killed in a

US airstrike on June 7. Bin Laden describes Zarqawi as a "knight ... the fierce lion of holy war", making some of the tributes in rhyming couplets. He speaks of giving Zarqawi "instructions" in an apparent attempt to claim the Jordanian-born terrorist—who was increasingly a rival in terms of status among extremists—was under his command. The Al-Qaeda leadership had disagreements with Zarqawi's strategy of attacking Shia to try and start a Sunni-Shia civil war.

Excerpts

"Abu Musab had clear instructions to focus his fight on the occupiers, particularly the Americans and to leave aside anyone who remains neutral. But for those who refused [neutrality] and stood to fight on the side of the crusaders against the Muslims, then he should kill them whoever they are, regardless of their sect or tribe."

2007

July 4, 2007

The footage of bin Laden himself does not appear to be recent; a Washington organization called the SITE Intelligence Group identifies it as 2003 footage. It is now that doubts arise about Osama being alive at all. This is one of the last videos that Al-Qaeda released before Abbottabad which actually features Osama bin Laden. Subsequent videos have shown the Qaeda deputy, Ayman al-Zawahri.

2007–2011

Zawahri and other leaders of Al-Qaeda keep appearing in the videos that are released but Osama bin Laden never does. A month after bin Laden's killing at Abbottabad Zawahri released another video in which he vowed to continue the work of the "martyred" leader. The Egyptian Al-Qaeda deputy is formally expected to take over as head of the organization.

APPENDIX 2

Timeline for Al-Qaeda Activities and Repercussions (accessed from WikiLeaks)

1988

Al-Qaeda founded in Afghanistan by Osama bin Laden

As Soviet troops withdraw from Afghanistan Osama bin Laden and other Arab fighters from the US CIA backed Mujihideen movement form a new organization called Al-Qaeda. This phrase in Arabic means "the base". The network begins looking for new "jihads" or holy wars.

1991

Bin Laden moves to Sudan where he sets up training camps

Sudan becomes Al-Qaeda's base for business operations and preparations for jihad. From here a number of attacks on Western targets are alleged to have been organised or supported. Bin Laden stays in the African country for five years. During this time it is believed he begins a search for nuclear material.

1993

26 February - Bomb explodes at the World Trade Center in New York

Six people are killed and more than 1000 injured by a 500kg bomb. Al-Qaeda's involvement is unclear but some analysts believe that after the attack the group sought out the plotter Ramzi Yousef and offered him money. Yousef is currently serving a life sentence for the attack. His uncle Khalid Sheikh Mohammed currently in custody is thought to have helped plan the 11 September attacks in 2001.

4 October - Eighteen US servicemen killed in Somalia

Members of a Somali militia shoot down two Black Hawk helicopters. The US believes that Al-Qaeda fighters helped train those responsible for the incident in which 18 American servicemen were killed. The movie "Black Hawk Down" is based on this true incident. This is also the incident that made America reluctant to meddle in affairs of Somalia in the future.

1996

May - Bin Laden leaves Sudan and returns to Afghanistan

In the mid1990s Sudan comes under growing international pressure to expel Osama bin Laden. It is not clear whether he is actually forced to leave the African country but in May 1996 he returns to Afghanistan. He has a solid base in Afghanistan which he has built up since 1979. This was even before the US stepped in to help the fraction protestors to fight the Russian forces which had marched into the country.

June - US military base in Saudi bombed 19 servicemen killed

A bomb rips through a US military housing complex near Dhahran, Saudi Arabia killing 19 Americans. The US believes Al-Qaeda may have been involved in this attack which has been blamed on the militant Hezbollah group.

1998

22 February - Bin Laden issues fatwa calling for attacks on US citizens

A statement signed by Bin Laden and four of his associates calls for the killing of Americans saying it is the "individual duty for every Muslim who can do it in any country in which it is possible to do it". The organization is growing its network and recruiting more people based on its fanatic ideology which uses terror as a tool to gain political goals.

7 August - US embassies in Kenya and Tanzania bombed

More than 220 people are killed when lorries laden with bombs drove into the US embassies in Kenya and Tanzania. On 20 August the US retaliates with air strikes against alleged training camps in Sudan and Afghanistan. Bin Laden is later indicted by a US court for the bombings in East Africa. He is now on his way to becoming public enemy number one for Americans.

2000

12 October - Attack on US warship in Yemen kills 17 sailors

Two suicide attackers ram a boat carrying explosives into the USS Cole in Aden port killing 17 American sailors. The impact is not as big as Al-Qaeda hoped for. In 2004 six suspected Al-Qaeda militants are charged in connection with the attack by a Yemeni court.

2001

11 September - The worst attack on US soil kills about 3000 people

Nineteen Al-Qaeda suspects hijack four planes and fly them into the

World Trade Center in New York, the Pentagon in Washington and a field in Pennsylvania. Six weeks later the US launches attacks on Afghanistan from where Bin Laden has been operating. After the war hundreds of suspected Al-Qaeda fighters are sent to America's base in Guantanamo Bay Cuba where they are held in US custody. Osama bin Laden is a household name and a wanted man. The American "war on terror" has now commenced.

12 December - First Al-Qaeda suspect charged over 9/11 in the US

A French citizen of Moroccan origin is charged with conspiring with Osama bin Laden and other suspects to kill thousands of Americans in the 11 September attacks. Zacarias Moussaoui was detained in the US on immigration charges in August after he aroused suspicion at a Minnesota flight school where he sought training. He admits being a member of Al-Qaeda but denies involvement in the plot to hijack planes and crash them.

14 December - US releases Bin Laden 911 video

The US government releases a video which it says proves that Osama bin Laden masterminded the 11 September attacks. In the West the tape is widely seen as strengthening the case against Bin Laden. In the Islamic world there is widespread skepticism and some claims that it is a fake.

23 December - Briton held after trying to blow up plane

A British man is arrested on a flight from Paris to Miami after trying to blow up the plane with explosives hidden in his shoes. During his trial in the US the British citizen named Richard Reid pledged allegiance to Osama bin Laden. He is now serving a life sentence.

2002

22 March - Senior alQaeda member captured in Pakistan

Abu Zubaydah believed to have served as Osama bin Laden's field commander and chief recruiter is captured during a raid on a house in Pakistan. Number three on America's list of most wanted Al-Qaeda suspects he is then handed over to the US authorities.

11 April - Blast at Tunisian synagogue kills 17 people

A fuel tanker is blown up outside a synagogue on the Tunisian island of Djerba killing 19 people including 14 German tourists. An Al-Qaeda spokesman later says the organisation was behind the suicide attack. The group seems keen on claiming responsibility for terror attacks all over the world.

11 June - Dirty bomb plot foiled says US

The US authorities announce the arrest of an American citizen they accuse of planning to build and detonate a bomb containing radioactive material. Jose Padilla was detained on 8 May at Chicago airport after arriving from Pakistan. The spread of volunteers in the Al-Qaeda cadre is seen as a worrying development.

11 September - 9/11 plotter captured in Pakistan

Ramzi Binalshibh is arrested in Karachi on the anniversary of the attacks on America. He is accused of being a leading member of Al-Qaeda and one of the main planners of the 11 September 2001 attacks carried out on the US.

12 October - Bomb attacks on Bali nightclubs kill 202

Two bombs rip through a busy nightclub area in the Balinese town of Kuta killing 202 people most of them foreign tourists. The Indonesian authorities believe the attacks were carried out by the South East Asian militant network Jemaah Islamiah which is said to have links to Al-Qaeda.

22 October - First 911 trial opens in Germany

Mounir alMotassadek a Moroccan citizen goes on trial in Hamburg accused of membership of a terrorist cell and of being an accessory to the murder of more than 3000 people. He denies any knowledge of plans to launch the attacks. In 2003 he is found guilty of assisting the hijackers and sentenced to 12 years in jail. Another court later orders a retrial.

28 November - Israeli targets come under attack in Kenya

Sixteen people including three suicide bombers are killed in a blast at an Israeli owned hotel in Mombasa. A missile fired at an Israeli plane misses its target. A message on a website purporting to come from Al-Qaeda says the group carried out the attack.

2003

1 March - Al-Qaeda kingpin captured

Khalid Sheikh Mohammed thought to be one of Al-Qaeda's most senior leaders is arrested in a joint Pakistani CIA operation near Islamabad. The US believes he helped plan the 11 September attacks. He was charged in February 2008 with war crimes and murder by a U.S. military commission and faces the death penalty if convicted.

12 May - Dozens killed in Saudi bombings

At least 34 people are killed in a series of bomb attacks in Saudi Arabia's capital Riyadh. The targets are luxury comdos housing foreign nationals and a US Saudi office. Al-Qaeda is the prime suspect Washington and Riyadh say. It is the first in a string of attacks over successive months in Saudi Arabia.

16 May - Morocco rocked by suicide attacks

Bomb attacks in Casablanca kill 45 people including 12 attackers. Targets include a Spanish restaurant, a five-star hotel, a Jewish community centre and the Belgian consulate. Four men later sentenced to death for the attacks are said by the Moroccan authorities to be members of the Salafia Jihadia widely believed to be linked to Al-Qaeda.

27 June - Mastermind of Riyadh attacks arrested

The man suspected of masterminding the series of bombings in Riyadh is detained in Saudi Arabia. The arrest of Ali Abdul Rahman alGhamdi also known as Abu Bakr alAzdi is described as a major blow to alQaeda's operations in Saudi Arabia. He was number two on the list of most wanted suspects in connection with the 12 May attacks. US officials asserted that he had been present in Afghanistan in late 2001, and that he had been present at the battle of Tora Bora.

15 December - Suicide bombers hit two Turkish synagogues

At least 23 people are killed and more than 300 injured in two devastating suicide attacks on synagogues in Istanbul. The government blames Al-Qaeda for the attacks. The organization does not formally claim the attacks for a while.

20 December - Two bomb attacks on British interests in Turkey

Attacks on the British Consulate and the HSBC bank offices in Istanbul leave 27 people dead and more than 450 wounded. There are separate claims of responsibility from two allegedly Al-Qaeda connected groups.

2004

9 February - US uncovers Al-Qaeda plans for Iraq violence

US officials say they have uncovered what they believe is a plot by an Al-Qaeda linked militant Abu Musab al Zarqawi to stir up sectarian violence in Iraq. This is the first major appearance of the Al-Qaeda deputy who will take over as the leader of the organization after the death of Osama bin Laden.

11 March - Madrid rocked by deadly train bombings

Ten bombs explode on four packed early morning commuter trains in Madrid killing 191 people and leaving at least 1800 injured. Spanish officials later say their investigations are focusing on the Moroccan Islamic Combatant Group which is said to support Al-Qaeda's war against the West.

15 April - Bin Laden offers Europe truce

An audio tape purported to be from Osama bin Laden is broadcast. In it he offers Europe a truce if it "stops attacking Muslims" and withdraws all its troops from Muslim countries. There is no such offer made to the US forces being rallied by President Bush.

17 May - Top Iraqi official killed in suicide attack

Ezzedine Salim head of the Iraqi Governing Council is killed when a bomber blows himself up near the headquarters of the US - led coalition in Baghdad. A group linked to Al-Qaeda suspect Abu Musab al Zarqawi says it carried out the attack. US officials believe Zarqawi was behind a number of attacks in Iraq and was responsible for the beheading of a US hostage.

29 May - Militant shooting spree and siege kill 22 in Saudi Arabia

Gunmen allegedly from a group linked to Al-Qaeda attack company offices in the eastern city of Khobar killing a number of people. The militants then move to the Oasis housing com£ where they seize several dozen people mostly expatriates. The 25hour crisis ends on 30 May when Saudi commandos storm the housing complex.

18 June - US engineer beheaded in Saudi Arabia

Suspected Al-Qaeda militants in Saudi Arabia behead Paul Johnson after holding him hostage for a week. The purported head of Al-Qaeda in the country Abdul Aziz al Muqrin is later killed by security forces.

30 July - Embassy bombings suspect arrest announced

The arrest of a key suspect in the bombings of two US embassies in East Africa in 1998 is announced by Pakistani officials. Days after Ahmed Khalfan Ghailani's capture Pakistan confirms the arrest of another man believed to be an Al-Qaeda computer and communications expert.

26 September - Pakistan Al-Qaeda suspect killed

Pakistani police shoot dead suspected Al-Qaeda militant Amjad Farooqi in a two hour gun battle. Farooqi was wanted in connection with the murder of US journalist Daniel Pearl and attempts to kill

Pakistani President Pervez Musharraf. He was said to be a close associate of Abu Faraj al Libbi described as the operational chief of Al-Qaeda in the region.

29 September - US warship bombers given death sentence

A Yemeni court sentences Abd al Rahim al Nashiri and Jamal Mohammed al Badawi to death over the bomb attack on the USS Cole which killed 17 people in 2000. Four others are given between five and 10 years in jail for the attack.

29 October - Bin Laden video threatens US

Four days before presidential elections in the US al Jazeera TV airs a videotape in which Osama bin Laden threatens fresh attacks on the US. The Al-Qaeda leader says the reasons behind the events of 11 September 2001 still exist.

2005

14 April - A UK court convicts alQaeda suspect Kamal Bourgass

AlQaeda suspect Kamal Bourgass who stabbed to death a policeman is jailed for 17 years for plotting to spread ricin and other poisons on the UK's streets. Bourgass 31 was already serving a life term after being convicted of murdering Detective Constable Stephen Oake during a 2003 raid in Manchester.

20 April - Judge allows 911 suspect Moussaoui to enter guilty plea

A US judge rules that Zacarias Moussaoui the only person to be charged in the US in connection with the 9/11 attacks can enter a guilty plea. Mr Moussaoui a French citizen of Moroccan origin tried to plead guilty in 2002 but retracted the plea a week later.

22 April - Alleged 911 planners go on trial in Madrid

Immad Yarkas Driss Chebli and Ghassub al Abrash Ghaylun appear in court in Spain charged with assisting in the planning of the 11 September attacks. The three are charged variously with assisting with planning and logistics of the attacks and reconnaissance of the World Trade Center and other US targets.

4 May - Pakistan says it has caught Al-Qaedas alleged number three

Pakistan announces it has arrested Libyan Al-Qaeda suspect Abu Faraj al Libbi thought to be third in the network's hierarchy. Pakistani investigators say detraction from suspects caught in 2004 led them to identify Libbi as a target and capture him. US President George Bush describes him as a "major facilitator and chief planner" for Al-Qaeda.

7 July - Rushhour bomb attacks strike the heart of London

Fifty two people die and 700 are injured as bombs explode on three underground trains and one bus in central London. Analysts say the attacks bear the hallmarks of groups linked to or at least inspired by Al-Qaeda. This is one of the biggest terror attacks since 9/11 to strike the heart of the world.

26 September - Al-Qaeda suspect jailed in Spain for role in 911 attacks

Syrian Imad Yarkas is jailed for 27 years by a court in Madrid after being convicted of conspiracy to commit murder in connection with the 11 September attacks. Prosecutors said Yarkas had run an Al-Qaeda cell in Spain which helped to organise the attacks. A further 17 men including an al Jazeera TV journalist receive sentences ranging from six to 11 years for various other terrorism offences.

2006

19 January - Bin Laden offers a long term truce

In what is believed to be his first new message since December 2004 Osama bin Laden offers the US a "long term truce". The offer quickly rejected by the US comes in an audio tape aired by Arabic TV station al Jazeera. The al-Qaeda leader also warns that new attacks on the US are being planned.

6 May - Zacarias Moussaoui jailed for life for role in 9/11 attacks

Zacarias Moussaoui is sentenced to life in prison after being found guilty of involvement in the 11 September attacks. Judge Leonie Brinkema tells Moussaoui 37 that he will "never get a chance to speak again and that's an appropriate ending". Moussaoui will serve his sentence in a maximum security jail in Colorado.

8 June - Al-Qaeda in Iraq leader Zarqawi killed in airstrike

Militant leader Abu Musab al Zarqawi is killed in a US airstrike in Iraq. The self styled head of Al-Qaeda in Iraq was linked to hundreds of attacks and killings including the videotaped executions of Western hostages Nick Berg and Ken Bigley.

29 June - US Supreme Court rules military tribunals illegal

In a major blow to President Bush's policy the American Supreme Court rules that Al-Qaeda and Taliban suspects held at Guantanamo Bay cannot be tried in closed military tribunals. The ruling was made after an appeal by a man alleged to be Osama bin Laden's driver who claimed that such proceedings violated the Geneva Convention.

Despite this the US says it will not close the controversial Guantanamo Bay facilities.

3 September - Al-Qaeda's number 2 in Iraq al Saedi arrested

He was captured during a joint raid by Iraqi and United States forces on June 19, 2006 either north or southwest of Baquba, Iraq. He was interrogated for over two months. Muwaffaq al-Rubaie, Iraq's national security adviser, said that information from Saedi after his capture resulted in the death or capture of 11 "top Al-Qaeda in Iraq figures" and nine "lower-level members."

7 November - Al-Qaeda plotter who planned attacks in UK and US is jailed for life

Dhiren Barot is told he must serve at least 40 years in jail after admitting conspiracy to murder. The court heard Barot prepared meticulous plans for a series of synchronised attacks in the UK. Barot a former Hindu who converted to Islam is also wanted by US authorities over charges of conspiracy to use weapons of mass destruction in the US and in Yemen

Index